Reading the Bible outside the Church

Reading the Bible outside the Church

A Case Study

David G. Ford

☙PICKWICK *Publications* · Eugene, Oregon

READING THE BIBLE OUTSIDE THE CHURCH
A Case Study

Copyright © 2018 David G. Ford. All rights reserved. Except for brief quotations in critical publications or reviews, no part of this book may be reproduced in any manner without prior written permission from the publisher. Write: Permissions, Wipf and Stock Publishers, 199 W. 8th Ave., Suite 3, Eugene, OR 97401.

Pickwick Publications
An Imprint of Wipf and Stock Publishers
199 W. 8th Ave., Suite 3
Eugene, OR 97401

www.wipfandstock.com

PAPERBACK ISBN: 978-1-5326-3681-3
HARDCOVER ISBN: 978-1-5326-3683-7
EBOOK ISBN: 978-1-5326-3682-0

Cataloguing-in-Publication data:

Names: Ford, David G., author.

Title: Reading the Bible outside the church : a case study / David G. Ford.

Description: Eugene, OR: Pickwick Publications, 2018 | Includes bibliographical references.

Identifiers: ISBN 978-1-5326-3681-3 (paperback) | ISBN 978-1-5326-3683-7 (hardcover) | ISBN 978-1-5326-3682-0 (ebook)

Subjects: LCSH: Bible—Hermeneutics | Christianity and the social sciences | Christianity—Sacred books—Hermeneutics | Bible and sociology

Classification: BS480 F672 2018 (print) | BS480 (ebook)

Scripture quotations are taken from the Holy Bible, New Living Translation, copyright ©1996, 2004, 2007, 2013, 2015 by Tyndale House Foundation. Used by permission of Tyndale House Publishers, Inc., Carol Stream, Illinois 60188. All rights reserved.

Scripture quotations marked (NIV) are taken from the Holy Bible, New International Version®, NIV®. Copyright © 1973, 1978, 1984, 2011 by Biblica, Inc.™ Used by permission of Zondervan. All rights reserved worldwide. www.zondervan.com The "NIV" and "New International Version" are trademarks registered in the United States Patent and Trademark Office by Biblica, Inc.™

Manufactured in the U.S.A.   07/06/18

Contents

Figures and Tables | vi
Acknowledgements | vii

Introduction: The Relational Nature of Reading | 1

Part One

Chapter 1: An Unheard Voice | 17
Chapter 2: Research Design—Methodology, Sample, and Texts | 42
Chapter 3: Data Production—Methods and Fieldwork | 65

Part Two

Chapter 4: The Transactional Theory of Reading | 89
Chapter 5: Reader-shaped Readings—Experience | 99
Chapter 6: Reader-shaped Readings—Identity | 118
Chapter 7: Reader-shaped Readings—Attitude | 135
Chapter 8: Reader-shaped Readings—Belief 1 | 148
Chapter 9: Reader-shaped Readings—Belief 2 | 169
Chapter 10: Text-shaped Readings | 185

Conclusion: Implications of Relational Bible Reading | 204

Bibliography | 219
Index | 241

Figures and Tables

Figures

Figure 1: Dave's Annotations on Proverbs 10:1–11 | 102

Figure 2: John's Annotations on 2 Samuel 5:17–25 | 121

Figure 3: Anthony's Annotations on 2 Samuel 5:17–25 | 128

Figure 4: Dave's Annotation on Proverb 10:9 | 131

Figure 5: Bob's Annotation on Proverbs 10:8 | 131

Figure 6: Victor's Annotations on Matthew 18:21–35 | 137

Figure 7: Paul's Annotations on Matthew 18:21–35 | 141

Figure 8: Sam's Annotations on Psalm 88 | 152

Figure 9: Annotation Content | 155

Figure 10: Questionnaire Content | 155

Figure 11: Interview Content | 155

Tables

Table 1: The Spectrum of Skeptical and Accepting Readings | 144

Acknowledgements

THIS WORK DOES NOT belong to me. Although I have written every word, it is the product of a much wider collective. Therefore thanks are due.

To Andy K, Andy G, Anthony, Bob, Dave, Derek, Ethan, Gary, John, Matty, Mick, Paul, Peter, Phil, Richie, Sam, Stuart, Tony, Victor and Zadok, the twenty men who volunteered to take part in this Bible-reading research. To George and the wider management at the Chemical Industrial Plant who facilitated my entry into that setting and to the *Mission in the Economy* and the *Salt of the Earth Network* who were also active in the establishing of my fieldwork. I am very grateful for all that these friends have done. Out of the kindness of their hearts they helped me, taking a risk when others would not. It is a privilege to have known them.

To the staff and students at International Christian College, Glasgow, who provided the stimulating environment that led me towards a PhD. In a similar way, colleagues at the University of Chester have been an encouragement over the past four years, especially David Shepherd and Wayne Morris who played pivotal roles at different times. My supervisor Dawn Llewellyn has fought my corner and persevered with a somewhat unwieldy PhD student. Her professionalism and thoroughness has pushed me to produce my best. My thanks go particularly to her. More recently Pete Phillips and the CODEC team have provided space for me to reflect upon my project. This, along with valuable feedback from Wendy Dossett, Mark Pike, Chris Crosby, David Robertson, Alex MacDonald, and Peter Brierley has all further refined my thinking.

To our friends and family at Kirkintilloch Baptist Church, who have supported us financially and in prayer, as too our friends and family at Matthew Henry Evangelical Church, who have journeyed with us over the past four years. These communities sustained us as a family, walking with us and sharing our load.

To the Mylne Trust, the British and Foreign Bible Society (the Bible Society in England and Wales, hereafter called "Bible Society"), and friends in Edinburgh, each of who provided me with a research grant. Their generosity, encouragement and interest enabled us to keep our heads above water.

To the Ford side of the family: my Mum and Dad; Aunty Margaret; the Scotts—Liz, Andy, Hannah, Julia, Martha and Naomi; the Mackays—Rebecca, Steve, Abi, Chloe, Lois, and Esther; Matt; John, Jo, Luke, Sam, and Mark. To the Dring side of the family: Robert and Christina; Pete, Jen, Daniel, and Joel. And friends like Oli and Susan Ward, Graeme and Emily Hamilton, and Will Thorburn. They have supported me, and us, not only for the duration of my doctorate but also for many years before. This has involved finances, proof reading, long discussions, Tesco shops, holidays, removals, visits, a car, coffee money, consistent encouragement, prayer, and a whole lot more. It has at times been overwhelming, often very timely and always with love. My heartfelt thanks for all you have done, but more importantly for all you are.

To Anna, Molly and Tom who have kept me sane and made sure my feet remained firmly on the ground. They have not shied away from the unknown and have coped with disappointment and less, bringing color to life by getting up every morning and choosing to laugh rather than cry (most of the time). Thank you for joining in the doctoral experience, and for your sacrificial love and patience.

My final word of thanks goes to my loving heavenly father, who in a world, and a life, of uncertainty and mess is my hope.

Introduction

The Relational Nature of Reading

SAM WAS SITTING AT his desk surrounded by papers. Aged twenty-four he is one of the younger engineers at the Chemical Industrial Plant and clearly enjoys his job. He is a Mechanical Engineer and the papers on his desk seem to be drawings for new pipe work. The Plant has been running for over sixty years and it requires constant redevelopment as the demands upon it change. It is located in North West England, an area with a long industrial heritage, and perhaps for this reason Sam is typical of the men who work here, most of whom are white, British, and raised in the local area.

I had been visiting the Plant for six months and was introduced to Sam four weeks ago. I was a researcher with a rather unusual research project. I was exploring how men, who neither read the Bible nor went to church regularly, might read the Bible; and in this Chemical Plant I had found such men. These were individuals who typically had little interest in religion but were willing to help by giving up five of their lunchtimes to read through five different biblical texts, sharing their readings with me. Sam was one of these men for he did not own a Bible, and had never regularly read it or gone to church. He did identify as "Christian" in the 2011 Census of England and Wales, but that was because he was christened as a baby, reflecting Abby Day's idea of "natal nominalism."[1] In this project though, Sam described himself as "not at all religious," but "slightly spiritual" because he hoped that "there's something out there."[2]

---

1. Day, *Believing in Belonging*, 182. Day describes this as "an ascribed identity they believe was conferred upon them at birth, one that has not engaged them often in later life, until asked." See also: Arweck, "'I've been christened but I don't really believe in it.'"

2. The label "spiritual but not religious" is one which scholars are aware of. For example see: Leonard, *Living in Godless Times*; Fuller, *Spiritual But Not Religious*; Marler and Hadaway, "'Being Religious' or 'Being Spiritual' in America"; Tacey, *The Spiritual Revolution*; Heelas and Woodhead, *The Spiritual Revolution*; Chandler, "The Social Ethic of Religiously Unaffiliated Spirituality"; Hamberg, "Unchurched Spirituality"; King, *The Search for Spirituality*; Beaman and Beyer, "Betwixt and Between. David Hay and

I was due to interview Sam, for over the past two weeks he had read through the different Bible passages I had given him, annotating them with his thoughts and completing a questionnaire on each. Today was an opportunity for Sam to talk about the Bible passages and add any concluding remarks. It was also my chance to raise some of my own questions about his reading of the texts, for something had caught my eye.

In the questionnaire which accompanied each text, the reader was asked if he thought the passage had a message, and if so what was it?

- For Proverbs 10:1–11, Sam wrote:[3] "Basically work hard, be good, be godly and you will live well and prosper, or be 'wicked' lazy and bad and you will fail."
- For 2 Samuel 5:17–25 he wrote: "The message is that David had God's backing and therefore his regime was good[;] anyone who opposed it was bad."
- For Matthew 18:21–35 he wrote: "Forgive or be punished/'tortured' and don't expect to be forgiven if you don't."
- For Psalm 88 he wrote: "Do as god says or you will suffer."
- And finally having read 2 John he simply wrote: "Love god or you are evil."[4]

In three out of the five texts, Sam's reply contained the formulaic answer: Do X or Y will happen. In the two passages where this did not occur (2 Sam 5:17–25 and 2 John), Sam's replies echo that formula. I brought these responses to Sam's attention during our interview and this was his reaction.

> Sam: Yeh they are all pretty similar aren't they?
>
> David: Yeah, both in terms of, kind of direction, but also in terms of the "do or something," em, thoughts?
>
> Sam: Em, I suppose that's, that the view of the Bible I have over all is, be godly and do as God says or you, or you won't prosper, bad things will happen to you. So

---

Kate Hunt undertook focus group research amongst British adults who did not regularly go to church in order to explore their sense of spirituality. Mirroring Sam's self-description, they point out that the commonest explanation given for having a sense of spiritual identity was "the conviction that there is 'something there.'" See: *Understanding the Spirituality of People Who Don't Go to Church*, 18.

3. Each of the five biblical passages is presented fully in chapter 2.

4. Throughout I present quotes from the participants as they were written or spoken, so at times God appears with a capital "G" and at others with a small "g."

> I suppose, yeah, without thinking about it, that's what I've put each time.

Sam's reading of the five biblical texts was one significantly influenced by his "view of the Bible," for it was that view which shaped how the texts were read and was in turn reaffirmed by his reading of the texts. Sam understood the Bible to have a central message, "do as God says or you, or you won't prosper" and a variation of this message was what he noted in every text, and so confirmed his view that the Bible had such a central message. Sam's readings were not unique, for in different ways, but consistently throughout this project, I found that what these readers associated with the texts significantly shaped their readings of them. In other words, the type of relationship which the reader had with the texts informed the subsequent reading transactions. This phenomenon highlights the influence of the reader in the act of reading, something known as reader-response criticism. I draw upon one particular reader-response theory, the transactional theory of reading, to explore and explain the readings that Sam and the other men undertook.

Overview of Argument

The catalyst for this study was a research question: How would a British person, who does not regularly read the Bible (or go to church), read the Bible? As a question it builds upon reader-response theory but also draws heavily from biblical studies and theology, where the role of real Bible readers has been considered. Much of this research however has focused upon those who are regular Bible readers.[5] Those who have been excluded from this research are those who rarely if ever read the Bible, and in Britain that is the majority of the population.[6] In particular, because men are the cohort of society least likely to read the Bible,[7] I focus on them.

Therefore, my use of the phrase "outside the church" should be understood to refer to the cohort of British society who do not regularly read the Bible or go to church. In using this phrase I am not principally concerned with the geographical location where the Bible is read, such as

---

5. For example see: Francis, "What Happened to the Fig Tree?"; Jennings, "Word and Spirit"; Lawrence, *The Word in Place*; Rogers, *Congregational Hermeneutics*; Todd, "The Interaction of Talk and Text"; Village, *The Bible and Lay People*.

6. Field, "Is the Bible Becoming a Closed Book?" 517; Theos, *Post-Religious Britain?* 20–21.

7. Field, "Is the Bible Becoming a Closed Book?" 518.

a restaurant,[8] a pub,[9] or in my case a Chemical Industrial Plant, although this will be touched upon in chapter 6. Neither am I exclusively referring to those who identify as "non-religious,"[10] or as having de-converted,[11] although the place of a reader's religious identity will also be reflected upon in chapters 6 and 7. My definition of "outside the church" is concerned with actions, that is, an individual's practice of neither going to church nor reading the Bible regularly.

The attempt to answer my research question took me to a Chemical Industrial Plant and to twenty men there who volunteered to read through five different biblical texts. They were invited to annotate the text, answer a short questionnaire on their reading of it and then discuss the text in a one-to-one semi-structured interview. My analysis of that data resulted in the central finding that my participants' relationships with the five biblical texts shaped their readings of those texts. By relationship, I am referring to all that a person is in relation to a particular text, including their attitudes, beliefs, memories, expectations and identities. In other words, a person brings all that they are to a text and different aspects of the reader will shape the reading that takes place, some informing it more than others. This can be seen in Sam's case, where his belief that the Bible had a particular message directly shaped his readings, whilst the influence of his natal Christian identity was less notable.

I argue for this central finding in three ways. First, by grounding my finding in Louise Rosenblatt's transactional theory of reading, I explain the mechanism behind these readings. Rosenblatt contends that texts and their readers are not independent entities which come together in the act of reading and move on potentially unaffected, instead they are part of the same dynamic matrix, co-existing.[12] Her focus is upon the reader and text as they come together in the act of reading, but I highlight the pre-existing nature of this co-existence. In my case, the men existed within a matrix in which the Bible and Christianity could also be found, and the nature of their co-existence became clear as they read the five texts, for it informed the sense of "meaning" which arose.[13]

Rosenblatt further argues that a reader brings all that they are to a text. She writes:

8. Bielo, *Words Upon the Word*, 47–72.
9. Lawrence, *The Word in Place*, 60–73.
10. Lee, "Secular or Nonreligious?"
11. Wright et al., "Explaining Deconversion from Christianity."
12. Rosenblatt, *Making Meaning with Texts*, 40.
13. Rosenblatt, *The Reader, the Text, the Poem*, 11.

> If we think of the total literary transaction, we must recognize that the reader brings to or adds to the nonverbal or sociophysical setting his whole past experience of life and literature. His memories, his present preoccupations, his sense of values, his aspirations, enter into a relationship with the text.[14]

From all of these memories, preoccupations, sense of values, and aspirations a reader decides which are of most relevance to the text. This is what William James called "selective attention,"[15] and Rosenblatt incorporates this into her theory of reading, for she argues:

> It became possible to show that the text stirred up, brought into the stream [of consciousness], a complex welter of sensations, thoughts, and feelings. "Selective attention" brings some elements into the center of attention and pushes others into the background or ignores them.[16]

Those elements that have been selected then play a greater role in shaping the subsequent reading that takes place.

Second, having grounded my central finding in the transactional theory of reading I then present four different ways in which my readers' relationships with the texts shaped their readings of those texts. Using the headings: "experience," "identity," "attitude," and "belief" I explore the influence of these factors upon the readings which took place. Moreover, in each of these cases the reader assumes a dominant position when reading the texts, resulting in their relationship with the texts being reaffirmed by their reading, as is seen in Sam's case.

The third part of my argument further evidences my central claim by demonstrating how a text is able to stimulate a reader into an unexpected reading, one which is shaped by, but does not conform to, their prior relationship with the text. In other words, their experiences, beliefs, or identity informed their reading but were not reaffirmed by it. In this way, these readers were seen to have a relationship with these texts, one that shaped the readings and often reaffirmed the readers' pre-existing dispositions, but not always.

To this end, the first part of this book (chapters 1–3) charts the formation and refinement of my research question, along with the designing and implementing of the research. The second part (chapters 4–10) then argues for my central finding by theorizing what took place and evidencing

---

14. Ibid., 81.
15. James, *Principles of Psychology*.
16. Rosenblatt, *Making Meaning with Texts*, xxv.

it through a series of examples. These examples not only demonstrate the veracity of my central claim but also nuance or challenge five different assumptions regarding Bible reading that can be seen in the academic or Christian world. These assumptions are:

1. That the geographical context significantly informs reading.[17]
2. That there is a skeptical/accepting binary found in Bible reading and readers.[18]
3. That the Bible is no longer a book of power in the West.[19]
4. That the Bible is a book of power able to transform the reader.[20]
5. That the text cannot stimulate a reader to a reading beyond their assumptions.[21]

The second part of the book also engages with these subthemes, each being addressed when the relevant data is engaged with.

The Readers and the Reading Site

Crucially though, it is the readings of twenty particular men which has enabled the production of this work. It is therefore appropriate to briefly mention each of them for they are at its heart. Chapter 2 will consider in more depth my sampling approach and criteria, but for the present it is sufficient to note that all of these men were white, British, and did not read the Bible or go to church (or take part in a religious activity) on a regular basis.[22]

- Andy K is a twenty-six-year-old welder, motorbike enthusiast, and identified as "not at all religious" in this project.
- Andy G is a forty-nine-year-old mechanic. He is an active Freemason, and for this reason identified as "moderately religious."

---

17. Lawrence, *The Word in Place*; Riches, *What is Contextual Bible Study?* 23–24.
18. Davies, *Whose Bible? Anyone's?*; Volf, *Captive to the Word of God*, 34–35.
19. Aichele, *The Control of Biblical Meaning*, 221; Vincent, "The Death and Resurrection of the Bible in Church and Society."
20. Detweiler, "What Is a Sacred Text?" 22; Engelke, *God's Agents*.
21. Fish, *Is There a Text in This Class?*
22. Throughout I use "regular" to mean, monthly or more often, as is common practice in religious surveys, for example see: Brierley, *Pulling Out of the Nose Dive*.

INTRODUCTION: THE RELATIONAL NATURE OF READING 7

- Anthony is a fifty-nine-year-old manager and tennis player. He identified as a Christian and "moderately religious" although at the time he neither attended church nor read the Bible.
- Bob is a sixty-one-year-old part-time manager who was also completing a computer science degree. He identified as "slightly religious" as he was neither overtly religious nor anti-religious.
- Dave is a forty-four-year-old welder and team leader for a group of welders. He identified as "not at all religious."
- Derek is a sixty-two-year-old welder, former rugby player and the oldest participant in this project. He identified as a non-practicing Catholic and so "moderately religious."
- Ethan is a forty-year-old engineer who was working on a new distillation system for the Plant. He was shortly to remarry, and identified as "not at all religious."
- Gary is a forty-eight-year-old utility technician with an interest in psychology. He described himself as a "lover not a fighter" and identified as "not at all religious."
- John is a twenty-two-year-old manager who enjoys socializing with friends and was the youngest participant. He identified as "not at all religious."
- Matty is a thirty-six-year-old scaffolder, rugby league fan, and was very family-orientated. In this project, he identified as "not at all religious."
- Mick is a thirty-year-old scaffolder who enjoys carp fishing. His wife was shortly due to give birth to their first child and he identified as "not at all religious."
- Paul is a thirty-six-year-old scaffolder who plays golf and at the time was trying to sell his house. He described himself as a non-practicing Catholic and identified as "moderately religious."
- Peter is a fifty-six-year-old electrician who had had a varied career, which included coalmining. He identified as "not at all religious."
- Phil is a forty-eight-year-old electrician who a year ago stopped riding motorbikes in favor of playing golf. He identified as "slightly religious," because he did not disbelieve in God.
- Richie is a forty-six-year-old mechanic and keen rugby league fan. He described himself as a lapsed Catholic and identified as "slightly religious."

- Sam is the twenty-four-year-old engineer whom I introduced at the start of this chapter. He enjoys playing football, lives with his parents, and identified as "not at all religious."
- Stuart is a forty-one-year-old welder who found that work and family consumed most of his time. He was unwell for three weeks during the project and identified as "not at all religious."
- Tony is a fifty-five-year-old engineer and had worked at the Plant for twenty years. He described himself as a Catholic and attended church every five or six weeks; for that reason he identified as "moderately religious."
- Victor is a thirty-one-year-old scaffolder who had worked for thirteen years as a delivery driver. He identified as "not at all religious."
- Zadok is a fifty-nine-year-old utility technician who was heading towards retirement. He was very contented with life and identified as "not at all religious."

These men's readings of five biblical texts make up the substance of this research. However, I am the one who designed the project, asked for their assistance, analyzed the data, and wrote this book. I do not consider myself to be an objective outsider, rather I am a figure within this research project and although this will be considered later, for the present a brief descriptor should suffice:

- David is a thirty-seven-year-old PhD student who previously worked as a Physiotherapist. In this project he identified as "very religious."[23]

I spent from October 2012 to July 2013 at the Chemical Industrial Plant where these twenty men worked. As a location it was one foreign to me, having its own dress code and culture. I had to wear a hardhat and safety glasses on most trips and was not allowed to visit the Plant unaccompanied until I had completed an induction process. There were some buildings that could only be entered with a security swipe card and others which were prefabricated portacabins without running water. However, the architecture of the Plant was its most striking feature; steel towers and miles of pipes, which to an untrained eyed looked like a maze of spaghetti. The Plant had opened in 1946 and I assume its location, close to a river and a now unused railway track, indicates that it was of some importance. Nowadays two global Chemical companies principally own the site and its

---

23. My self-identifying as "very religious" reflects the description I was given by my participants, that of being "a religious guy."

products are used in household goods such as fabric detergent. Over two hundred men work at the Plant and are employed by one or other of the two main companies, or one of the smaller firms that are subcontracted there. All of my participants had their own base, be that an office or a staff room, which they shared with the rest of their team. Each of these small teams had their own sense of identity and atmosphere. Some groups were noisy and the room was filled with banter, whilst others were quieter with each man reading his own newspaper. It was at lunchtimes, in these staff rooms that these participants individually read through and commented on the five Bible passages.

Overview of Chapters

What was produced in those lunchtimes makes up what follows. The subsequent chapters have not been set out to conform to any one pre-established structure advocated by qualitative researchers.[24] In my case, aware of the qualitative methodology that I assume and its emphasis on transparency, I have adopted a chronological and thematic approach to my chapters. This should not only result in a coherent argument but also allows for the inductive nature of my project, and the open-endedness which that brings, to shape what follows, something potentially lost in the adoption of a pre-established framework. Thus each chapter builds on the preceding as a single narrative is constructed.

However, I am aware that some people read selectively, skipping or skimming sections of little interest and concentrating on others. I provide a thorough retelling of a doctoral project, for some however there might be too much information about the research methods, whilst others might feel there is too much discussion of literary theory. What I hope I have achieved is a stimulating and detailed case study that is written in an accessible way but allows readers to skim sections they consider less interesting, if they choose to do so. With this in mind, the main themes are continually signposted and each chapter is framed accordingly.

Chapter 1 primarily deals with the prompts and formation of my research question: how would a British person, who does not regularly read the Bible (or go to church), read the Bible? I begin by considering the "turn to the reader" in literary studies and how the role of the Bible reader has also been studied within biblical studies and theology. In doing so, I highlight that most of the work undertaken so far has focused upon regular

---

24. For example see: Bell, *Doing your Research Project*; Swinton and Mowat, *Practical Theology and Qualitative Research*.

Bible readers and as a consequence the majority of the British population have been excluded from this enquiry. Three lesser-known pieces of research are considered which all involved some participants who could be labeled "outside the church," (in that they were not regular Bible readers or churchgoers).[25] These studies explored how selected biblical texts were engaged with, but their methods and objectives differed from my own, demonstrating the need for this research.

Chapter 2 considers the methodological underpinnings that I build upon, arguing for a qualitative case study. It also addresses two issues that further refine my research enquiry. First, in light of my focus upon non-regular Bible readers and noting that men are less likely to read the Bible than women,[26] I decide to limit my selection to men. Second, it seemed unlikely that men who were not regular Bible readers would be willing to read the entire Bible, so I chose five biblical texts which I would ask them to read. This was the maximum number I thought I could include without negatively affecting how many men would be willing to participate. In this way then a broad research question was refined to ask: How would a British man, who does not regularly read the Bible (or go to church), read five biblical texts?

Chapter 3 then documents how I went about answering this question. I begin by reflecting on my own identity and position within this research, for it would influence the readings the men would undertake. I then trace the decision to assume a mixed method approach utilizing three different research tools: annotation, questionnaire and interview. I recount the experience of undertaking the pilot study and how it informed the subsequent fieldwork. The chapter ends by describing the fieldwork and subsequent data analysis that took place. In this way the first part of this book provides a platform upon which my presentation and discussion of the findings is situated.

Chapter 4 presents Rosenblatt's transactional theory of reading. In particular I trace her explanation of the way in which a reader's relationship with a text shapes their reading of that text.[27] I acknowledge that this literary theory is not without its limitations, but nonetheless argue it provides a clear framework for understanding the readings that took place, as is demonstrated in the subsequent chapters. In this way the theoretical

---

25. Le Grys, *Shaped by God's Story*; Macdonald. "The Psalms and Spirituality"; Webster, "When the Bible Meets the Black Stuff."

26. Field, "Is the Bible Becoming a Closed Book?" 518.

27. Rosenblatt, *Making Meaning with Texts*, 30.

underpinnings are put in place as I go on to explore in more depth some of the findings from my case study.

Chapter 5 is the first of four working examples of this theory. Specifically, it explores how a reader's prior experiences can mold their reading. Dave is presented as someone who read skeptically focusing on the parts of the text with which disagreed and he directly linked this reading style to his childhood experiences of church. In order to consider his readings in more depth, insights from the fields of Bible reception and social psychology are brought into conversation with them. Gary's detached readings of the five biblical texts are then considered, for once again his prior experiences of religion shaped them. Matthew Engelke's ethnography of a community of Christians who have rejected the Bible, the Masowe weChishanu Church, is compared with Gary's rejection of the Bible.[28]

Chapter 6 explores a second aspect of a reader's relationship with a biblical text, that is their sense of religious identity. This is done by presenting John, an atheist, and Anthony, a Christian, both of whose readings were not only informed by their sense of religious identity, but resulted in a strengthening of that identity. Once again, I draw on insights from social psychology to examine these particular readings. Moreover, the impact of the reader's religious identity, rather than their workplace identity or setting, suggests that some social locations are more significant than others.[29] This troubles an assumption within contextual Bible reading methods, that the reader's geographical location shapes their reading,[30] for the Chemical Industrial context was hardly ever linked to the readings that took place in it.

However, by noting the prominence of the reader's religious identity, it could be supposed that there are principally two types of readings, atheist or Christian, skeptical or accepting, a binary that has been promoted by some scholars.[31] Chapter 7 addresses this assumption by demonstrating the influence of a reader's attitude towards the texts. Victor, a nonreligious man, is considered, for he was aware of the potential to read the texts skeptically, but chose to "be fair" resulting in skeptical and accepting readings. Paul is also presented. He is a moderately religious non-practicing Catholic, whose doubting attitude resulted in him reading the texts skeptically, as most of the

---

28. Engelke, *A Problem of Presence*.

29. The term "social location" has come to describe the various influences upon a reader and their reading which distinguish one reading community from another. These include: gender, class, nationality, personality, geographical location and employment. For example see: Powell, *Chasing the Eastern Star*; Segovia and Tolbert, *Reading from this Place* (Vol. 1 and 2).

30. Riches, *What is Contextual Bible Study?* 23–24.

31. Davies, *Whose Bible? Anyone's?*; Volf, *Captive to the Word of God*, 34–35

nonreligious men did. In light of these findings, this chapter ends by showing that a spectrum, rather than a binary, of readings took place. Moreover, although there was a link between a reader's sense of religious identity and their reading, there were exceptions.

Chapters 8 and 9 consider the place of the readers' beliefs about the Bible, in their reading of the five biblical texts. In chapter 8, I note that the texts were usually read for information, which the reader then critiqued and typically rejected. Once again I build upon the transactional theory of reading, for it contends that every reader is situated upon an efferent/aesthetic continuum. To read efferently is to read for information, as one does a handbook. Whereas to read aesthetically is to read in such a way as to become absorbed in the world of the text, as one does a novel.[32] I argue that my participants assumed an efferent standpoint towards the texts and so read them for information. According to Rosenblatt, such a reading stance is appropriate for a selection of proverbs, but not for poetry, like Psalm 88.[33] Nonetheless no matter the genre, my participants typically engaged with the texts from an efferent standpoint. I suggest that there are three reasons for this: that the research materials encouraged the participants to assume this stance, that the reader's personality and gender meant they were predisposed to this stance, and that the men believed the Bible to be a guidebook or manual and so read these texts efferently. Ultimately I suggest that all three factors played a part, but the most significant was the reader's belief that the Bible is a guide.

In chapter 9 I explore a further reason why the texts were predominantly read skeptically and conclude that most of the men believed the act of reading these Bible passages had the potential to convert them. In other words, even though these men indicated that they did not believe the Bible to be the word of God or of any relevance to them, when it came to reading the texts, they did so demonstrating a belief in the transformative potential of these texts. This is seen in the act of "counter-reading," my term to describe a skeptical engagement with a text so as to disempower the assumed threat posed by its reading. In treating these five texts as texts of power, but a power they were able to disarm, these men trouble the views that the Bible is now a powerless book in the West,[34] or that its agency-like qualities will transform a reader.[35]

---

32. Rosenblatt, *Making Meaning with Texts*, 10–12.

33. Ibid., 11.

34. Aichele, *The Control of Biblical Meaning*, 221; Macdonald, "Engaging the Scriptures," 193.

35. Engelke, *God's Agents*, 4–5.

Chapter 10 begins by recounting the ways in which these four different aspects of the readers' relationships with the texts shaped their readings of the texts. Having done so, I note that so far the reader has dominated the reading, for it was their experiences, identities, attitudes, or beliefs that shaped the subsequent readings. However, there were a few occasions in which the text stimulated the reader to an unexpected or atypical reading. Three examples are given where the reader's relationship with the texts shaped their reading of it but did not result in the affirmation of that prior relationship. In these cases, the reader's experiences, preconceptions, or beliefs informed a reading but did not bring about a reading that conformed to them. This is the third strand of my argument. Such a finding is at home with the transactional theory and its understanding that the reader and the text are capable of shaping the reading. However, it challenges literary theories that contend that the text has no influence upon the reading, like that proposed by Stanley Fish,[36] for in my case study the text provoked the reader to an unforeseen reading.

The concluding chapter retraces my central argument and the ways in which my case study problematizes five assumptions found within the academic and Christian world. I also highlight the uniqueness of this piece of work as one engaging a previously unexplored people group in this way, one which draws together the "guidebook" view of the Bible noted in biblical literacy and the efferent standpoint from literary theory, and one which has named and explored the phenomenon of "counter-reading." I then reflect upon four implications of my work for the practice and study of Bible reading, before concluding with three main limitations of my work and the subsequent stimulus that they are for future research. What I hope I have achieved is the weaving together of a central theme and various subthemes without losing the particularity of each aspect nor the voices of the twenty participants. As a body of work however, it all begins with a research question.

---

36. Fish, *Is There a Text in This Class?*

Part One

Chapter 1

An Unheard Voice

THIS CHAPTER EXPLORES THE prompts which led to the formation of my research question. I argue that within Britain, study into how the Bible is read has typically concentrated on regular Bible readers, such as the clergy, laity, or biblical scholars. Non-regular Bible readers, those outside the church, are missing from this field of inquiry, raising the question: How would a British person who does not regularly read the Bible (or go to church), read the Bible?

In order to situate present-day Bible reading research within a wider context, I begin by briefly noting the shift from the author to the reader in literary theory and the related emphasis seen in the philosophy and hermeneutics of Hans-Georg Gadamer.[1] However, this "turn to the reader" is not just seen in literary and hermeneutical theory but also in biblical studies and theology. Accordingly, I consider three subfields within these disciplines that demonstrate this new focus on the role of the Bible reader. What these subfields illustrate is that within Britain this research has typically concentrated on regular Bible readers. However, with national surveys indicating that most people in Britain do not regularly read the Bible, or go to church, I conclude that the majority of the population has been excluded from this research.

In bringing together the current focus on the role of the Bible reader and the lack of research into how the majority of the population may read the Bible, I provide the theoretical foundation for my study. The chapter concludes by highlighting three recent works that involved non-regular Bible readers. However, these works do not directly address my research question, reaffirming the need of my enquiry.

---

1. Gadamer, *Truth and Method*.

The "Turn to the Reader" in Literary Theory

Reader-response criticism is a term given to describe a collection of literary theories that are united in their emphasis on the role of the reader. The rise of reader-response criticism is usually described as a two-step process. First, literary scholars shifted their attention from the author of the text to the text itself, and then they turned their attention from the text to the reader of the text. This two-step recounting of recent literary history is a simplified one, ignoring counter movements and alternative trajectories.[2] For instance, in *Validity in Interpretation,* the literary critic E. D. Hirsch Jr. responded to the shift from author to text, by arguing for the centrality of the author and their intent. However, for my purposes a brief overview of these two steps is sufficient to locate reader-response criticism within its wider context.

In the mid-twentieth century scholars moved away from focusing on the author's motivation and purpose for writing, to concentrate on the text and its structure, this became known as new criticism. New critics, such as William Wimsatt and Monroe Beardsley, claimed that "the design and intention of the author is neither available nor desirable as a standard for judging the success of a work of art."[3] This rejection of the author was neatly condensed into the phrase "the intentional fallacy" which Wimsatt and Beardsley coined in 1946. New critics took up this phrase as they argued against the idea that the reader was able to understand the mind or purpose of the author. In so doing, these scholars moved away from considering the author's intention behind the text, to focus instead on the text as an entity in itself. They argued for the autonomy of the text, describing it "as an object of specifically critical judgment."[4] However, what new criticism also emphasized was that a text (such as a poem) and its results (its impact upon a reader) were in danger of being confused. Accordingly, they also rejected "the affective fallacy" which valued the reader's response to a text, arguing that it would result in "impressionism and relativism."[5] Thus, "what readers brought to each text–including thoughts and feelings–was deemed extraneous to meaning-making."[6]

Nevertheless, the new critics' "affective fallacy" was found wanting, as is seen in the first essay in Jane Tompkins's anthology *Reader-Response Criticism.* This essay, by Walker Gibson, is entitled "Authors, Speakers, Readers,

2. Davies, *Biblical Criticism,* 11–35; Aichele et al, *The Postmodern Bible.*
3. Wimsatt and Beardsley, "The Intentional Fallacy," 3.
4. Wimsatt and Beardsley, "The Affective Fallacy," 21.
5. Ibid., 21.
6. Damico et al., "Transactional Theory and Critical Theory in Reading Comprehension," 179.

and Mock Readers" and is situated within new criticism because it principally concerns textual analysis. However, it focuses on the role of the "mock reader" in this analysis, by which Gibson is referring to the way a reader identifies with and responds to a text. Thus, Tompkins describes it as,

> The first step in a series that gradually breaks through the boundaries that separate the text from its producers and consumers and reconstitutes it as a web whose threads have no beginning and no end.[7]

It was not long before scholars had turned their attention from the text to the reader, theorizing the role of the reader and the reader/text relationship in the reading process. The reader-response critic Norman Holland argues for such a focus:

> Let us open up the text by assuming the person brings to it something extrinsic. It could be information from literary history, biography, or an archaic ritual like the flyting between primitive bards. [. . .] It seems to me not only possible but likely that whenever we read, we are associating such extratextual, extraliterary facts to the supposedly fixed text. Now rather than strip those associations away, what will happen if we accept these things outside the text and try to understand the combination of the text and personal association?[8]

This shift in emphasis from the author, to the text, and then to the reader is one well documented and perhaps most famously argued by Roland Barthes who wrote that "the birth of the reader must be requited by the death of the Author."[9] In writing this, Barthes is contending that meaning is not, and never has been, found in the authorial intent, but rather is located in the reader.

At present there is a wide variety of reader-response critics and associated theories which attempt to explain the reader's role in reading.[10] Having approached the subject from a variety of angles, scholars have aired contrasting theories to explain the role of the reader in reading. In *The Postmodern Bible*, reader-response critics are divided into three camps.[11] First

7. Tompkins, *Reader-Response Criticism*, xi.
8. Holland, "Re-Covering 'the Purloined Letter,'" 363–64.
9. Barthes, "The Death of the Author," 55.

10. Three edited collections that present a range of reader-response theories are: Bennett, *Readers and Reading*; Suleiman and Crosman, *The Reader in the Text*; and Tompkins, *Reader-Response Criticism*.

11. Aichele et al., *The Postmodern Bible*, 27.

there are those like Norman Holland and David Bleich who assume a psychological or subjective approach.[12] Holland for instance, builds on Freudian developmental psychology suggesting that the reader's identity theme (something akin to their personality or character) is the dominant influence on their reading of a text. Employing the acronym DEFT, he suggests that every reader responds defensively to a text and their identity theme shapes their expectations of that text. The reader projects their fantasies on to a text but these are transformed and so a coherent reading can take place, one "associated with this person's particular identity theme."[13] Accordingly, each text can have multiple meanings/readings but their scope is limited by the reader's identity theme and its response to the text.

Second, there are those who assume an interactive or phenomenological approach: Wolfgang Iser, Wayne Booth, and Louise Rosenblatt could be identified in this way.[14] Iser, for example, upholds both the objectivity of the text and the subjectivity of the reader by suggesting that there is a relationship between both parties. The reader is able to follow the flow of a text and fill in any textual "gaps" which exist from their own expectations or imagination, in this way reading becomes stimulating:

> Whenever the flow is interrupted and we are led off in unexpected directions, the opportunity is given to us to bring into play our faculty for establishing connections-for filling in the gaps left by the text itself.[15]

Therefore, he too claims that there are multiple meanings/readings of a text, but they are constrained by the text.

Finally, the third group, which includes Stanley Fish[16] and Jonathan Culler, consists of social or structural approaches.[17] Fish, for instance, argues that a reader's "interpretive community" nurtures them to read in a certain way. That community validates their reading by deciding if it is acceptable or not, and it also limits the reading, for a reader cannot read in a

---

12. Bleich, *Subjective Criticism*; Holland, *The Nature of Literary Response*; Holland, *Poems in Persons*.

13. Holland, "Unit Identity Text Self," 127.

14. Booth, *The Rhetoric of Fiction*; Iser, *The Act of Reading*; Iser, *The Implied Reader*; Iser, *Prospecting*; Rosenblatt, *Literature as Exploration*.

15. Iser, "The Reading Process," 55.

16. Stanley Fish's earlier work (*Surprised by Sin*) assumed that there was a reader/text relationship and that the text was able to lead the reader. His later work (*Is There a Text in This Class?*), however, argues that there is no such relationship, and it is this work that I engage with.

17. Culler, *The Pursuit of Signs*; Fish, *Is There a Text in This Class?*

way they have not been taught. For Fish then, multiple meanings/readings of a text also exist, however it is the reader's "interpretive community, rather than either the text or the reader, that produce meanings" and also restrict them.[18] The difference noted between these three groups of scholars demonstrates something of the diversity seen in reader-response criticism.

This "turn to the reader" should not be thought of as something solely emerging from new criticism and limited to literary theory, for there were other works that contributed to this focus on the reader.[19] The philosophical and hermeneutical theories of Hans-Georg Gadamer are examples of this.[20] In particular, his emphasis on the role of the reader's preconceptions in the reading process helped to theorize the subjective nature of reading vital to reader-response criticism. Gadamer acknowledges Martin Heidegger's influence, for it was Heidegger who contended that all interpretation starts with an individual's "foreconceptions" (that is preconceptions) which are molded by their life experience.[21] Gadamer, in turn, draws attention to the word "prejudice" and its original meaning of "pre-judgments" to develop his own theory of interpretation:

> What is necessary is a fundamental rehabilitation of the concept of prejudice and a recognition of the fact that there are legitimate prejudices, if we want to do justice to man's finite, historical mode of being.[22]

Having so framed the word, he points out that prejudices are vital for any reading, that is, for the creation of meaning, because the reader must have some prejudices or fore-meanings of what certain words placed in a certain order mean. The meaning that is generated is then constantly reviewed as the reading continues, with the reader engaging their prejudices.[23]

This directly challenged the Enlightenment idea that preconceptions, or prejudices, were negative and a reader must strive to engage with a text

---

18. Fish, *Is There a Text in This Class?* 14.

19. Walter Brueggemann, in "The Re-Emergence of Scripture," highlights the influence of the theologian Karl Barth. Barth moved away from the established historical-critical approach towards a post-liberal one, under which present day contextual Bible readings would fall. Kevin Vanhoozer, in "The Reader in New Testament Interpretation," traces this turn to the reader back to Immanuel Kant and his "Copernican Revolution," whilst the George Aichele et al., in *The Postmodern Bible*, link it to postmodernity.

20. Fiorenza, "Systematic Theology," 11; Osborne, "Hermeneutics/Interpreting Paul."

21. Heidegger, *Supplements*, 77.

22. Gadamer, *Truth and Method*, 246.

23. Gadamer is not alone in highlighting the role of the reader's prejudices, Rudolf Bultmann also asked *Is Exegesis without Presupposition Possible?*

in a prejudice-free way. For example, famously Heinrich Meyer, in his 1829 *Critical and Exegetical Commentary on the New Testament*, writes:

> The area of dogmatics and philosophy is to remain off limits for a commentary. For to ascertain the meaning the author intended to convey by his words, impartially and historico-grammatically-that is the duty of the exegete.[24]

Gadamer described the Enlightenment as having a "prejudice against prejudices."[25] He countered the assumption that the Bible reader (or exegete) is able to set aside their prejudices in order to handle the text impartially by arguing that meaning could only emerge if the reader engaged with her or his prejudices.

Gadamer acknowledges that some prejudices are helpful in the construction of meaning, whilst others may lead to misunderstanding. Furthermore, he highlights two sources of influence upon a reader's prejudices. The first is authority, such as a knowledgeable person whose advice they may follow, and the second is the tradition of which the reader is part.[26] Moreover, Gadamer understands that as the reader engages with a text the prejudices which make the reading possible have the potential to be challenged, for the text may cause the reader to reject or adjust certain prejudices. Therefore the reader is not trapped by their prejudices for the text has the potential to "assert its own truth" against the reader's preconceptions and so change them.[27] Accordingly, prejudices are not a stable or fixed aspect of a reader but are constantly in flux.[28] In these ways then within literary, philosophical, and hermeneutical theory the attention of many scholars has turned to the reader. Unsurprisingly these developments have impacted biblical studies and Bible reading research.

The "Turn to the Reader" and the Bible

The impact of reader-response criticism upon biblical studies and theology is growing. Eryl Davies comments:

---

24. Kümmel, *The New Testament*, 111; Porter and Clarke "What is Exegesis?" 8; Silva, *Has the Church Misread the Bible?* 22; Waters, *Justification and the New Perspective*, 4.

25. Gadamer, *Truth and Method*, 242.

26. Ibid., 262.

27. Ibid., 238.

28. Ibid., 266–67.

> It has become something of a cliché to claim that developments in biblical studies lag behind those in secular literary criticism by some 20 or 30 years, but it is nevertheless a cliché that contains an element of truth.[29]

It is therefore no surprise that in recent years biblical scholars and theologians have started to draw upon insights from reader-response theory and apply them to Bible reading.[30] For example, in light of a postmodern context, Walter Brueggemann argues for a different way of reading the Bible within the church. He does not reject the historical critical tools associated with modernity, but his main emphasis is on the need to prioritize and engage the reader's or hearer's imagination. He describes a reader's imaginative engagement with a biblical text as:

> that operation of receiving, processing, and ordering that transpires when my mind wonders in listening to a text, a reading, in praying, or in any other time. In that wondrous, liberated moment, I take the material and process it in ways that are useful to me, about which only I know.[31]

Accordingly, he argues that the contextual, local, and pluralistic nature of such readings be valued and respected.[32] Brueggemann is not advocating the wholesale adoption of any particular reader-response theory rather he is indirectly drawing on different reader-response critics to advocate for the role of the reader's imagination. Thus, he echoes Fish's idea of an interpretive community,[33] Holland's use of Freudian psychology,[34] and Iser's claim that the text has a degree of objectivity.[35] In elevating the reader and their subjective engagement with the Bible, Brueggemann is affirming core elements of reader-response theory.

There are two ways in which biblical scholars' engagement with reader-response criticism should be qualified however. First, contrasting the earlier threefold division of reader-response criticisms,[36] some biblical scholars

---

29. Davies, *Biblical Criticism*, 22.

30. For example see: Briggs, *The Virtuous Reader*; Clines, *What Does Eve Do to Help?*; Darr, *On Character Building*; Fowler, *Let the Reader Understand*; McKnight, *Postmodern Use of the Bible*; Powell, *Chasing the Eastern Star*.

31. Brueggemann, *The Bible and Postmodern Imagination*, 62.

32. Ibid., 9.

33. Ibid., 62

34. Ibid., 59–63

35. Ibid., 67.

36. Aichele et al., *The Postmodern Bible*, 27.

divide them into two groups, "moderate" and "radical."[37] At the heart of this division is the degree to which each reader-response critic understands the text to play a role in the production of meaning. Subsequently, those theorists who argue that the text has a significant degree of influence on the reading are labeled "moderate," and those who suggest it has little or no influence are labeled "radical." For instance, Iser's reader-response theory is typically viewed as "moderate" for he affirms the objectivity of the text, understanding the text to guide the reader, correcting their tentative interpretation.[38] Fish though is presented as a "radical" reader-response theorist because he plays down the role of the text. He contends that all the reader can really claim to know is their interpretation of the text and this interpretation is itself constructed by the reader, who has been shaped by their interpretive community.[39]

Second, as John Barton points out, reader-response theory is still considered a "fairly hot topic" within biblical studies.[40] Traditionally, and today, the focus of biblical scholars is principally on the author's intent and the text, accessed through a historical-grammatical approach.[41] This is evidenced by the majority of Bible commentaries assuming a historical-grammatical approach to the text, with little emphasis on the reader. Accordingly, David Clines assessment is that "historical criticism is the most salient form of biblical scholarship today."[42]

For my purposes however, three specific subfields within biblical studies/theology will be reviewed to show the way in which the role of the Bible reader is being considered, and who the Bible readers under consideration are. First, there are those who have made use of social scientific tools to consider how real readers read the Bible. Second, scholars have considered biblical texts in light of their own social location. Third, some have described and promoted particular Bible reading methods that consciously consider the role of the reader. There are other subfields that can assume a

---

37. Osborne, "Hermeneutics/Interpreting Paul." Other comparable labels are "soft" and "hard" e.g., Barton, "Thinking about Reader-Response Criticism," or "conservative" and "radical" e.g., Petric, "The Reader(s) and the Bible(s) 'Reader Versus Community' in Reader-Response Criticism and Biblical Interpretation"; and Vanhoozer, "The Reader in New Testament Interpretation."

38. Iser, *The Act of Reading*; Iser, *The Implied Reader*.

39. Fish, *Is There a Text in This Class?*

40. Barton, "Thinking about Reader-Response Criticism," 147.

41. Barton, "Historical-Critical Approaches"; Patte, "Critical Biblical Studies from a Semiotic Perspective"; Porter, "Why hasn't Reader-Response Criticism Caught on in New Testament Studies?".

42. Clines, "Historical Criticism," 542.

reader centered approach, such as Bible reception, however the empirical and contextual nature of my case study corresponds to the three subfields noted above, thus I concentrate on them.

Social-Scientific Approaches

Anthropology, a subfield within social science, has been fruitful in considering how the Bible is read or engaged with by faith communities all over the world. James Bielo's edited collection *The Social Life of Scriptures* gives a flavor of the diversity of this work. However, although there are examples of such research globally, including that by Eva Keller in Madagascar,[43] and Matthew Engelke in Zimbabwe,[44] much of the research has been based in the USA.[45] Bielo himself built upon this body of work when he undertook nineteen months studying different evangelical Bible study groups in Michigan.[46] Anna Strhan's ethnographic work in London with evangelical Anglican students is, in part, a British example of this anthropological enquiry into Bible engagement.[47] What is common to all these works is that those being researched are either regular Bible readers or active members of faith communities.

Theologians are also using social scientific tools to consider how British people read the Bible, this includes: feminist,[48] practical,[49] and contextual theologians.[50] Once again though, those being studied are regular Bible readers. For example, ordinary theology is as a subfield of practical theology that seeks to chart the "theological beliefs and processes of believing that find expression in the God-talk of those believers who have received no scholarly theological education."[51] Over the past ten years there has been a small but growing body of research which has assumed the label "ordinary theology," including "ordinary Christology,"[52] "ordinary Pentecostal

43. Keller, *The Road to Clarity*.
44. Engelke, *A Problem of Presence*.
45. Ammerman, *Bible Believers*; Ault, *Spirit and Flesh*; Crapanzano, *Serving the Word*; Davie, *Women in the Presence*; Malley, *How the Bible Works*; Wuthnow, *Sharing the Journey*.
46. Bielo, *Words upon the Word*.
47. Strhan, *Aliens and Strangers?*
48. For example see: Llewellyn, *Reading Feminism, and Spirituality*.
49. For example see: Francis, *Personality Type and Scripture*.
50. For example see: Morris, *Theology without Words*.
51. Astley, *Ordinary Theology*, 1.
52. Christie, *Ordinary Christology*.

theology,"⁵³ and is most recently seen in the edited collection: *Exploring Ordinary Theology: Everyday Christian Believing.*⁵⁴

Under the umbrella of "ordinary theology" Andrew Village, Andrew Rogers, and Ruth Perrin have all considered how lay British Christians interpret the Bible, something known as "ordinary hermeneutics." Andrew Village assumed a quantitative approach, designing a questionnaire that over four hundred Anglicans completed from eleven different churches. He focused on one text, Mark 9:14–29, and considered the participants' reading of it in light of various readerly issues, such as the influence of the participants' personality or church affiliation.⁵⁵ Andrew Rogers undertook ethnographic research to consider the use of the Bible at two evangelical churches in England, one charismatic and the other conservative.⁵⁶ Assuming a multi-method approach, Rogers spent over six months at each church, acting as a participant observer at services and Bible study groups, along with undertaking a questionnaire and interviewing church attendees.⁵⁷ Ruth Perrin principally used focus groups to explore how eighteen-to-thirty-five-year-olds⁵⁸ evangelicals read the Bible, (she briefly attend the churches they represented as well). In her case, she explored how they responded to three narratives that may be problematic to some as they contained elements of the supernatural, acts of divine violence and leading female characters (2 Kings 5, 1 Samuel 25 and Acts 12). By dividing the focus groups by age and evangelical tradition she explored how these two factors influence the readers' responses to the texts.⁵⁹ Where Village's research shed light on preselected areas he chose to investigate, Rogers' qualitative approached provided more flexibility, allowing the data to shape the lines of enquiry. In Perrin's case, she is able to set her findings into a wider context due to her also interviewing the relevant church leaders and undertaking participant observation in the churches.

Once again though, those being studied are regular Bible readers. Positively, this empirical approach employed by theologians and ethnographers

---

53. Cartledge, *Testimony of the Spirit.*
54. Astley and Francis, *Exploring Ordinary Theology.*
55. Village, *The Bible and lay People.*
56. Over time Rogers has distanced himself from the phrase "ordinary hermeneutics" e.g., Rogers, "Ordinary Hermeneutics and the Local Church," preferring the label "congregational hermeneutics." E.g., Rogers, "Congregational Hermeneutics: A Tale of Two Churches," which he borrows from Stuart Murray, *Biblical Interpretation in the Anabaptist Tradition.*
57. Rogers, *Congregational Hermeneutics.*
58. This age group is known as "Generation Y" or "Millennials".
59. Perrin, *The Bible Reading of Young Evangelicals.*

is one I will draw upon, for although my anticipated participants will be different, many of the methods these scholars have used are valid for my work. This is the first of the three examples demonstrating the influence of reader-response criticism within Bible-reading research and the narrowness of the sample being studied.

Social Locations and Bible Reading

Recently there has also been global interest in the contextual nature of Bible reading, with scholars often use the term "social location" to describe a particular context or setting that is understood to directly shape the reading. In some cases the role of the researcher is to note the different ways in which certain social locations are unconsciously informing a reader's response to a text, such as the influence of the reader's personality,[60] or geographical location.[61] In others, the reader is consciously allowing a specific social location, standpoint or ideology to inform their engagement with the Bible. The exact nature of the context which is said to shape the reading often varies, but examples include: feminist;[62] third world;[63] African, Asian or Latin American;[64] disabled;[65] postcolonial;[66] liberationist;[67] queer;[68] postmodern;[69] Rabbi;[70] sinner;[71] exile;[72] and various alternatives (such as an Oceania context,[73] or combinations of the above like a postcolonial feminist standpoint.[74] To a greater or lesser degree, reflexivity is a part of all these approaches. In other words, the author(s) has considered an individual passage, or the entire Bible, in light of a particular ideology, social location or

---

60. For example see: Francis, *Personality Type and Scripture*.
61. For example see: Powell, *What Do they Hear?* 11–27.
62. For example see: Brenner and Fontaine, *A Feminist Companion to Reading the Bible*.
63. For example see: Sugirtharajah, *Voices from the Margin*.
64. For example see: Levison and Pope-Levison, *Return to Babel*.
65. For example see: Avalos, et al., *This Abled Body*.
66. For example see: Sugirtharajah, *Exploring Postcolonial Biblical Criticism*.
67. For example see: Gottwald and Horsley, *The Bible and Liberation*.
68. For example see: Guest et al., *The Queer Bible Commentary*.
69. For example see: Castelli et al., *The Postmodern Bible*.
70. For example see: Magonet, *A Rabbi's Bible*.
71. For example see: Rowland and Roberts, *The Bible for Sinners*.
72. For example see: Brueggemann, *The Bible and Postmodern Imagination*.
73. For example see: Havea et al., *Bible, Boarders, Belonging(s)*.
74. For example see: Dube, *Postcolonial Feminist Interpretation of the Bible*.

life experience. Indeed, these three factors often inter-twine in the Bible reading that they present. Nevertheless, as I will shortly demonstrate some tend to assume a form of ideological criticism, others consider themselves to be doing contextual Bible readings, whilst still others identify with autobiographical criticism.

The studies listed above have generally been undertaken by academics who have been underrepresented in the field of biblical studies. Unfortunately the reflexivity that they employ is often missing from the white western males who have historically dominated this field, for they too have a social location that will have influenced their own engagement with the biblical texts.[75] As Brueggemann points out, "what was taken to be 'objective' was in fact the aggressive practice of privileged interpretations, mostly white, mostly male, mostly adherent to Enlightenment rationality."[76] However, even though many of the white males who have dominated biblical studies have come from Britain, there are those who have engaged with the Bible reflexively in light of their ideological standpoint, social location, or life experience.

David Clines argues for the place of ideological biblical criticism in *Interested Parties: The Ideology of Writers and Readers of the Hebrew Bible*,[77] and David Horrell is a specific example of this in his ecological reading of the Bible.[78] In other words, ecology is the ideology through which various biblical texts are engaged. Horrell is aware that the Bible is somewhat ambivalent towards environmental issues, but argues that it should be read in light of contemporary science, for such a reading would challenge a traditional Christian anthropocentric view of the world, and so:

> Reading the Bible afresh in light of the environmental issues that face us involves reconfiguring the landscape, recasting the story, seeing the whole thing differently, and at the same time seeing ourselves and our world differently too.[79]

Horrell's ideological criticism is a recuperative one where the Bible continues to play a positive role in his thinking. He notes though that this

---

75. Patte, "Acknowledging the Contextual Character of Male, European-American Critical Exegesis."

76. Brueggemann, "The Re-Emergence of Scripture," 155.

77. Ideological criticism also explores the ideology promoted by the text itself or emanating from the historical interpretation of the text, typically undertaken by the church, see: Davies, *Biblical Criticism*, 61–80. See also West, "Taming Texts of Terror," for a wider discussion on whether texts do or do not have ideologies.

78. Horrell, *The Bible and the Environment*; Horrell et al., *Ecological Hermeneutics*; and Horrell et al., *Greening Paul, Rereading the Apostle in a Time of Ecological Crisis*.

79. Horrell, *The Bible and the Environment*, 128.

need not always be the case, for in some instances it is rejected as being incompatible with the ideological stance of the reader, such as was the case for Daphne Hampson.[80]

There are also British contextual readings of the Bible where the author has consciously chosen to consider the text in light of their social location. The results of this are readings that are informed by and inform their context. For example, in Lloyd Pietersen's *Reading the Bible After Christendom* he reflects on how the Bible could be read in a British post-Christendom context. John Hull's book *In the Beginning There was Darkness* is another example of this. Hull is a British scholar who reads the Bible acutely aware of his blindness and its impact upon that reading. He describes the content of his monograph in this way:

> In these chapters I will enter into conversation with the Bible from my point of view as a blind person. I describe these as conversations because I am conscious of the fact that what the Bible says to me has changed since I lost my sight. This is not only true of the places where there is specific reference to blindness, but of the text as a whole: when I realized that the Bible was written by sighted people, I felt alienated from it.[81]

This book not only contains Hull's reflections on certain Bible passages, it also discusses wider philosophical and practical issues regarding blindness, the biblical text and the author's experiences. For example, reflecting on the actions of two anonymous blind men going to Jesus for healing (Matt 9:27–31), Hull recounts the only occasion when he sought "faith healing" and the lasting impression it left upon him.[82]

Hull's example overlaps with autobiographical biblical criticism, which is a way of reflecting on a Bible passage with the reader consciously aware of his or her own sense of identity and life experience. There are a number of international edited collections,[83] but I am unaware of many British examples of this approach to Bible reading. Stephen Moore's essay "Revolting Revelations" is one, as is Hugh Pyper's "The Bible as a Children's Book." Pyper recalls growing up in a Presbyterian Church in Edinburgh in the 1960s and the impact which singing metrical psalms had upon him as a child, and still does. His essay reflects on this and another childhood experience, reading

---

80. Hampson, *After Christianity*.
81. Hull, *In the Beginning There was Darkness*, 3.
82. Ibid., 34–39.
83. Anderson and Staley, *Taking it Personally*; Black, *The Recycled Bible*; Kitzberger, *The Personal Voice in Biblical Interpretation*; Kitzberger, *Autobiographical Biblical Criticism*.

Carol Kendall's *The Gammage Cup*. He notes that these experiences are ones which "I think, affected, or at least confirmed, my attitude to texts and still have repercussions in my approach to biblical reading."[84] For instance he, recalls some of the colorful, evocative and mysterious language used in the Psalms, commenting on Psalm 24 that:

> The tune was stirring, but the words have stuck because even then I felt their fascination. The personification of the doors singing and lifting up their heads was a curious excitement, as does the implied power of apostrophe in that weird word "Ye."[85]

Other poetry, such as Lewis Carroll's *Jabberwocky*, had a similar effect. In the case of the Psalms, this was language (or poetry) that some scholars regarded as childish or simple. In Pyper's experience however, it was a "gateway to a sense of language as a field of fantasy and imaginative construction."[86] Accordingly, he argues that "there is a childlike wonder in the possibilities of language that open up and deeper sense that there may be truths that are too much for language at its most eloquent."[87]

These then are some of the examples, where professional Bible readers, such as a biblical scholar, or members of faith communities, have engaged with the Bible consciously aware of their role as the reader. This may involve engaging with the text through a particular ideological lens, with reference to a particular context, or in light of their past experiences. What is common to them all is that the reader understands him- or herself as informing the reading and those missing from this inquiry are non-regular Bible readers.

Bible Reading Methods

My final example of the way in which the "turn to the reader" has influenced biblical studies and theology, is in the promotion of certain Bible reading methods which have gained a following amongst academics. Two such methods are Scriptural Reasoning and the Contextual Bible Study method (CBS). The practice of scriptural reasoning involves Christians, Jews, and Muslims reading and discussing their scriptures together, usually focusing on a particular topic or individual.[88] This method emerged in mid-1990s

---

84. Pyper, "The Bible as a Children's Book," 143.
85. Ibid., 144.
86. Ibid., 150.
87. Ibid., 150.
88. Higton and Muers, *The TEXT in PLAY*.

North America with Peter Ochs coining the term "scriptural reasoning."[89] In Britain, David Ford and the Cambridge Inter-Faith Program have championed it.[90] CBS on the other hand traces its roots back to 1950s and 1960s Latin America and Liberation Theology. It parallels my own work most and so is the final example.

In the mid-twentieth century an evangelization and education drive by the Roman Catholic Church, along with a shortage of priests within Latin America (and in particular Brazil) led to the training up of lay readers who would lead small community Bible studies, known as "Base communities."[91] In this way lay people were given the tools, opportunity, and authority to read the biblical text for themselves. These small groups followed a see, judge, act approach, whereby their own context (see) was brought to the biblical text and considered (judge), with a practical result anticipated (act).[92] These stages have remained central to the CBS method that emerged from it.[93] So significant was this movement that in 1968 the Latin American Episcopal Council (CELAM) in Medellín acknowledged and affirmed it.

The South African Gerald West adapted this approach and gave it the name Contextual Bible Study (CBS) method. He described it as having four aspects:

1. A commitment to read the Bible from a poor and oppressed perspective.

2. A commitment to read the Bible in community.

3. A commitment to read the Bible critically.

4. A commitment to read the Bible for individual and social transformation.[94]

In practice, CBS is a setting whereby a group of people can openly discuss a biblical text and its outworking for their lives and community. In an attempt to provide space for those on the margins to speak, the Bible reading and discussion is facilitated rather than led and everyone's contribution is noted down. Unsurprisingly those who typically participate are Christians

---

89. Higton, "Scriptural Reasoning."

90. Ford, "An Interfaith Wisdom."

91. Dawson, "The Origins and Character of the Base Ecclesial Community"; Muskus, *The Origins and Early Development of Liberation Theology in Latin America*, 12–13.

92. Brown, *Gustavo Gutierrez*, 118.

93. West, "Do Two Walk Together?"

94. West, *Contextual Bible Study*, 12.

or on the margins of Christianity and have something in common, such as geographical location.[95] CBS does incorporate aspects of historical and grammatical criticism, but also considers the reader and their context,[96] understanding that each reading community will engage with the biblical texts in a unique way.[97]

CBS has gained prominence within the British Church and amongst academics that have an interest in real readers and the Bible.[98] Much like the Bible readers studied by anthropologists, CBS readers are often active members of faith communities. However, it has also been used with those on the margins of the church and society. For example, Alison Peden recounts its use in Cornton Vale Women's prison, Stirling. As a prison chaplain she led a weekly CBS session, adapting the method for that setting. She reflects:

> CBS provided a wonderful way for women to make some sense of imprisonment and to give language to their experience. They often recognized their lives in the Bible and so felt validated in their identities.[99]

Susannah Cornwall and David Nixon have also used CBS with a group of homeless people,[100] and John Riches writes of its use amongst male prisoners and ex-offenders in Scotland.[101] Once again though, those taking part have some connection to Christianity. In Peden's case, the participants were prisoners linked to the chaplaincy, for Cornwall and Nixon they were clients at a Christian run soup kitchen. So although these Bible readers could be identified as being outside the church, they had a personal and practical link with Christianity.

---

95. Lawrence, *The Word in Place*.

96. Riches, *What is Contextual Bible Study?* 37–45.

97. There are similarities between CBS and ordinary theology, for both are principally concerned with the views and insights of non-professional Christians, (that is, not clergy or academics), and Astley's phrase "ordinary theology" (see: Astley, *Ordinary Theology*) echoes Gerald West's "ordinary readers" (see: West, *Contextual Bible Study; The Academy of the Poor*).

98. Lawrence, *The Word in Place*; Riches, *What is Contextual Bible Study?*

99. Peden, "Contextual Bible Study at Cornton Vale Women's Prison, Stirling," 18.

100. Cornwall and Nixon "Readings from the Road."

101. Riches, *What is Contextual Bible Study?* 13–15. Others have facilitated similar Bible reading approaches with those at the margins of society. For example see, Andrew Curtis "An Encounter with Ordinary Real Readers Reading the Gospels" and Avaren Ipsen, *Sex Working and the Bible,* who have both considered how sex workers read certain Bible passages.

Summary

This short survey demonstrates that "the turn to the reader" has not just occurred in literary theory, but has influenced the shape and content of present day biblical studies and theology. Practical theologians are using tools from social science to consider how "ordinary" Christians are reading the Bible and biblical scholars are becoming more aware of their social location and its influence on their reading of the Bible. Moreover, some have then invested in Bible reading methods that allow lay Christians to do the same. However, as I have consistently demonstrated, those missing from this research are those who are not regularly exposed to the Bible, either in an academic or religious setting. In light of the decline of Christianity in Britain, most of the population make up this cohort.[102]

An Unheard Voice

In 2012, Theos, a Christian think-tank, published *Post-Religious Britain? The Faith of the Faithless*. This report drew on three different surveys that had been taken over the last four years to gain a better understanding of non-religiosity in Britain.[103] It concluded that 81% of those sampled were not regular Bible readers.[104] A 2010 survey of England and Wales conducted by Christian Research concluded that 87% of those polled were not regular Bible readers.[105] In 2008 CODEC undertook an earlier survey of the public's Bible reading habits and knowledge, and concluded that 74% of those interviewed were not regular Bible readers.[106] These results must be handled

---

102. What follows considers the adult population. There has been significant research into children and young people's engagement with the Bible, for example see Freathy "Gender, Age, Attendance at a Place of Worship and Young People's Attitudes Towards the Bible" and Briggs, *How Children Read Biblical Narrative*.

103. "Non-religion" is an emerging phenomenon. In Britain this is principally due to the significant increase in people identifying in this way, 25% of the population of England and Wales identified as having "no religion" in the 2011 Census, a 10% increase from 2001 (Office of National Statistics, "Religion in England and Wales 2011").

104. Theos, *Post-Religious Britain?* 20–21. The exact figures were as follows: 61% never read the Bible, 10% read it once a year, 10% read it several times a year, 4% read it once a month, 3% read it several times a month, 3% read it once a week, 3% read it several times a week, 5% read it once a day and 1% read it several times a day.

105. Christian Research, *Bible Engagement in England and Wales*, 44. The exact figures were as follows: 67% never read the Bible, 10% hardly ever read it, 3% read it once a year, 7% read it a few times a year, 2% read it once a month, 1% read it once a fortnight, 4% read it once a week and 5% read it daily/almost daily.

106. The exact figures were as follows: 13.3% never read/use the Bible, 21.4% can't remember reading it, 26.5% read it more than a year ago, 12.8% read it in the last year,

cautiously, for different surveys word questions differently and the public often respond by giving more socially acceptable answers. Furthermore, all these figures do not refer solely to people's personal Bible reading habits some include reading the Bible in a church service, wedding, or other setting. However it consistently suggests that the majority of the British population are not regular Bible readers. Clive Field recently reviewed over 123 national and thirty-five local surveys undertaken since the Second World War concerning the Bible and the British public. He concluded that: "Readership in the Bible has declined, with only around one in ten reading it at least weekly and three-quarters less than once a year or never."[107] These findings suggest that the majority of the British population have been excluded from Bible reading research.

In light of this decline in Bible readership, some may be tempted to conclude that biblical literacy in Britain is also diminishing. Certainly research shows a similar decrease in Bible ownership, knowledge, and belief.[108] However, the term "biblical literacy" and its assumed downturn are contested.[109] For instance, the decline in Bible readership noted, lends itself to the claim that the Bible is now less of an influence upon British people and culture than it once was. However, the recent edited collection by Katie Edwards, *Rethinking Biblical Literacy*, in part argues that biblical images and tropes continue to be found throughout British (and global) culture, something Yvonne Sherwood refers to as the "afterlives" of the Bible.[110] Accordingly, one of the contributors to this volume, Matthew Collins, writes:

> rumours of the Bible's "loss" to modern society are greatly exaggerated. It may no longer play such an explicitly prominent role in daily life, yet nevertheless continues to saturate our culture and heritage.[111]

Two points are worth noting in this discussion. First, some of the evidence used to argue for or against a decline in biblical literacy is not longitudinal in nature, but rather provides a snapshot of one or more aspects

---

8.6% read it in the last month and 17.1% read it in the last week. My thanks to Pete Phillips, the Director of Research at CODEC who provided this information (personal communication, October 30, 2012).

107. Field, "Is the Bible Becoming a Closed Book?" 517.

108. Ibid., 503–28.

109. Avalos, "In Praise of Biblical Illiteracy"; Crossley, "What the Bible Really Means"; Hine et al., "Practicing Biblical Literacy"; and Rodriguez, "Bible Illiteracy and the Contribution of Biblical Higher Education."

110. Sherwood, *A Biblical Text and Its Afterlives*.

111. Collins, "Loss of the Bible and the Bible in *Lost*," 90.

of biblical literacy at a particular point in time. For example, Philip Davies argues for a decline in biblical literacy quoting figures from the CODEC survey I noted earlier, even though that survey only refers to one-off data gathered in 2008.[112] This is not always the case, a few works have incorporated a longitudinal component,[113] or purposefully gathered data from different age groups in society, as seen in the research behind the 2014 *Pass it On* campaign by Bible Society. Second, some suggest that their research addresses the issue of biblical literacy, but in truth it only deals with one aspect of biblical literacy, such as Bible ownership, as Davies does,[114] or a selective cultural manifestation of biblical images and tropes, as is seen with Christopher Meredith.[115]

There is still no consensus regarding what should or should not be understood as biblical literacy or indeed if it is more accurate to speak of biblical literacies. The broadest definition I am aware of is given by Pete Phillips, and encompasses seven areas.[116] They are an ability to read the Bible, knowledge of its content, awareness of its significance, ability to apply it, recognition of biblical allusions in a culture, an ability to embed biblical knowledge back into a culture, and playful use of biblical tropes and images. There has also not been a longitudinal study that has addressed the topic of British biblical literacy in all its breadth, demonstrating the need for further research on these issues. However, for my purposes I will refrain from using the term "biblical literacy." Instead I will use "Bible reading," which overlaps with the subject of biblical literacy, but better describes the phenomenon I am concentrating upon.[117]

The figures I presented earlier on Bible reading are part of a wider trajectory where church attendance and other Christian activities and identities are also seen to be in decline.[118] Therefore, not only do the majority of the population not read the Bible regularly but they also do not attend church

---

112. Davies, "Whose Bible? Anyone's?"
113. Crossley, *Harnessing Chaos*.
114. Davies, "Whose Bible? Anyone's?"
115. Meredith, "A Big Room for Poo."
116. This was in personal communication, June 10, 2015.

117. The word "biblicism" has been used to describe the Bible, its role, function, symbolism, and identity within a particular community or setting (e.g., Malley, *How the Bible Works*). However, it is also used to describe a particular view of the Bible that emphasizes its unity, clarity, infallibility and centrality to the Christian life (e.g., Smith, *The Bible Made Impossible*). To avoid confusion, I do not use the term.

118. Although the decline I have focused upon is well documented, there are counter-trends challenging it, such as a growth in Pentecostal and Charismatic churches. For a recent overview of religious change in Britain, see Davie, *Religion in Britain*.

on a regular basis either. The 2012 Theos report concluded that 73% of those polled do not attend a religious service regularly.[119] The 2010 Christian Research survey found that 85% of those sampled did not attend church regularly.[120] The CODEC survey indicated that over 75% of people did not regularly attend a place of worship.[121] The figure that Peter Brierley arrived at following the church Census in 2005 was that 92.7% of the English population did not attend church on a regular basis.[122] Reflecting on the decades of decline in church attendance along with the corresponding decline of other Christian rituals like baptism and activities such as Sunday school attendance, Callum Brown entitled his book *The Death of Christian Britain*.[123] Echoing this, Lloyd Pietersen describes present-day Britain as a society where "it can no longer be assumed that ordinary people know the contents of the Bible or even the basic outline of the Christian story."[124]

Thus, the bulk of the British population, perhaps around 75%–93%, do not regularly attend church and, similarly, 74%-87% do not regularly read the Bible. Unsurprisingly, it is those who do not regularly attend church, or do not identify with a particular religion that read the Bible least.[125] Christian Research notes this overlap,[126] as does Theos who found that 96% of those who self-designated as not belonging to a religion did not read the Bible regularly.[127] One conclusion from this data is that most

---

119. Theos, *Post-Religious Britain?* 19. The exact figures were as follows: 45% never attend a religious service, 13% attend yearly, 15% attend several times a year, 6% attend monthly, 4% attend several times a month, 10% attend weekly, 4% attend several times a week, 3% attend daily.

120. Christian Research, *Bible Engagement in England and Wales*, 25. The exact figures were as follows: 69% never/hardly ever attend church, 5% attend yearly, 11% attend a few times a year, 2% attend monthly, 3% attend fortnightly, 10% attend weekly, 1% attend daily.

121. The exact figures were as follows: 48% never attend a place of worship, 25% attend once to six times a year, 3% attend seven to twelve times a year, 3% attend thirteen to twenty-five times a year, and 19% attend twenty-six times a year or more (personal communication, October 30, 2012).

122. Brierley, *Pulling Out of the Nose Dive*, 151. The exact figures were as follows: 85.5% never attend church, 4.6% attend yearly, 1.9% attend twice a year, 0.7% attend quarterly, 0.4% attend monthly, 1.7% attend fortnightly, and 5.2% attend weekly.

123. For a good summary of this subject and associated data see Bruce, "The Demise of Christianity in Britain."

124. Pietersen, *Reading the Bible After Christendom*, 5–6.

125. Field, "Is the Bible Becoming a Closed Book?" 520.

126. Christian Research, *Bible Engagement in England and Wales*, 15.

127. Theos, *Post-Religious Britain?* 20–21. The exact figures were as follows: 82% never read the Bible, 7% read it once a year, 6% read it several times a year, 1% read it once a month, 2% read it several times a month and 1% read it several times a week.

of the British adult population have been excluded from academic research into the role of the reader in Bible reading. It is something of a paradox therefore that many who promote contextual readings of the Bible, do so understanding that those taking part are often unheard voices from the margins of society or the church. However, in Britain, it is the *largest* group within society who have not been given the opportunity to voice their readings of the Bible.

Comparable Research

In light of the near singular focus upon regular Bible readers, demonstrated in this chapter, a research question emerged: How would people, who are not regular Bible readers, in other words the majority of the British population, read the Bible if given the opportunity? As I have just shown, there are various surveys into the British public's use of, views on, beliefs about or attitudes towards the Bible.[128] Smaller qualitative pieces of work have also been undertaken. Nick Spencer interviewed sixty people who did not regularly attend church and discussed various aspects of life and faith, including their views on the Bible.[129] F. Morgan undertook a case study exploring the opinions and biblical awareness of young adults who do not attend church.[130] Dawn Llewellyn interviewed post-Christian women and found that some still selectively read the Bible as an aid for their spiritual development.[131] James Crossley also interviewed people, in his case thirty individuals from Barrow-in-Furness, and contrasted their views on the historical role of the Bible in British culture with that of David Cameron's.[132] Significantly though, none of these works actually involved people reading a biblical text. Although different methods have been used and a variety of approaches can be seen, there still remains a lack of research into how most British people would actually read the Bible.

I am aware of three lesser-known pieces of research that involved non-regular Bible readers reading different sections of the Bible. As I will show, all three had different aims and none sought to consider the act of Bible reading in the way I do. In Edinburgh, Fergus Macdonald undertook a qualitative project, which in part considered "how far can meditative

---

128. Other surveys include Gill et al., "Is Religious Belief Declining in Britain?"; and the Catholic Biblical Federation, *Scriptures Reading*.
129. Spencer, *Beyond the Fringe*.
130. Morgan, "Raising Awareness of the Bible in Contemporary British Society."
131. Llewellyn, *Reading, Feminism, and Spirituality*, 65–87.
132. Crossley, "Brexit Barrow."

engagement with specific psalm texts facilitate the spiritual quest of young adults for personal meaning and spiritual enlightenment?"[133] Thirteen university students volunteered to take part, all who had a deep interest in spirituality and varying degrees of religious affiliation and practice.[134] They were all under the age of thirty, and only three were British. Although Macdonald does not explicitly state it, three of the participants may have been regular Bible readers as they attended church on a regular basis. The others, it is assumed, were not regular Bible readers.[135] The participants took part in six *Lectio Divina* meditations each based on a different psalm.[136] The students committed themselves to spending at least ten minutes a day meditating on the respective psalm and journaling their interaction with it for a week. At the end of which members of the group met together for a *Lectio Divina* based on the psalm and shared excerpts from their journals. This process was repeated for each of the six psalms. Macdonald concluded that the participants had a

> meaningful conversation with the Psalms. In exploring the extent to which the conversation is theological, i.e. is referenced to God, [. . .] the less religiously active respondents moved nearer to contemplating a relationship with God, although none claim to have had an encounter with Ultimate Being.[137]

This work is located within the field of practical theology and reflects Macdonald's interest in scripture engagement, but the aims of this study were different to the emerging research question I have identified. He considered if meditating on the Psalms was of spiritual benefit for these young adults, whereas I am more interested in the act of Bible reading. His participants were from a variety of nationalities whilst my focus is upon British people.

Alan Le Grys considered how twenty-two people might read Psalm 23 and Psalm 36.[138] Two participants were Jewish, fifteen were Christian (five Pentecostal, five Anglican, and five Catholic) and five identified as "non-churchgoers."[139] All of them lived in England, although not all the Pentecostal and Catholic participants were born in England. Of the five

---

133. Macdonald, "The Psalms and Spirituality," 2.

134. Macdonald, "Engaging the Scriptures," 197.

135. The other participants were from a variety of faiths (or none) and five attended church on a yearly or twice yearly basis.

136. Pss 22, 30, 55, 73, 74 and 126 were used as they were considered to have values or subject matter that the participants could easily relate to.

137. Macdonald, "The Psalms and Spirituality," 186.

138. My thanks to Andrew Rogers who alerted me to this study.

139. Le Grys, *Shaped by God's Story*.

non-churchgoers four of them had been brought-up attending church and none actively practiced another religion. Le Grys compared and contrasted how these different groups read the Psalms.[140]

In a one-to-one interview setting, each of the twenty-two participants discussed their up-bringing and various subjects related to the Christian faith, one being the Bible.[141] They were also invited to read through the Psalms and discuss them. In contrast to Macdonald, Le Grys concluded:

> There appears to be little expectation that Bible reading might be drawing the reader into a closer relationship with God. This finding is confirmed by the evidence from the non-church goers, who also appeared to regard the Bible primarily as a resource for moral and doctrinal teaching. Scripture is essentially a guidance manual for right belief and right behavior.[142]

In part, the difference in conclusions reflects the differing aims and methods of each piece of work. Ultimately, Le Grys' research did not address my research question for he principally explored how Christians from different traditions read the Bible and to what extent their reading was normative, formative and transformative.[143] The inclusion of non-churchgoers was as a source of comparison.[144] Furthermore, the majority of the non-churchgoing participants had grown up attending church regularly, which influenced their attitude towards, and reading of, the Bible.

The final research project I am aware of was undertaken by Tiffany Webster, and is entitled *When the Bible Meets the Black Stuff: A Contextual Bible Study Experiment*.[145] Webster carried out ten CBS sessions over a ten-month period with a group of five South Derbyshire coalminers. In light of her identity as a pagan, and her participants being men who do not regularly attend church or read the Bible, she adapted CBS, eliminating the need for the facilitator and participants to be Christians or consider themselves marginalized.[146] She also removed the need for the facilitator to

---

140. He found the interviews became too long if both Psalms were discussed, so he focused on Psalm 23.

141. There were other components to his research, such as a series of Bible studies that he led and a questionnaire distributed amongst his own church members.

142. Ibid., 60.

143. Ibid., 132–34.

144. Ibid., 13.

145. Much of what follows was detailed in email correspondence with Webster (personal communication July 2014).

146. A few did describe themselves as "cultural Christians but not practicing Christians."

ask questions and amended the final "Action Plan" phase of CBS to include therapy and self-growth.

Her aim was not only to see what contextually sensitive readings would emerge in light of their social location as coalminers.[147] She also planned to critically refine CBS in order to widen its future scope and inclusivity, with specific emphasis on adapting CBS for use in the West. Unfortunately the men were all made redundant whilst undertaking the research and the subsequent CBS sessions became a pseudo-therapeutic setting where they were able to verbalize their feelings associated with the pit closure.

Webster's research did examine how people who do not regularly read the Bible would read it but she located this engagement within a CBS setting, and part of the purpose of her study was to redesign CBS for a new context. Thus, there still remains the need to undertake a piece of research that primarily addresses the question: How would a person who does not regularly read the Bible or go to church, read the Bible?

Conclusion

This chapter began by noting the "turn to the reader" which had occurred in literary theory and hermeneutics. I then suggested that this "turn" had impacted biblical studies and theology, demonstrating this by presenting three diverse subfields within these disciplines. I noted that in practical theology, scholars are using social scientific tools to consider how lay people read the Bible. In biblical studies, scholars are writing themselves into their textual analysis, aware that their ideology, social location and/or life experience informs their reading. Finally, some of these scholars have also promoted Bible reading methods, such as CBS, which acknowledge and value the reader's contribution.

However, what this survey demonstrates is that most of the research being carried out into Bible reading concerns regular Bible readers be they clergy, laity, or academics. In Britain, the majority of the population cannot be described as regular Bible readers and are missing from this field of study. Finally, three recent research projects were presented that to some degree involved non-regular Bible readers, but these projects either did not directly addressed how the Bible was being read or did so but within an established Bible reading framework, showing the need for my own inquiry.

---

147. She chose biblical texts dealing with subjects pertinent to coalmining, such as Employee-Employer relationships (Jer 18:1–12 and Matt 20:1–16) or Hell/Darkness/Death/Condemnation (Job 17:1–16 and Rev 20:1–15).

The following chapter turns to consider the methodological options available, for the nature of the research question informs the methodology which is adopted.[148] I argue for the use of a qualitative case study and for the narrowing of the research in two ways. First, the profile of the participants is considered, for the type of sample would influence the results of the study. Second, it seemed improbable that people would read the entire Bible, so I had to select individual passages that my participants would read. In this way, my initial research question was further refined and a bespoke research project began to emerge.

---

148. David and Sutton, *Social Research*, 13–15.

Chapter 2

Research Design—Methodology, Sample, and Texts

Research often begins with a broad research question or topic that is refined over time. In my case, there were three aspects of the proposed enquiry that now required consideration: the methodological underpinning, the participant profile, and the biblical texts. In this chapter I argue that because of the inductive nature of my research enquiry a qualitative methodology and case study approach are best suited to my project. In light of this decision, my participant selection is then considered. I revisit some of the surveys presented in chapter 1, highlighting the gender differences that they found, for it was men who were least likely to read the Bible regularly. Accordingly, I decide to focus on British men rather than the population in general. Finally, I suggest the use of five particular texts for it is unlikely that my volunteers would be willing to read the whole Bible. In this way, the foundations of my research project are put in place.

Methodology—A Qualitative Case Study

Quantitative and qualitative methodologies are two approaches commonly used by social scientists. One difference between these two avenues of research lies in the kind of knowledge they are trying to access about the social world.[1] A quantitative methodology is concerned with general patterns and trends, often assuming a deductive approach. It has a more objective view of the social world, and deals with numbers and percentages, thus the size and representativity of the sample are crucial.[2] The surveys I highlighted in chapter 1 are based on this methodology, for they involved large numbers of British people answering questions concerning their views of the Bible,

---

1. Sarantakos, *Social Research*, 29.
2. Ibid., 365–403.

religion or Christianity. Andrew Village's study into lay Anglicans' reading of Mark 9:14–29 assumed a quantitative methodology, using a questionnaire which over four hundred participants completed.[3]

A qualitative methodology focuses more on particular experiences and processes. It often takes an inductive approach, a subjective and relational view of the social world, and deals with words and meanings, thus depth of analysis rather than sample size is key.[4] This methodology is more commonly used by those who are exploring the nature of Bible reading practices, for they are usually undertaking research which seeks to detail processes or shed light on implicit practices which are not easily accessed through a quantitative approach. For example, Brian Malley adopts a qualitative methodology to explore the "cognitive and social processes that cause evangelical Christians to feel that the Bible is 'living and active' in their lives."[5] Andrew Rogers also chooses a qualitative methodology in order to study "the shape of ordinary hermeneutics within English evangelical churches."[6] These two scholars limit their research to one (Malley) or two (Rogers) churches rather than hundreds, as might be the case if they had used a quantitative methodology. However, what is lost in sample size is gained in depth of analysis, for a more holistic perspective can be gained and the different interlocking aspects of Bible engagement identified and teased out.

Like Malley and Rogers, my own research is best suited to a qualitative methodology for I too am not attempting to prove a particular hypothesis or challenge an established theory, rather I am seeking to understand and describe how the Bible is read. My research question is an open one and assumes that an in-depth investigation of the complex activity of reading will be required. This inductive approach lends itself to a smaller sample, from which rich detailed data can emerge and shape the subsequent lines of enquiry.

Although I have presented quantitative and qualitative methodologies as distinct approaches, they are not mutually exclusive. Matthew David and Carole Sutton argue that all research contains both quantitative

---

3. Village, *The Bible and Lay People*.
4. Snape and Spencer, "The Foundations of Qualitative Research," 3–5.
5. Malley, *How the Bible Works*, 1.
6. He also asked: "How are ordinary hermeneutics mediated both internally (from within the church) and externally (from without the church)? How transformative of congregational horizons are these configurations of ordinary hermeneutics? How might these configurations be more transformative?" See: Rogers, "Ordinary Biblical Hermeneutics and the Transformation of Congregational Horizons within English Evangelicalism," 15.

and qualitative elements,[7] and Colin Robson highlights the emergence of "multi-strategy research" which consciously incorporates both elements into the research design.[8] With reference to the study of religion, and in particular ordinary theology, Jeff Astley argues for the inclusion of both methodologies:

> Where qualitative research adopts what has been described as an "inner perspective" on the phenomena being studied, quantitative research facilitates an "outer perspective." I believe that each has its own contribution to make in the study of ordinary theology.[9]

An example of this methodological blurring is Fergus Macdonald's work, which I described in the preceding chapter. He assumes a deductive approach, linked to a quantitative methodology, because he is testing a hypothesis regarding people's spiritual engagement with certain psalms. However, he uses methods commonly identified with qualitative research because he wants to capture the personal, subjective element of these readings.[10] In my case, there are two instances where elements of a quantitative approach can be found. First, as I will later describe, in the questionnaires used to explore my participants' readings of the texts I include a series of questions that are deductive in nature, in that they stem from contemporary Bible reading research. For instance, asking the participant if he thought the meaning of the text was located in the world of the author, the text, or the reader? Second, in this book I will on occasion use tables (Table 1) or charts (Figures 10, 11 and 12) to present my data, and will refer to numbers and percentages on occasion. My use of these devices normally associated with quantitative research does not reflect the introduction of an alternative methodology, but rather is an attempt to present certain parts of my data in an accessible way, for at its heart this is a qualitative piece of research.

Under "qualitative research" different research methods and approaches can be used. One of those growing in popularity is the case study.[11] There is no single agreed definition of "case study," however it usually "refers to research that investigates a few cases, often just one, in considerable depth."[12] The objective is "a deep understanding of the actors, interactions,

---

7. David and Sutton, *Social Research*, 96.
8. Robson, *Real World Research*, 29–30.
9. Astley, *Ordinary Theology*, 98.
10. Macdonald, "The Psalms and Spirituality," 45.
11. Yin, *Case Study Research*.
12. Hammersley and Gomm, "Introduction," 3.

sentiments, and behaviors occurring for a specific process through time."[13] This focus on depth and detail correlates closely with the qualitative methodology I have adopted and by choosing to undertake a case study my research is provided with an appropriate boundary for it enables me to focus on one particular reading site. Case studies are also particularly sensitive to the context of the research,[14] thus I decided to define my project as a case study and so locate my fieldwork at one site rather than multiple sites. Such a decision fits with the contextual nature of reading that understands every site to inform the readings hosted there,[15] and so by focusing on one site I should gain insights particular to it.

I am not alone in undertaking a case study to explore how a particular individual or group reads the Bible, James Bielo also did.[16] He researched the place and function of Bible study groups in the lives of American evangelical Christians, and in part I follow his example. Bielo undertook an ethnographic study involving nineteen different Bible study groups (attending 324 Bible study meetings), but only reflects on five of them in *Words Upon the Word: An Ethnography of Evangelical Group Bible Study*. The five that he discusses are each presented as individual case studies that form a single study which has one central claim, that "Evangelical Bible study is organized by a series of practices, logics and tensions that are deeply embedded in the broader cultural scene of American Evangelicalism."[17] Each of the five groups is used to highlight a different aspect integral to evangelical Bible study. These are: biblical authority/ideology and the related interpretive practice, developing intimacy in Bible study, the role of shared interests for a group, using Bible study to prepare to witness, and the place of Bible study in the formation of religious identity.

Bielo's decision to present five of his nineteen groups was an attempt to balance the need for breadth and depth in his research. He could have focused upon one group and so produce something of considerable depth but limited breadth, or he could have incorporated all nineteen groups into a much broader piece, but one where no one group was extensively considered. Some scholars who have explored Bible reading practices have assumed a "narrow and deep" approach. For instance, Mike Jennings studied nine emerging adults' spiritual engagement with the Bible.[18] However, in

13. Woodside, *Case Study Research*, 16.
14. Harding, *Qualitative Data Analysis From Start to Finish*, 16.
15. Riches, *What is Contextual Bible Study?* 23–24.
16. Bielo, *Words upon the Word*.
17. Ibid., 5.
18. Jennings, "Word and Spirit."

order to adequately chart the interweaving nature of Bible reading he did not consider all nine participants in depth but focused upon one reader (Simon), who Jennings presents as representative of the group. This approach provides a rich description of a particular reader, and is valued by qualitative research on account of its thoroughness. The attention to detail increases the validity of the claims made regarding Simon's reading, however it does result in the other eight participants being side-lined and a lack of evidence that Simon was representative of the wider group.

Other scholars, like Fergus Macdonald,[19] or Alan Le Grys,[20] adopted a "broad and shallow" approach. They present their participants as one unit, often providing quotes from different readers to demonstrate either the centrality of a theme or the divergence found within the group. This approach enables all the participants to be represented within the thesis and the use of multiple members to evidence key findings is an established technique used to demonstrate the validity of the themes presented. However, by giving voice to all the participants less depth and context is given to each, and so there is the danger of misrepresentation.

There is no perfect approach and I will attempt to navigate a middle road, as Bielo does. I will present my data as one case study, with one central claim, which is comprised of a series of mini arguments. At times these are made using individual readers that I present as mini-case studies, reflecting a "narrow and deep" approach. For example, when arguing for the influence of the reader's experiences upon their reading of the biblical texts, I present two readers who illustrate the point. By focusing upon two men in depth, I can provide the thick descriptions that are required. These participants should be understood to represent a wider group of men within this case study, but not the whole cohort. However, on the occasion that the findings relate to all the participants, such as the influence of their beliefs upon their readings, I present data from a much wider number of readers, which leans towards the "broad and shallow" approach. In this way then I attempt to balance the need for breadth and depth.

Qualitative case studies have a particular weakness: inappropriate generalizing or comparing of cases. George Steinmetz unpacks the multifaceted argument that the findings from one case study should not be compared with another (or other research findings) for they are incommensurable.[21] At its heart this view stems from an understanding that different terms or traits found in one context cannot be naïvely matched to corresponding

---

19. Macdonald, "The Psalms and Spirituality."
20. Le Grys, *Shaped by God's Story*.
21. Steinmetz, "Odious Comparisons," 384–90.

terms or traits from another. Furthermore, comparing cases can lead to misappropriation, misrepresentation, exoticization, essentialization, romanticizing, and other-ing. The result of comparing cases can be distortion.[22] Nonetheless, comparing cases has also produced insights that were not obvious prior to the comparison and contribute to a greater awareness of the topic being considered.[23] To that end, aware of the dangers mentioned above, I have chosen to bring my data into conversation with other case studies, ethnographies, surveys, insights from literary theorists, social psychologists, and others. The result of this should be a strong and expansive interdisciplinary piece with links made across academic disciplines and my findings being further illuminated.

There are other weaknesses associated with this approach, for example a lack of reflexivity on the part of the researcher can detract from the study and a desire for thick rich descriptions can produce too much data and so swamp the researcher. However, these potential pitfalls do not mean that undertaking a qualitative case study is a fraught process, rather aware of these dangers I hoped that what was produced could accommodate them. Indeed, one of the strengths of a case study is that by focusing on one setting in greater depth, they have been useful in problematizing commonly held assumptions.[24] Thus, my case study will contribute to the on-going discussion on real readers reading the Bible in Britain by giving voice to some people from a particular subgroup of society who have never been heard.

Theoretical Sampling—A Focus on Men

The implication of a qualitative methodology upon my sampling approach is that I will not attempt to gain a large, representative cohort of the British population but instead will concentrate on a small select group who meet the required criteria.[25] The Bible reading surveys mentioned in the previous chapter were instrumental in guiding this process, for they showed that men were less likely to have an interest in the Bible than women.[26] For example, Christian Research found that 83% of men compared with 73% of women either hardly ever or never read the Bible and men were less likely to have

22. Povinelli, "Radical Worlds."
23. Handler, "The Uses of Incommensurability in Anthropology."
24. Flyvbjerg, "Case Study"; Gerring, *Case Study Research*, 37–63.
25. Snape and Spencer, "The Foundations of Qualitative Research," 3–5.
26. This gender difference has been seen in young people as well, see: Freathy, "Gender, Age, Attendance at a Place of Worship and Young People's Attitudes towards the Bible."

a Bible at home (45% compared with 59% of women).[27] Other research has produced similar findings. For instance, David Clines also noted that men (61%) are less likely to own a Bible compared with women (81%), and they are more likely to have a dismissive attitude towards the Bible (35% compared with 18% of women).[28] Ben Clements similarly highlights this gender difference when considering people's beliefs about the Bible as found in national surveys from 1979 onwards. He concludes that women are more likely to believe the Bible is the word of God and that the Old and New Testaments have divine authority.[29] In light of much of this data, Field concludes: "On all measures women are somewhat more Bible-centric than men."[30] He goes on to suggest that the present-day profile of the person least likely to read the Bible is male, does not go to church, is under the age of twenty-five and comes from social band DE.[31] Jan Harrison concluded something similar approximately thirty years ago,[32] when she noted that the person least likely to own a Bible was male, seldom or never attended church, was under the age of thirty-four and came from social class C2 or DE.[33] She further adds that they left school at fifteen, had children under ten years of age in the household, were not working, lived in a city, were single, had an unfavorable attitude to the church, found God unimportant in their lives and identified as Roman Catholic.

These figures are comparable with the gender difference noted amongst churchgoers, for within Britain, it is also men who are least likely to attend church. A nationwide survey by Tearfund in 2007 concluded that:

> Women are more regular churchgoers than men (19% vs. 11%) and also more likely to be infrequent attendees or open dechurched (18% vs. 12% men). Men are much more likely to be closed non-churched i.e. with no prior experience of church and unlikely to change their ways.[34]

---

27. Christian Research, *Bible Engagement in England and Wales*, 31, 44.

28. Clines, *The Bible and the Modern World*, 68.

29. Clements, *Surveying Christian Beliefs and Religious Debates in Post-War Britain*.

30. Field, "Is the Bible Becoming a Closed Book?" 518.

31. Ibid., 507, 518. Field also notes that men from social group DE are more likely to personally own a Bible and view it as true, although they are least likely to read it, know its content or have one at home.

32. Harrison, *Attitudes to Bible, God, Church*.

33. Social class has been graded A, B, C1, C2, D and E, with DE referring to the working class (D) and those on the lowest income in society (E).

34. Tearfund, "Churchgoing in the UK," 8.

These differences are part of a much wider phenomenon, for in post-industrial countries it has been consistently found that men are less religious than women.[35] Sociologists are presently exploring the reasons for this. For example, Grace Davie suggests it may be due to women being more closely involved with aspects of life that, to some degree, have a sacred status, such as birth and death.[36] On the other hand, Marta Trzebiatowska and Steve Bruce argue the primary cause is a time lag, where men rather than women were influenced earlier by secularizing forces and so are further ahead in their marginalizing of religion.[37] Whatever the reason, the lack of male Bible readers should be understood as being part of this bigger context.

The gender difference in Bible reading must be qualified though, for the data is not as clear cut as might be assumed and there are settings where the gender divide disappears. For instance, although Christian Research noted a 10% difference between those men who hardly ever or never read the Bible and their female counterparts, when the figures were collated to measure the percentage of people who were regular Bible readers, the divide was reduced to 2%. That is, 12% of men and 14% of women said they were regular Bible readers. Indeed, more men (6%) than women (5%) indicated that they engaged with the Bible on a daily basis.[38] A recent survey in Scotland also found that there was little difference between male (11%) and female (10%) regular readers of the Bible.[39] Similarly, following the 2005 church Census, Peter Brierley noted the obvious male/female divide, concluding that 57% of those attending church were female and 43% were male. However, he then highlighted that women are leaving the church faster than men and that there are certain denominations: New Churches, Pentecostals and Independents, where there is either no gender difference or a minimal one of 1 or 2%.[40]

On account of my interest in those who are not regular Bible readers or churchgoers, and because of the gender difference I highlighted earlier, I decided to limit my sample to men. I did so aware of, and sensitive to, the qualification I have just noted. This decision does not mean that this is a study principally exploring the impact of gender upon reading, although in chapter 8 I will reflect upon the influence of my participants' gender. Tiffany

---

35. Davie and Walter, "The Religiosity of Women in the Modern West"; Trzebiatowska and Bruce, *Why Are Women More Religious Than Men?*

36. Davie, "Vicarious Religion."

37. Trzebiatowska and Bruce, *Why Are Women More Religious Than Men?*

38. Christian Research, *Bible Engagement in England and Wales*, 44.

39. Barna, *Transforming Scotland*, 94.

40. Brierley, *Pulling Out of the Nose Dive*, 131–36.

Webster's CBS research focused on the readings of five men and she chooses to directly reflect on how their gender shapes their engagement with the texts.[41] However many studies that principally address the issue of gender and reading do so by comparing and contrasting male and female readers,[42] or exploring readings by those who do not fit the male/female binary such as transsexuals,[43] or those with intersex conditions.[44] This leaves the door open to further research that could incorporate a comparative element if the subject of gender was going to be directly addressed. In this way then, the gender difference that is typically seen in Bible reading practices resulted in a further refinement of my research. I was no longer exploring how British people would read the Bible but was focusing on British men.

My decision to concentrate on men is an example of theoretical sampling. This is a form of sampling where the researcher is

> selecting groups or categories to study on the basis of their relevance to your research questions your theoretical position and analytical framework, your analytical practice, and more importantly the argument or explanation you are developing.[45]

In my case, because studies show that men are less inclined to read the Bible and so more likely to meet my research criteria, I concentrate solely on them. Theoretical sampling is a form of sampling closely related to Grounded Theory,[46] and is compatible with snowball sampling, an approach I also use (as chapter 3 will show).

There were two further ways in which I could have narrowed my participant selection. First, I could have concentrated on those who fitted the earlier profile of the person least likely to read the Bible: young men from social band DE who do not go to church.[47] Second, I could have followed the example of Theos and others,[48] by focusing exclusively on men

---

41. Webster, "When the Bible Meets the Black Stuff."

42. See for example: Bleich, "Gender Interests in Reading and Language"; Crawford and Chaffin, "The Reader's Construction of Meaning"; Hartley, *Reading Groups*, 25–71; Summers, "Adult Reading Habits and Preferences in Relation to Gender and Difference."

43. Curtis, "An Encounter with Ordinary Real Readers Reading the Gospels."

44. Cornwall, "British Intersex Christians' Accounts of Intersex Identity, Christian Identity and Church Experience."

45. Mason, *Qualitative Researching*. 124.

46. Glaser and Strauss, *The Discovery of Grounded Theory*.

47. Field, "Is the Bible Becoming a Closed Book?"; Harrison, *Attitudes to Bible, God, Church*.

48. Theos, *Post-Religious Britain?* See also: Bullivant and Lee, "Interdisciplinary Studies of Non-Religion and Secularity"; Lee, "Research Note: Talking about a

who identify as "not religious." However, it seemed reasonable to assume a degree of difficulty in getting people to participate in this project, for I would be asking men who probably had no interest in the Bible to read it. Unsurprisingly Christian Research found that when asked if they could be encouraged to read the Bible more, only 8% of those surveyed said "yes" (77% said "no" and 15% said "don't know").[49] I therefore decided not to limit my selection process in either of these two ways, as it may have made recruitment too difficult.

These decisions highlight three potential avenues of further research. First, although women read the Bible more and Christian women's reading practices have been explored,[50] there is a lack of Bible-reading research amongst women who are not regular Bible readers. Second, the significant overlap between Harrison's and Field's profiles of those least likely to read the Bible,[51] suggests that studying this subgroup of society and their views and readings of the Bible would be important. Such a study could shed light on contemporary issues of biblical literacy and Bible engagement. So too, exploring Bible readings by those who identify as "nonreligious" would contribute to the emerging research on this growing cohort of society. Callum Brown and Gordon Lynch note that "for younger people born since the 1960s, a position of 'non-religion' became not so much a conscious choice, but the default position."[52]

Five Biblical Texts

Selection Criteria

Having decided to narrow down my research to men, a further refinement concerned the Bible, for it was unlikely that any of my anticipated participants would be willing to read it in its entirety. Other scholars who undertook empirical research into how the Bible was being read focused

---

Revolution"; Sheard, "Ninety-Eight Atheists"; Voas and McAndrew, "Three Puzzles of Non-Religion in Britain." See also the Nonreligion and Secularity Research Network (nsrn.net) and its recently established *Secularism and Nonreligion* journal.

49. The two top reasons given by those who said that they could not be encouraged to read the Bible more were a lack of interest, and not considering themselves religious enough. See: Christian Research, *Bible Engagement in England and Wales*, 57–59.

50. Neal, *Romancing God*; Radway, *Reading the Romance*; Weaver-Zercher, *Thrill of the Chaste*.

51. Field incorporated Harrison's findings into his own data set, so they are not a true comparison.

52. Brown and Lynch, "Cultural Perspectives," 337–38.

on one or two preselected texts,[53] or a series of passages.[54] In a similar fashion, I too would have to choose one or more texts for my own study and in doing so the research question would be nuanced, for I would no longer be exploring how people read the Bible, rather how they read (a) particular text(s). As I began to consider which, and how many, biblical texts should be used, nine principles guided my selection. These principles were identified in light of the ethical, practical, and theoretical considerations associated with this research.

First, a variety of genres should be represented. Unlike Webster who specifically chose texts which she believed coalminers could relate to or Macdonald who identified the Psalms as a genre well suited to a postmodern context,[55] I wanted to uncover how the Bible would be read. To that end, the texts I chose should cover as wide a biblical spectrum as possible, including passages that appear relevant and others that do not, ones that accord with Christian doctrine and those that some consider "sub-Christian."[56] However, the genres included should be ones that the men, to some degree, were familiar with. This increases the accessibility of the texts, resulting in a greater understanding of them and greater confidence for the reader. This was important, as some participants may have never read the Bible and so might have felt apprehensive about the actual task of reading, unsure as to what to expect. Accordingly, apocalyptic material was excluded, for although terms like "apocalypse" and "Armageddon" are in common use the genre is unfamiliar to most people.

Second, the readers would need to engage with at least two biblical texts, in order to accommodate different genres. Indeed, the more texts they would be willing to read, the more data would be produced and the greater degree of comparison and analysis which could take place. The imagined location of the fieldwork contributed to this decision, for by choosing to study those who are outside the church I wanted to avoid the use of an ecclesial reading site, for the nature of the site may inform the readings which take place there. One possibility was to locate the fieldwork in a workplace where men could undertake the research during their lunch breaks. To that end, I decided that five biblical texts, one text per lunchtime, would be the optimum number. The project could be presented as one that would involve

53. For example see: Le Grys, *Shaped by God's Story*; Village, *The Bible and Lay People*.

54. For example see: Macdonald, "The Psalms and Spirituality"; Webster, "When the Bible Meets the Black Stuff."

55. Ibid.

56. Vincent, "The Death and Resurrection of the Bible in Church and Society," 162.

reading a different biblical text each day for one week. This seemed a reasonable request and time frame. It was not too onerous for the participants, which would have discouraged uptake, and it had the potential to produce a large amount of data.

Third, although the genres should be familiar to the reader, the texts should not. Village found that readers who were familiar with the text were more likely to see it as relevant to their life whilst those who were unfamiliar with it "tended to perceive it as more distant and opaque."[57] To minimize this variable I decided to use texts that were probably unfamiliar to all my participants. In light of my selection criteria it was unlikely that my participants would have a good knowledge of the Bible, but it was not impossible. Most, if not all, would have been exposed to the Bible through British culture and media, at school and at any Christian festivals or services they may have attended, such as a carol service or a wedding. Some may even have regularly attended church or Sunday school in the past. Therefore, the texts should be unfamiliar, even to the participants who might have attended church in the past.

Fourth, although I wanted the texts to be unfamiliar, the language and the subject matter needed to be accessible. This was of particular importance, for if any participants felt anxious about taking part and then were faced with a text whose language they found unfamiliar and content confusing, they might decide to withdraw. Susannah Cornwall and David Nixon faced a similar challenge when facilitating four CBS sessions with a group of homeless and vulnerably-housed people. In their case they decided to read the Bible passage aloud to address issues of accessibility and literacy.[58] However, I was exploring how men would read the Bible and for this reason the text could not be read to them, they would have to read it for themselves.

To that end I surveyed English translations of the Bible, in an attempt to find one that was accessible to the general population by using contemporary language and having a low reading level. Of the options available, the New Living Translation (NLT) stood out as it had been revised in 2007 and had a reading level of 6.3,[59] so a person aged eleven or older should be able to read it.[60] This, I hoped, would mean that men with high and low literacy

---

57. Village, *The Bible and Lay People*, 86–87, 94.

58. Cornwall and Nixon, "Readings from the Road," 13.

59. Mardel, "Bible Translation Guide." Other possible translations included the New Century Version (published in 1991 with a reading level of 5.6), the Contemporary English Version (published in 1995 with a reading level of 5.4), and The Message (published in 2001, with a reading level of 5.5 to 10 depending upon the passage).

60. By comparison, someone aged nine or older is said to be able to read the *Sun* newspaper, and a person aged sixteen or older is thought to be able to read the *Guardian*

levels could engage with the texts, without anyone feeling disadvantaged. Mardel describes the NLT as sitting in the middle of the formal/dynamic equivalence translation scale,[61] others however place it more towards the dynamic equivalence side.[62] I viewed this positively, for it lends itself to a more accessible translation thereby giving the readers greater confidence as they engaged with the texts. The main concern regarding this translation was its language, for it was principally written for a North American readership, which might result in the use of colloquialisms or phrases that are uncommon in Britain. Nonetheless I decided to proceed with the NLT as my choice of translation.

Fifth, each text should be, as far as possible, a complete literary unit so that the reader could make sense of it without its wider literary context. Sixth, the texts must have some content with which the reader could engage, but should not be too dull, or acutely provocative. Therefore, I avoided potentially boring passages, such as a list of Benjamin's descendant's (1 Chr 8:1–40), and overly provocative texts, for instance dealing with rape and murder (Judg 19:1–30). Furthermore, a provocative text may lead the readers to exclusively focus on the issue presented in the text rather than the actual act of reading and so skew the data and findings. It may also raise issues and emotions within the participants to which as a researcher I would be ill equipped to respond. For this reason, Alison Peden also avoided using provocative texts in her CBS sessions with a group of women prisoners, even though she was a chaplain.[63] Seventh, all the texts should be of similar length so as to provide a degree of uniformity and routineness to the research task. Again, this sense of routineness would be important so that over time the participants would feel more relaxed and confident, aware that there were no unexpected surprises.

Eighth, so far I have referred to the Bible as a single, uncontested text, even though this is not the case.[64] There are a number of Bibles, each acting as a unified collection of sacred texts for different communities. For example, with reference to the Old Testament, the Protestant Church has thirty-nine books, the Roman Catholic has forty-six, the Orthodox has forty-nine and

---

newspaper, see: Guy, *Transforming Reading Skills in Secondary School*, 29.

61. Mardel, "Bible Translation Guide." This is a scale used by translators to indicate the degree to which the translation is word for word (formal equivalence) or thought for thought (dynamic equivalence). For further discussion see: Fee and Strauss, *How to Choose a Translation for All its Worth*, 26–28, 145–57; Nida and Taber: *Theory and Practice of Translation*.

62. Zondervan, "Bible Translation Chart."

63. Peden, "Contextual Bible Study at Cornton Vale Women's Prison, Stirling."

64. Carroll, *Wolf in the Sheepfold*, 14–21.

the Ethiopian has between forty-six and fifty-four.⁶⁵ In my case, the texts should be found in both the Roman Catholic and Protestant Bibles for they are the two Christian traditions most commonly found in England.⁶⁶ This therefore excluded books found in the Apocrypha, as those participants from a Protestant background may not consider them to be biblical. Ninth, there were various ethical parameters that guided both the research design and the subsequent fieldwork, and these are considered in greater depth in chapter 3. However, with reference to the text selection criteria, a need to ensure that the project was not proselytism in the guise of research, meant that the texts must not be concerned with conversion to Christianity such as the story of Lydia's conversion in Acts 16:11–15. Likewise it should not have a popular historical role in evangelizing, like John 3:16. Furthermore, not all the texts should present God or religion in a favorable light, as this could also be considered an attempt to proselytize.

Having these criteria in place I then undertook a survey of the Bible. My own practice of regularly reading the Bible and going to church, along with the theological education I had received, meant that I had a good grasp of the Protestant canon. This provided me with the ability to navigate through this Bible in search of suitable texts. In the end though, to my surprise, I found my choice to be limited. Only two letters were of suitable length, 2 John and 3 John. Psalm 88 is unique in its hopeless outlook and there were few parables and narratives which were sufficiently self-contained and the required length. Therefore, more often than not I had to pick one text from a choice of two or three, and the passage chosen was the one that most closely corresponded with the nine criteria I have outlined. The texts I selected were: 2 John, Proverbs 10:1–11, 2 Samuel 5:17–25, Psalm 88, and Matthew 18:21–35.

2 John

¹This letter is from John, the elder.

I am writing to the chosen lady and to her children, whom I love in the truth—as does everyone else who knows the truth—²because the truth lives in us and will be with us forever.

---

65. Wooden, "The Role of 'the Septuagint' in the Formation of the Biblical Canons," 130–31.

66. Brierley, *Pulling Out of the Nose Dive*, 156.

³Grace, mercy, and peace, which come from God the Father and from Jesus Christ—the Son of the Father—will continue to be with us who live in truth and love.

⁴How happy I was to meet some of your children and find them living according to the truth, just as the Father commanded.

⁵I am writing to remind you, dear friends, that we should love one another. This is not a new commandment, but one we have had from the beginning. ⁶Love means doing what God has commanded us, and he has commanded us to love one another, just as you heard from the beginning.

⁷I say this because many deceivers have gone out into the world. They deny that Jesus Christ came in a real body. Such a person is a deceiver and an antichrist. ⁸Watch out that you do not lose what we have worked so hard to achieve. Be diligent so that you receive your full

reward. ⁹Anyone who wanders away from this teaching has no relationship with God. But anyone who remains in the teaching of Christ has a relationship with both the Father and the Son.

¹⁰If anyone comes to your meeting and does not teach the truth about Christ, don't invite that person into your home or give any kind of encouragement. ¹¹Anyone who encourages such people becomes a partner in their evil work.

¹²I have much more to say to you, but I don't want to do it with paper and ink. For I hope to visit you soon and talk with you face to face. Then our joy will be complete.

¹³Greetings from the children of your sister, chosen by God.

(New Living Translation)

I was keen to include a letter because it would be a familiar genre. The letter of 2 John is one of the shortest books of the Bible, its length corresponds "to the conventionally brief length of a private letter which, at the time, would have been written on a single papyrus sheet of standard size."[67] In my context it fitted comfortably onto an A4 page with room for annotation.

Even though the genre was one I felt the readers would recognize, I did not think this was a text they would easily relate to, for it is addressed to a first century group of Christians responding to a particular situation they faced. 2 John presents itself as a letter from "John, the elder" to "the chosen

---

67. Smalley, *1, 2, 3 John*, 314.

lady and to her children"[68] and its content deals with issues related to church life. Raymond Brown describes it as: "A letter from the Presbyter to a church warning against any reception of secessionist teachers who are spreading christological and moral errors."[69] I did not imagine that these issues would be of interest to my participants, but because the relevance of the passage was not important to my study, this did not disqualify it.

The text fulfilled all the criteria set out earlier, but there were two phrases that may have been viewed as offensive by some of the readers. First, the word "antichrist" is used to describe someone who denies that "Jesus came in a real body."[70] Second, the directive not to invite a person into your home if they do "not teach the truth about Christ" is also present.[71] Nevertheless, these comments principally seem to address false teachers within a church, not those outside it,[72] and for this reason I did not consider it to be inappropriately provocative for my participants. This then was the first passage that I included in my study and it resulted in the subsequent texts needing to be of a similar length.

Proverbs 10:1–11

1 A wise child brings joy to a father;

a foolish child brings grief to a mother.

2 Tainted wealth has no lasting value,

but right living can save your life.

3 The Lord will not let the godly go hungry,

but he refuses to satisfy the craving of the wicked.

4 Lazy people are soon poor;

hard workers get rich.

5 A wise youth harvests in the summer,

but one who sleeps during harvest is a disgrace.

---

68. 2 John 1.
69. Brown, *The Epistles of John*, 643.
70. 2 John 7.
71. 2 John 10.
72. Brown, *The Epistles of John*, 69–71; Marshall, *The Epistles of John*, 68–75; Thompson, *1–3 John*, 14–18.

⁶ The godly are showered with blessings;

    the words of the wicked conceal violent intentions.

⁷ We have happy memories of the godly,

    but the name of a wicked person rots away.

⁸ The wise are glad to be instructed,

    but babbling fools fall flat on their faces.

⁹ People with integrity walk safely,

    but those who follow crooked paths will slip and fall.

¹⁰ People who wink at wrong cause trouble,

    but a bold reproof promotes peace.

¹¹ The words of the godly are a life-giving fountain;

    the words of the wicked conceal violent intentions

(New Living Translation)

Proverbs were chosen as this is another genre in use today and their content may have been more relevant to the lives of the men than that of 2 John. The book of Proverbs, as its name suggests, primarily contains lists of short, pithy sayings, exhortations, warnings and expressions.[73]

Proverbs 10:1–11 may be considered a literary unit. That is not to say it has a beginning, middle, and end, rather that it includes complete sections. Duane Garrett suggests that aside from the introduction in 10:1a, it contains two main sections 10:1b–5 and 6–11,[74] Roland Murphy, on the other hand, describes three main sections in 10:1–5, 6–7, and 8–11.[75] Not everyone agrees with these divisions. Some contend that there is no clear structure and that the individual proverbs are placed in a more random fashion,[76] whilst others suggest the division is 10:1–5 and 6–21.[77] Although there is an on-going disagreement regarding the exact structure of these verses, following Murphy and Garrett I selected Proverbs 10:1–11, understanding that in a tentative way it formed a literary unit.

---

73. Longman III, *Proverbs*, 21.
74. Garrett, *Proverbs Ecclesiastes Song of Songs*, 59.
75. Murphy, *Proverbs*, 72–74.
76. Longman III, *Proverbs*, 229; Perdue, *Proverbs*, 163–64.
77. Koptak, *Proverbs*, 283.

Compared with 2 John, I thought the content of this passage would be much more relevant to my potential participants. These eleven verses consider practical subjects such as wealth, work ethic and wise living all of which are contemporary issues. Finally, this section of Proverbs begins with an introduction: "The proverbs of Solomon."[78] For stylistic purposes I decided to exclude this phrase but added it to the short descriptor provided for the participants, as chapter 3 details.

2 Samuel 5:17–25

[17]When the Philistines heard that David had been anointed king of Israel, they mobilized all their forces to capture him. But David was told they were coming, so he went into the stronghold. [18]The Philistines arrived and spread out across the valley of Rephaim. [19]So David asked the Lord, "Should I go out to fight the Philistines? Will you hand them over to me?"

The Lord replied to David, "Yes, go ahead. I will certainly hand them over to you."

[20]So David went to Baal-perazim and defeated the Philistines there. "The Lord did it!" David exclaimed. "He burst through my enemies like a raging flood!" So he named that place Baal-perazim (which means "the Lord who bursts through"). [21]The Philistines had abandoned their idols there, so David and his men confiscated them.

[22]But after a while the Philistines returned and again spread out across the valley of Rephaim. [23]And again David asked the Lord what to do. "Do not attack them straight on," the Lord replied. "Instead, circle around behind and attack them near the poplar trees. [24]When you hear a sound like marching feet in the tops of the poplar trees, be on the alert! That will be the signal that the Lord is moving ahead of you to strike down the Philistine army." [25]So David did what the Lord commanded, and he struck down the Philistines all the way from Gibeon to Gezer.

(New Living Translation)

The third text I selected was 2 Samuel 5:17–25. It is a narrative which recounts the Philistines twice going to fight the newly appointed king David, who with God's help defeats them on both occasions. This short section was the appropriate length and is viewed as a literary unit by many

---

78. Proverbs 10:1a.

commentators.[79] There are three main characters: David, the Philistines, and the "Lord." Two battles feature in the text, which is part of a much wider narrative and some of my participants may know the story of David and Goliath which is found earlier in the book of 1 Samuel. This text however is relatively unfamiliar, and because it focuses only on three characters and situates the events in one location, I assumed my reader's would be able to easily engage with it.

As a text where God is seen to give David victory in a series of battles, a phenomenon that may be considered a type of "holy war,"[80] this text had the potential to provoke, for there is a popular distrust of those who claim divine help or sanction when undertaking armed conflict. Especially as during the fieldwork there were on-going conflicts in the Middle East and North Africa with some claiming divine sanction for their actions. Importantly though, this text is different to those which recount people invading lands and killing the inhabitants at God's command,[81] for in this passage the Philistines are presented as the aggressors who come and challenge the newly crowned king. Therefore, I hoped that this text was not an overly provocative one.

Matthew 18:21–35

[21]Then Peter came to him and asked, "Lord, how often should I forgive someone who sins against me? Seven times?"

[22]"No, not seven times," Jesus replied, "but seventy times seven!"

[23]"Therefore, the Kingdom of Heaven can be compared to a king who decided to bring his accounts up to date with servants who had borrowed money from him. [24]In the process, one of his debtors was brought in who owed him millions of dollars. [25]He couldn't pay, so his master ordered that he be sold—along with his wife, his children, and everything he owned—to pay the debt.

[26]"But the man fell down before his master and begged him, 'Please, be patient with me, and I will pay it all.' [27]Then his master was filled with pity for him, and he released him and forgave his debt.

---

79. Anderson, *2 Samuel*, 89; Bergen, *1, 2 Samuel*, 324–27; Brueggemann, *First and Second Samuel*, 247.

80. Brueggemann, *First and Second Samuel*, 247.

81. For example see: Joshua 1–12.

[28]"But when the man left the king, he went to a fellow servant who owed him a few thousand dollars. He grabbed him by the throat and demanded instant payment.

[29]"His fellow servant fell down before him and begged for a little more time. 'Be patient with me, and I will pay it,' he pleaded. [30]But his creditor wouldn't wait. He had the man arrested and put in prison until the debt could be paid in full.

[31]"When some of the other servants saw this, they were very upset. They went to the king and told him everything that had happened. [32]Then the king called in the man he had forgiven and said, 'You evil servant! I forgave you that tremendous debt because you pleaded with me. [33]Shouldn't you have mercy on your fellow servant, just as I had mercy on you?' [34]Then the angry king sent the man to prison to be tortured until he had paid his entire debt.

[35]"That's what my heavenly Father will do to you if you refuse to forgive your brothers and sisters from your heart."

(New Living Translation)

It seemed appropriate to include a text that made reference to Jesus for he is a central character within Christianity. Therefore, the fourth text was Matthew 18:21–35. The main part of this pericope is a parable that Jesus tells in response to the question: How often should I forgive someone who sins against me?[82] This text is again a complete literary unit,[83] of a suitable length and in a genre that the men would be familiar with, in so far as it is a story with a purpose.

This parable is not overly provocative nor about conversion to Christianity, but it does have a sting in the tail, ending with a warning directed at Jesus' disciples that they must forgive or they too will face punishment. Once again, because the warning is made to Jesus's disciples I thought my reader's would not feel threatened by it, as they would probably not identify with, or as, disciples of Jesus. The main concern I had was the NLT's use of the word "dollars" in place of the words "talents" and "denarii" which are typically used.[84] This was the only distinctly North American word that any of the five texts had, but I anticipated my participants would be familiar with the term.

---

82. Matt 18:21.
83. Hagner, *Matthew 14–28*, 534; Nolland, *The Gospel of Matthew*, 751.
84. Davies and Allison, *Matthew*, 309; Hagner, *Matthew 14–28*, 539.

Psalm 88

¹O Lord, God of my salvation,

> I cry out to you by day.

> I come to you at night.

²Now hear my prayer;

> listen to my cry.

³For my life is full of troubles,

> and death draws near.

⁴I am as good as dead,

> like a strong man with no strength left.

⁵They have left me among the dead,

> and I lie like a corpse in a grave.

I am forgotten,

> cut off from your care.

⁶You have thrown me into the lowest pit,

> into the darkest depths.

⁷Your anger weighs me down;

> with wave after wave you have engulfed me.   *Interlude*

⁸You have driven my friends away

> by making me repulsive to them.

I am in a trap with no way of escape.

> ⁹   My eyes are blinded by my tears.

Each day I beg for your help, O Lord;

> I lift my hands to you for mercy.

¹⁰Are your wonderful deeds of any use to the dead?

> Do the dead rise up and praise you?   *Interlude*

> ¹¹Can those in the grave declare your unfailing love?
>
>> Can they proclaim your faithfulness in the place of destruction?
>
> ¹²Can the darkness speak of your wonderful deeds?
>
>> Can anyone in the land of forgetfulness talk about your righteousness?
>
> ¹³O Lord, I cry out to you.
>
>> I will keep on pleading day by day.
>
> ¹⁴O Lord, why do you reject me?
>
>> Why do you turn your face from me?
>
> ¹⁵I have been sick and close to death since my youth.
>
>> I stand helpless and desperate before your terrors.
>
> ¹⁶Your fierce anger has overwhelmed me.
>
>> Your terrors have paralyzed me.
>
> ¹⁷They swirl around me like floodwaters all day long.
>
>> They have engulfed me completely.
>
> ¹⁸You have taken away my companions and loved ones.
>
>> Darkness is my closest friend.
>
> (New Living Translation)

The final text was Psalm 88, which again met the required selection criteria. In light of the other four texts portraying God, religion, or Jesus positively, I wanted to include a text where this was not the case. As a psalm of lament, Psalm 88 is one where the author cries out to God but God does not reply; the text concludes with the phrase, "Darkness is my closest friend."[85] Walter Brueggemann notes that in "this Psalm, there is no hint of an answer, response, or resolution from God. The speaker addresses what is apparently an empty sky and an indifferent throne."[86] The main issue with this psalm is its length, as it normally requires forty-one lines of text, which was significantly longer than the other passages. However, if the psalm is printed with each phrase directly proceeding from the next, then it appears of similar

---

85. Ps 88:18.
86. Brueggemann, *The Psalms & the Life of Faith*, 56.

length to the other texts. By doing so the psalm could be included in this research, but its poetic structure would not be as clearly seen. In light of its negative and hopeless tone towards God I included it and sought to compensate for its layout by describing it as a "song" in the short descriptor I provided for the participants.

Prior to the actual psalm commencing there is a short directive "For the choir director: A psalm of the descendants of Korah. A song to be sung to the tune 'The Suffering of Affliction.' A psalm of Heman the Ezrahite." I decided to omit this directive for two reasons. First, there was no space to accommodate it in light of the psalm's length. Second, I was concerned that the inclusion of names like "Korah" or "Heman the Ezrahite" would obscure the text for the readers. The psalm also contains a probable musical directive that the NLT renders as "interlude," and is more commonly translated "Selah" occurring at the end of verses 7 and 10. Again, it did not appear to add to the psalm's accessibility, rather I thought it might confuse the participants, and it was omitted.

Conclusion

Therefore, this chapter has argued for three foundational layers that will shape my subsequent study. First, I suggested that a qualitative methodology was best suited to addressing my research question, and by identifying it as a case study I could concentrate on one reading site in depth. Then, by assuming a theoretical sampling approach I decided to focus solely on men who were not regular churchgoers or Bible readers. Finally, I would not be considering how they read the whole Bible but five specific texts: 2 John, Proverbs 10:1–11, 2 Samuel 5:17–25, Matthew 18:21–35, and Psalm 88. These developments resulted in a refined research question asking: how would a British man, who does not read the Bible or go to church, read five biblical texts? Chapter 3 now unpacks the designing of my research tools, along with recounting the fieldwork and data analysis that took place, but first it considers my place within this research.

Chapter 3

Data Production—Methods and Fieldwork

Having highlighted the prompts for my research question and then traced its development and refinement, this chapter now recounts the research methods I constructed and the fieldwork that was undertaken. I begin by considering my position within this research and some of the ways in which I have influenced it. In particular, I suggest that as a Christian, some people may assume that this research is really an attempt to evangelize and I outline three different areas demonstrating this not to be the case: my conduct, the research materials and the content of this book. Having located myself and acknowledged my role in this work, I then argue for a mixed method approach, utilizing annotation, a questionnaire and a semi-structured interview. This section ends by describing my use of biographical Entrance and Exit questionnaires and how these tools were refined in a pilot study. The chapter then recounts the fieldwork, noting the importance of George, my gatekeeper, who not only made my entrance into the Chemical Plant possible, but also introduced me to some of the men. I then chart the effectiveness of snowball sampling with one group introducing me to another, so that after ten months seven groups (twenty men) had completed the project. The chapter ends by briefly describing my analysis of the data, which the following chapters will build upon.

Reflexivity and Ethical Considerations

Underpinning the concept of self-reflection is the assumption that the researcher is part of the research process not an objective outsider peering in, as David Gray notes:

> Reflexivity involves the realization that the researcher is not a neutral observer, and is implicated in the construction of knowledge. Far from being a disinterested bystander, the researcher is

seen as someone whose observations are by their very nature, selective, and whose interpretations of results are partial.[1]

By acknowledging this, it becomes incumbent upon the researcher to reflect upon their thoughts, actions, feelings, ideologies, and presuppositions, in order to examine their influence upon the research. Nicola Slee argues that this self-reflection should be viewed as a source of "empirical evidence" within the research matrix, evidence that "must be open to critical scrutiny no less than what is traditionally defined as relevant evidence."[2] In doing so a clearer understanding of the research process and accompanying results is gained, for the researcher's influence is also accounted for.[3]

Therefore, it should be assumed that I have influenced this research in ways I am aware of and in ways I am not. For example, following Sam Porter in regards to social enquiry, I am a critical realist.[4] Critical realism emerged in the 1970s,[5] and understands there to be a reality outside (or independent) of my knowledge base and consciousness, one which can be known (or experienced) but in a culturally conditioned way, thus making any conclusions in some way provisional. Andrew Rogers writes: "a critical realist stance sees our knowing as partial, provisional and mediate."[6] Furthermore, with Terry Eagleton I would add that "a certain capacity for critical self-distancing is actually part of the way we are bound up with the world."[7] Therefore, with reference to my research, unlike someone who assumes a constructivist approach and so only refers to their "interpretation of the data" and not to "findings,"[8] I will refer to my "interpretation of the data" and my "findings," both of which fit with critical realism. This then is one way in which I shape my research, and other examples could include the influence of my personality, interests and motivations.

The claim that I influence my research does not nullify its findings, but it does reinforce the particularity of them, for I am an integral part of what took place. In noting my influence within the research processes a

1. Gray, *Doing Research in the Real World,* 498.
2. Slee, *Women's Faith Development,* 51.
3. Mason, *Qualitative Researching,* 4–8; Simons, *Case Study Research in Practice,* 91–93.
4. Porter, "Critical Realist Ethnography."
5. Archer et al., *Critical Realism*; Sayer, *Realism and Social Science.*
6. Rogers, *Congregational Hermeneutics,* 120.
7. Eagleton, "The Estate Agent," 10.
8. This is because a constructivist approach presupposes that all engagement with reality is interpreted and so it "rejects the idea that there is objective knowledge in some external reality for the researcher to retrieve mechanistically," see: Costantino, "Constructivism," 118.

more honest and balanced description of the research emerges, one that acknowledges this subjective aspect of it. My aim is not to establish a claim of being "objective," but to ensure that the research process is transparent, the coding and analyzing accurate and the presentation of findings fair.[9] This openness allows for greater scrutiny of my work by others, and should result in a detailed and trustworthy account.

In light of this need for transparency, it has become common practice for the researcher to disclose their own sense of identity relevant to their research. In the introduction I briefly described myself, but a more thorough depiction is required. I am a thirty-seven-year-old white British male, who worked as a Physiotherapist prior to studying theology and beginning a PhD. I presently live in Northern England with my wife and two children. Perhaps most significantly, I am a Christian and was brought up in a church-going, Bible-reading family. Moreover, as I indicated in chapter 2, I have continued to regularly read the Bible and go to church throughout my adult life. In particular, I have an interest in contextual Bible readings possibly due to growing up in Latin America where my parents were missionaries. To that end, I affirm Stuart Murray's suggestion that in light of the declining influence of Christianity in Britain:

> We may also find surprising new insights from reading Scripture with those in post-Christendom who have no church background and read the Bible without traditional assumptions and interpretations.[10]

Furthermore, as a Christian, I believe that God is outward-looking and that Christians should be outward-looking as well.[11] Part of that outward-looking-ness could involve providing those who do not read the Bible with the opportunity to do so, in a meaningful setting and format. An awareness of how the Bible is read by those who do not normally read it may help inform this. This was part of my motivation when I began to undertake this research, and as I will highlight conflicts with the ethical guidelines my research adheres to.

Helen Simons suggests that the "fundamental ethical principle in research, whatever methodology you choose, is to 'do no harm.'"[12] She does not present this as a simple concept but goes on to document the various

---

9. Creswell, *Research Design*, 201.

10. Murray, *Post-Christendom*, 297.

11. Within Christian theology the phrase *Missio Dei* has been used to express the idea that God is outward looking. For a recent example and exploration of God as a missional God see Wright, *The Mission of God*.

12. Simons, *Case Study Research in Practice*, 96.

difficulties, grey areas, and ethical dilemmas that can occur. My own research was accepted by a University's Faculty of Humanities Research Ethics Committee and followed the ethical guidelines outlined by the British Sociological Association.[13] For instance, all the data collected was kept secure and confidential. The participants were told that any data particular to them would be anonymized prior to being included in a presentation, publication or other works. Having completed the research though, eighteen of the twenty men directly indicated that they did not want their details to be anonymized and so their personal details have been included.

In light of my Christian identity however, it was important to demonstrate that this project was not evangelism in the guise of research. Within Britain, Christians have been thought of as undertaking certain tasks or roles with the aim of proselytizing.[14] Gordon Lynch, for instance, notes that there are many Christians involved in charity work, and in particular counseling (an area in which he worked). He comments that some people viewed this with suspicion suspecting "that counselling was being exploited by some Christians as a way of inflicting the gospel message on vulnerable and unsuspecting clients. In general, though, I didn't find that to be the case."[15] This demonstrates both the suspicion which some have towards a Christian's motivation, but that those fears may be unfounded.

As a researcher interested in the subject of Bible reading, I anticipated that the participants would assume I was "religious" and so view me as an "outsider."[16] Moreover, I also suspected that I would be treated with a degree of suspicion, due to the reputation Christians have for evangelizing, as Lynch highlighted. Suspicion of field researchers is not uncommon.[17] In my case, I employed various strategies to demonstrate that this project was not concerned with proselytizing, and by doing so hoped to gain the trust of my participants. Importantly, although various techniques could be employed, as chapter 9 recounts, I was not wholly successful in this endeavor.

---

13. British Sociological Association, "Statement of Ethical Practice for the British Sociological Association."

14. Bickley, *The Problem of Proselytism*, 9, 14–19.

15. Lynch, *Losing My Religion?* 3–4.

16. McCutcheon, *The Insider/Outsider Problem in the Study of Religion.*

17. Agar, *The Professional Stranger*, 134–39; Goldstein, "Desconfianza and problems of Representation in Urban Ethnography"; Pearson, "'Going Native in Reverse.'"

The Researcher

In an attempt to both minimize my influence in the research process and show that the research was not concerned with evangelism I sought to limit the impact of my presence and associated Christian identity upon the fieldwork in four ways. First, I was concerned that by identifying as a Christian my potential participants would assume that I was mainly interested in their conversion. Such an assumption would both shape the data to emerge, but may also result in men refusing to volunteer. Issues of access are not uncommon in fieldwork. Contrasting my own context, but echoing my experience, Nadège Mézié was unable to gain access to an American evangelical missionary organization in Haiti, as she was not a Christian. Therefore she decided to pretend to convert to Christianity and in doing so found that access was granted.[18] If possible however, deception in fieldwork should be kept to a minimum and I did not want to undertake covert research or use deception by claiming to be nonreligious myself.[19] Furthermore, I lacked the time that others have had to build up trust with their participants, such as the three years Daniel Wolf spent with a Biker gang.[20] Therefore I decided that I would principally present myself as a researcher from a local University and not actively refer to my own religious identity whilst the men were completing the project. William Shaffir notes that:

> Field research requires some measure of role-playing and acting. In order to be granted access to the research setting and to secure the cooperation of his or her hosts, the researcher learns to present a particular image of himself or herself.[21]

If the participants were interested and asked about my religious affiliation or motivation, I indicated that I would answer all their questions regarding my identity and motivation once they had completed the project. This limited disclosure addressed my concern that knowledge of my identity would put people off participating, but also upheld the rights of the participants. This compromise was one the men seemed to appreciate, for the majority of the groups I approached at the Chemical plant were willing to take part and most would also ask about my religious identity having completed the research. When asked, I usually provided a brief answer indicating that I am a religious person, do read the Bible and do go to church. Typically the participants were content with that reply and the conversation ended.

18. Mézié, "'Wi, se kretyènn mwen ye' (Yes, I am Christian)."
19. Hammersley and Atkinson, *Ethnography*, 57.
20. Wolf, "High-Risk Methodology."
21. Shaffir, "Managing a Convincing Self-Presentation," 77.

Second, I continually reaffirmed that my role as the researcher was to listen and that the purpose of this project was to see how people read the five biblical texts. I would not reject any of their readings nor would I attempt to impose my views of the texts upon them. More often than not I emphasized that I simply sought their thoughts and opinions on these texts, valuing their honesty and willingness. So although most of the participants went on to express confusion, frustration, anger, bitterness, disagreement, and disbelief towards the texts, these were views that I accepted and valued without challenge.

Third, I kept a reflexive journal throughout the fieldwork. This is a recognized method that is employed by researchers to chart and reflect on their role in the research.[22] My field notes did not simply contain an account of what took place, but also my perceptions of how the participants responded to me and I to them. My hopes, fears, frustrations, and other feelings were also documented, and the content of my journal would become one of the data sources that informed the findings.

Finally, I abstained from answering any indirect questions that were raised about religion or the Bible. For example, during my interview with Zadok, a fifty-nine-year-old utility technician who identified as "not at all religious," he said:

> I'd like to find out the, when we say the Bible is a collection of stories, but in it is a core piece and I need to know what that core piece is. Or I'd like somebody to tell me what that core piece is so I can read it.

I did not reply by suggesting that in my opinion the "core piece" of the Bible is the person Jesus, rather I acknowledged his comment with a nod, but said nothing and the conversation moved on.

There were two instances where I responded to a participant's direct questioning in such a way that it could be argued I was attempting to evangelize. Andy G is a forty-nine-year-old mechanic, who identified as "moderately religious" because he is a Freemason. By completing the project he realized that he was unaware of much of the Bible's content, a book that he affirmed as "a guide to life." Therefore, towards the end of our interview, he asked what version of the Bible was best to read. I indicated that the Good News Bible was a popular version, written in simple language and so might be worth a try. The second occasion concerned Anthony, a fifty-nine-year-old manager, who identified as a Christian and so "moderately religious." He had enjoyed the project and indicated that during the course of the research

---

22. Gray, *Doing Research in the Real World*, 499; Janesick, "'Stretching' Exercises for Qualitative Researchers," 141–155.

he had accepted an invitation to attend a Bible reading course at the church his wife attended. In this instance I replied positively, saying such a course would seem to suit him. These two occasions are the only times I am aware of consciously affirmed a participant's interest in the Bible or religion. In doing so however I do not believe I stepped beyond the ethical boundaries of this project for both men initiated the question/comment, I answered or affirmed a decision which they had already made and did not pursue either matter further. Therefore, as a Christian who was undertaking research I attempted to carry myself as a professional researcher, comfortably within the ethical parameters of this research.

The Research Materials

The research materials were not concerned with proselytizing either, for instance I avoided using texts which were concerned with conversion to Christianity. Furthermore, as a way of double-checking for any potential bias within the research materials, I approached three different academics who acted as "critical friends." The use of a critical friend (or three) is common practice in educational research,[23] and has also been used in contextual Bible reading research.[24] Having these three critical friends enhanced the transparency and integrity of my work. In my case, I specifically asked them to review the materials in light of my Christian identity. These scholars were familiar with small scale qualitative projects and identified with a variety of religions and none. In this way the research materials that I used were all reviewed with an eye to excising any apparent Christian bias. As it was, although there were various comments made regarding certain questions or phrases, none concerned the issue of proselytizing.

Moreover, I decided not to give the participants an actual Bible to read from. There is the argument that the individual texts should be presented in a physical Bible, for my research question sought to consider how people read the Bible. In this way, many of the associations the Bible has for the reader would more readily influence their reading of the text. Brent Plate argues that the visible form of the words on the page, their layout and setting informs the reading and "the way words appear to their readers will change the reader's interaction, devotion, and interpretation."[25] However, in light of the possible accusation that this research was trying

---

23. Wachob, "Critical Friendship Circles, the Cultural Challenge of Cool Feedback."
24. Cornwall, "Contextual Bible Study."
25. Plate, "Looking at Words," 67.

to put the Bible into the hands of those who do not regularly read it, it was decided to provide the participants with the texts printed on a single sheet of A4 paper so that they would never see or handle an actual Bible. I attempted to compensate for this by including a short description of the text's literary position within the Bible and its implied historical context in an introductory sheet preceding the text. I am not alone in adopting this format, the CBS method of Bible engagement also advocates that the Bible passage is given to the readers on a single A4 sheet of paper. In their case it is done because it "encourages the group members to focus on the chosen passage rather than becoming side-tracked by other passages, related or unrelated."[26] For CBS, this decision is made for practical reasons; in my case the ethical consideration took priority.

My research is also part sponsored by two Christian organizations: Bible Society and a Christian trust fund. The two main conditions for receiving the grants were that I provide them with regular progress reports and a copy of the final thesis. The participants were informed about these two sponsors, verbally and in the Participant Information Sheet. Although researchers, such as ethnographers, have found that relationships with sponsors can develop into a "patron-client" type of relationship with consequences for their fieldwork,[27] this was not my experience. I had a minimal relationship with both organizations, who assumed a very hands-off approach and had no input into the design of the research, fieldwork, data analysis, or findings.

This Book

Finally, those same ethical decisions have implications for this book, what is produced is not an evangelism guide. Andrew Curtis reflected upon the Bible readings of transsexual sex-workers in Australia and concludes by considering the implications of his research for Christian mission (2000).[28] I will not develop my work in this way because my project is not concerned with proselytizing. Instead I will utilize reader-response criticism and assume a more sociological approach. This is similar to James Bielo and Brian Malley, who also identified as "Christian," and use reader-response

---

26. Riches, *What is Contextual Bible Study?* 60.

27. Hammersley and Atkinson, *Ethnography,* 58–60.

28. Others who have undertaken qualitative or quantitative research amongst those who do not attend church and in light of their findings suggested ways in which the church can engage such people, include: Bissett, *Outside In*; Hay and Hunt, "Understanding the Spirituality of People who don't go to Church"; Spencer, *Beyond Belief?*; and Stetzer *et al., Lost and Found.*

criticism and social science to reflect on how fellow Christians read the Bible. Malley writes:

> I assume [. . .] that the authority and relevance of the Bible today are less a function of properties specific to the Bible than a consequence of the ways in which Bible believers encounter this ancient text. I do not deny either that the Bible has special properties or that these may in some measure account for its durability, but in this book I attempt to understand the longevity of the Bible as a function of the social and psychological elements of Bible-users' traditions.[29]

My decision to use reader-response criticism and assume a sociological approach should not be viewed as reductionistic. I am not claiming that my findings fully explain the readings that took place, but instead am presenting one perspective on them. There are other approaches from philosophy, theology, biblical studies, psychology, and history that are also valid. Indeed, because my work is interdisciplinary I will engage with some of these in a secondary way, and the opportunity remains for similar research to be undertaken from one or more of these approaches.

This research faced various ethical challenges as every piece of research does. However, the concern that this project was an attempt to evangelize needed to be addressed. To that end, my conduct in the field, the research methods, and this book demonstrate that my aim was not to proselytize.

Methods

Having put in place the foundations of my research, and located myself within it, I then considered the research tools. What follows presents the rationale behind the mixed method approach I employed and describes the individual research methods. Two other components of the research are also considered; the construction of two questionnaires and the piloting of these materials.

---

29. Malley, *How the Bible Works*, 10.

A Mixed-method Approach

Some qualitative research examining real readers has used a single method, such as a written response,[30] or an interview.[31] Many though have chosen to use a mixed-method approach.[32] They do so understanding that the data gained from one research method can be reviewed in light of data from a second or third. For example, Lynn Neal examined women's readings of evangelical romance novels, and based her research upon a series of semi-structured interviews with fifty readers and twenty authors of such books. However, she also analyzed around one hundred letters sent from readers to authors, and writes: "Together, the interviews and letters provided an array of views on inspirational romance novel reading, and the story of why some women read these novels emerged."[33]

Therefore, I too decided to adopt a mixed method approach, for the triangulation of different data sources should result in the findings having greater validity. Furthermore, it is not only anticipated that the different methods would confirm a particular finding, but that each one would highlight different aspects of it and so a fuller picture would emerge. David Silverman warns that a mixed-method approach must be kept simple, for it could overcomplicate and confuse the research process.[34] Nonetheless, I chose three different research methods to consider how the men in my study read the biblical texts: annotation, a questionnaire, and a semi-structured interview. These three tools are suited to the individual nature of this research, with each participant expected to read the text for himself.

Annotation

My decision to include annotation borrows from Yvonne Sherwood who explored the annotations made upon a Bible displayed in the Modern Art Gallery in Glasgow.[35] This Bible was part of an exhibition entitled *Sh[out]*:

---

30. Bleich, *Subjective Criticism*; Flynn, "Gender and Reading"; Pearce, *Feminism and the Politics of Reading*.

31. Hermes, *Reading Women's Magazines*; Holland, *Poems in Persons*; Llewellyn, *Reading, Feminism, and Spirituality*; Radway, *Reading the Romance*.

32. Ammerman, *Bible Believers*; Crapanzano, *Serving the Word*; Jennings, "Word and Spirit"; Le Grys, *Shaped by God's Story*; Malley, *How the Bible Works*; Macdonald, "The Psalms and Spirituality."

33. Neal, *Romancing God*, 7.

34. Silverman, *Doing Qualitative Research*, 63–64.

35. Sherwood, *Biblical Blaspheming*. My thanks to Andrew Davies who alerted me to this study.

Contemporary Art and Human Rights, at which the public were invited to annotate any part of the biblical text they desired. The resulting annotations became part of the data that Sherwood used in her reflections on the reception of the Bible in that context.[36] The annotation of a text, or similar strategy, has been suggested as an aid to research or learning: David Bleich argues for the use of a response statement by the reader,[37] Lauren Leslie and JoAnne Caldwell suggest thinking out loud by the reader as they read,[38] and Mike Jennings provided his participants with a "Bible Reading Comment form" to complete whilst reading.[39]

In my case, the annotating of a text is a research method that adheres to the qualitative methodology assumed by this project for it allows a breadth of engagement with the text. It also fits with my research aim of considering the reading that takes place, and my research task, which involves reading a short text. I therefore designed a "Manual" where the text the participants would read was printed, preceded by instructions for its possible annotation. The first page of the Manual explained and reinforced various aspects of the research task. In particular, this page contained explicit instructions regarding the reading and annotating of the text:

1. Please read the passage through twice.

2. On the second reading underline words, phrases, or concepts which stand out for any reason, and use the blank space on either side of the passage to write down why they stood out.

3. Finally, use that same space to write down any thoughts, feelings, ideas, images, memories, concerns, or insights which you have about the passage. Don't forget, there are no "right" or "wrong" answers; your honest impressions are what count.

In line with the qualitative underpinnings of this research, the phrase "there are no 'right' or 'wrong' answers" appeared twice on this introductory page. This attempted to reaffirm that the participants' personal engagement with the text was what I valued, no matter its tone or substance. Of course, a blank unannotated text was just as valid and valuable as one full of comments. I also did not want to guide the participants to read in a particular way, so to communicate that any type of annotation was

---

36. In chapter 5 I will engage with Sherwood's work in greater depth.

37. Bleich, "The Identity of Pedagogy and Research in the Study of Response to Literature."

38. Leslie and Caldwell, "Formal and Informal Measures of Reading Comprehension."

39. Jennings, "Word and Spirit."

acceptable I used a list of seven nouns: "thoughts, feelings, ideas, images, memories, concerns or insights." My choice of language was borrowed from Mike Jennings' Bible Reading Comment form, where he asked his participants to respond to the following:

> *What strikes you about these verses?* Pay attention to any ideas, feelings, images, memories, or current concerns that may come to you as you read. Write them down. Highlight words or phrases in the verses that trigger your responses.[40] (emphasis in original)

On the second page of the Manual the passage was printed. The layout was similar to that used in the manuscript method of Bible study.[41] It was located towards the middle of the page, with wide margins available for annotation and one-and-a-half line spacing allowing for clear underlining. The printed text excluded verse numbers and the layout was typically in the form of one large section of text with no divisions.[42] Having completed the annotation exercise, the participant was invited to complete an accompanying questionnaire that made up the second half of the Manual.

Questionnaire

Research into Bible reading has also, at times, made use of a questionnaire. For example, Andrew Village used a questionnaire with over two hundred questions to explore how Mark 9:14–29 was read by Anglican lay people.[43] Susan Loman and Leslie Francis also used a questionnaire to investigated biblical literalism amongst UK school children.[44] In their case, over 3,400 pupils were asked to read a series of Bible passages and indicate in the questionnaire how they viewed them. When questionnaires have been used in qualitative projects they have often been part of a mixed method approach along with interviewing and participant observation,[45] providing the researcher with a further avenue of enquiry. I decided to make use of a questionnaire principally because I anticipated that on some occasions the

---

40. Jennings, "Word and Spirit," 226.
41. Olesberg, *The Bible Study Handbook*, 14–18.
42. The two exceptions to this were Proverbs 10:1–11 where each proverb was set as a couplet and Psalm 88 which was divided into three sections guided by the *interlude* (Ps 88:1–7, 8–10, 11–18).
43. Village, *The Bible and Lay People*.
44. Loman and Francis, "The Loman Index of Biblical Interpretation."
45. Malley, *How the Bible Works*; Rogers, *Congregational Hermeneutics*.

participants would not annotate the biblical text and I wanted an immediate opportunity to consider why this was the case. The inclusion of a questionnaire in the Manual ensured that this was so.

This questionnaire comprised fifteen open and closed questions that were primarily formulated in light of the research question. They attempted to consider it from a variety of angles, for instance asking: What, if anything, "jumped out at you" as you read through the passage? Or: What, if anything, was your "gut reaction" to this passage? (i.e., how did it make you feel?) And another example asked: Please write a one line summary of the passage.

However, at this stage I was also working with three secondary research questions. First, in light of the trifold division of the world of the author, text and reader which is seen in contemporary CBS methods,[46] and Village's work,[47] I asked: Where do my readers locate the meaning of the text? Second, with Le Grys,[48] and Schneiders,[49] I considered what the transformative potential of these readings were. Finally, in light of the contextual nature of reading,[50] what particular influences can be noted in the reading? These secondary research questions were helpful in constructing the questionnaire, but once the data was collated it was the emerging themes that I focused on rather than these secondary questions. The questionnaire concluded with the opportunity for the participant to note down any other thoughts or comments, reflecting standard questionnaire practice.

Semi-structured Interview

The third research method I chose was a semi-structured interview. This is perhaps the most popular research tool used to explore real readers. At times it has been used as the sole research method,[51] while at others as part of a mixed method approach.[52] A semi-structured interview allows the participant to speak to an issue using their words and for a conversation to develop between them and the researcher. Robert Weiss emphasizes

---

46. Riches, *What is Contextual Bible Study?*
47. Village, *The Bible and Lay People.*
48. Le Grys, *Shaped by God's Story.*
49. Schneiders, *The Revelatory Text.*
50. Davies, *Biblical Criticism,* 4–7.
51. Hermes, *Reading Women's Magazines*; Llewellyn, *Reading, Feminism, and Spirituality*; Radway, *Reading the Romance.*
52. Ammerman, *Bible Believers*; Bielo, *Words upon the* Word; Crapanzano, *Serving the Word*; Malley, *How the Bible Works*; Neal, *Romancing God*; Rogers, *Congregational Hermeneutics.*

the value of interviewing by arguing that it is one of the contexts most suited to the sharing of personal thoughts, feelings and experiences.[53] As a research method, the semi-structured interview sits comfortably within a qualitative methodology and in light of the previous two methods involving some form of written response, it provided the opportunity for the participants to respond verbally.

Having read the five texts, annotating and completing the related questionnaires, each participant would be invited to discuss the texts in a one-to-one semi-structured interview. The interview contained some questions that everyone was asked, for example, I always gave the participants a copy of each text, asking them, "What did you make of that one?" Other questions were specific to the participant and emerged in light of my analysis of their annotations and responses in the questionnaires. It was also in this setting that I could clarify answers and annotations that the participants had provided or raise some of the emerging themes related to their responses. This provided them with the opportunity to respond and if necessary clarify any misunderstanding on my part, which in turn further validated the findings.[54] As is standard interview practice I typically began by asking the participants to tell me a bit about themselves and concluded by offering them the opportunity to ask me any questions or add a further comment.[55] The interviews were recorded using a digital recording device and once completed, transcribed. A set transcription protocol was followed and I emailed the participants a copy of the transcript with the invitation to contact me if they felt there were any errors or wanted certain excerpts kept from publication,[56] but nothing was ever raised.

Entrance and Exit Questionnaires

There were two other tasks I asked my participants to complete. First, in order to gain some background information about them, along with a sense of their religious affiliation and attitudes towards the Bible, I designed a two-part Entrance Questionnaire. The first part requested basic biographical data about the participant and their religious affiliation, which was achieved by asking them how religious and spiritual they considered themselves to be.[57] Their past and present religious practice was also explored before con-

---

53. Weiss, *Learning from Strangers*, 1–2.
54. Creswell, *Research Design*, 201–2.
55. Kvale and Brinkmann, *InterViews*, 128–29.
56. Swinton and Mowat, *Practical Theology and Qualitative Research*, 119.
57. There was little difference between the participants' religious and spiritual

sidering their exposure to the Bible. These questions were developed in light of other surveys, in particular David Clines' two surveys in Sheffield,[58] and the British Social Attitudes survey on religious identity.[59]

The second part of the Entrance Questionnaire contained twenty-two statements related to the Bible and were designed to reveal the participants' attitudes to and beliefs about the Bible. Using a five-point Likert scale the participants had to indicate how strongly they (dis)agreed with each statement. Five statements considered the Bible's content, five its role or impact upon society, and five dealt with the participant's attitude towards the Bible. These areas were most significant for my research and so five statements were dedicated to each. Three statements were also included which considered the issue of interpretation and three dealt with the Bible and other faiths. Likert scales are recognized tools for measuring attitudes. Bram Oppenheim notes that they are not designed to yield subtle insights, rather they produce "reliable, rough ordering of people with regard to a particular attitude."[60] Mike Jennings used a five point Likert scale to assess his Bible readers' views on church and the Bible.[61] Christian Research also used a five point Likert scale to explore people's attitudes to the Bible.[62] In my case, the twenty-two statements were phrased positively and negatively and placed randomly throughout the three tables that held them, as is considered best practice.[63] The information gleaned from these tables was important in providing a fairly clear, if rough, measure of the participants' attitudes towards and beliefs about the Bible, which were then clarified during the semi-structured interview.

The Entrance Questionnaire was undertaken at the start of the research, prior to reading any of the texts. At the end, having read all five passages but not before the semi-structured interview, the participants

---

identities, someone who identified as "not at all religious" would also typically identify as "not at all spiritual." Moreover, the men predominantly spoke about "religion" and rarely "spirituality," because of this I focus on the men's sense of religious identity. There were four exceptions to this, Sam, Ethan and Zadok all described themselves as "spiritual but not religious" and Andy G, identified as "moderately religious" and "not at all spiritual" due to his active membership with the Freemasons. On analysis of the data no distinctive qualities could be seen in these four men's readings that I could attribute to the difference between their religious and spiritual identity.

58. Clines, *The Bible and the Modern World*.
59. British Social Attitudes, "British Social Attitudes 28."
60. Oppenheim, *Questionnaire Design, Interviewing and Attitude Measurement*, 200.
61. Jennings, "Word and Spirit," 74–75.
62. Christian Research, *Bible Engagement in England and Wales*.
63. Sapsford, *Survey Research*, 225.

completed an Exit Questionnaire. It contained the same twenty-two statements as the Entrance Questionnaire and comparing the results was one way of identifying any significant change in the readers' attitudes to or beliefs about the Bible. It also asked them directly whether or not they had been affected by reading the texts.

Pilot

Having thus designed my research methods I sought to pilot them. Such practice is a valuable part of the research design and is an opportunity not only to trial the newly constructed research tools, but also to test the wording of certain questions.[64] I approached nine, local, male dominated workplaces before the staff at the tenth agreed to take part. I had only begun to explain to this group of grounds and gardening staff that I was a researcher looking for participants for a research project when the only female in the group indicated that she would volunteer. In light of the difficulty in getting people to participate I said that although the main study would focus solely on men, for the purposes of the pilot men and women would be accepted. Thus three people from a group of five took part, two men (Rob and Mark) and one woman (Emily). As anticipated all the research tasks were conducted during the participants' lunchtimes at which I provided them with lunch. The use of an incentive is one method of encouraging participant uptake, and is common when there is difficulty getting volunteers.[65] In my case, the provision of lunch was less of an incentive and more of a thank you, as the participants had agreed to volunteer prior to being told about it.

Aside from the inclusion of a woman, there were four main differences between the pilot study and the fieldwork. First, in the fieldwork the men indicated that lunch would not be required, so I took them cream cakes instead. Second, where I had initially chosen five texts in the order of 2 John, Proverbs 10:1–11, 2 Samuel 5:17–25, Matthew 18:21–35, and Psalm 88, following feedback from the pilot participants I reordered them so as to begin with a more accessible text. Thus, the order given at the Chemical Industrial Plant was Proverbs 10:1–11, 2 Samuel 5:17–25, Matthew 18:21–35, Psalm 88, and 2 John. Third, I trialed different wordings of questions in the pilot study and was then able to gauge the participants' response to them. That informed my decision as to which questions would be included in the main fieldwork. Finally, the interviews with the pilot study participants were

---

64. Silverman, *Doing Qualitative Research*, 197.

65. Oppenheim, *Questionnaire Design, Interviewing and Attitude Measurement*, 104.

longer as they also included questions regarding any changes they would suggest to the research materials or process. The data that was produced in the pilot study was not added to the data from the main fieldwork for that was neither the purpose of the pilot nor did it correspond to the case study nature of my research. Only after having undertaken the pilot study and reviewed all the material did I turn to consider the actual fieldwork.

Fieldwork

In light of the difficulty getting participants for the pilot study, I expected the fieldwork to be no different. One technique that is commonly used by researchers to access a difficult field is the use of a gatekeeper.[66] This is usually someone who can act as a go-between and facilitate the researcher's entry into a particular research field, or introduce them to potential participants. Accordingly, I approached two workplace chaplaincy organizations to see if they would be able to facilitate my entry into a male dominated workplace. One of them was Mission in the Economy (MITE),[67] which sought to be a faith presence in the economic communities of North West England. Importantly evangelism was not one of their aims, so they were unlikely to see my own research as a proselytizing opportunity.

MITE put me in contact with George, a member of one of their local groups. He was in his early sixties and had worked as the health and safety coordinator at a local Chemical Industrial Plant for twenty-four years. George was a Christian and so was sympathetic to my project. We met in the summer of 2012 at the Chemical Plant where he worked, and when I described the project to George, he said he was happy to act as a gatekeeper, believing the Plant to be a good site for my fieldwork. It had a large male dominated workforce who typically returned to their staffrooms and portacabins during their forty-minute lunch breaks, so it could provide both the setting and the time for my project, if the men were willing to volunteer.

George was also part of a local initiative called *The Salt of the Earth Network*.[68] This was established by a local Bishop to facilitate discussion and action on the part of local industries and their communities. Typically they organized quarterly meetings at which issues like corporate social responsibility, fracking, or apprenticeships were discussed. This network was one known to the Chemical Plant and George suggested that my research

---

66. Burgess, "Sponsors, Gatekeepers, Members, and Friends"; Stewart, "Case Study."

67. http://www.missionintheeconomy.com

68. http://www.saltoftheearthnetwork.net

would fit within its broad vision of encouraging partnerships across agencies, industries and communities. Thus, in a very loose way my project was adopted by this network. This had two practical implications. First, over the next few weeks George raised my project with a member of the senior management team at the Plant. He presented it as a piece of doctoral research which had links with the *Salt of the Earth Network*, a network known to the manager, who subsequently agreed to the fieldwork taking place. Second, with my agreement, once the fieldwork had been completed the *Salt of the Earth Network* coordinated a feedback evening at the Chemical Industrial Plant where the participants and others were invited to hear the results.[69] These were the main roles that MITE and the *Salt of the Earth Network* played in the fieldwork. They consistently encouraged me in my research and their input was vital in providing access to a suitable workplace without pressurizing me to modify or alter my project in any way.

Not only did George facilitate my entry into this site, he also took me through the induction process enabling me to visit the site unaccompanied and introduced me to two groups of potential participants. It became clear that George had a particular talent for stimulating people's interest in the uninteresting. Further, having worked on the site for twenty four years, he had built up decades of good will with many workers. I was to benefit from this good will, for these two groups of men, most of who identified as "not at all religious," indicated that they would be willing to participate.

By the time the fieldwork started, in October 2012, George had retired. This meant that the fieldwork could take place free from any direct influence from him. George and I continued to meet throughout the fieldwork however, and I kept him updated on my progress. In order to maintain the participants' confidentiality and anonymity, George never asked any direct questions about them and the project was always discussed in general terms.

The first group of men began the project in October 2012. They were a group of welders who had lunch together in their portacabin and four out of the five men took part. Over a period of two weeks these men read through the five texts and completed the various research materials. Due to two of the participants falling ill it was a further two weeks before all the participants had been interviewed. This group was then able to recommend another small group and introduced me to them. Snowball sampling is an accepted and common sampling technique especially in settings that are unfamiliar to the researcher or difficult to access.[70]

---

69. Significantly, only one of the men came: Anthony. This perhaps indicates that although most of the men were willing to volunteer, ultimately they were not that interested in the project.

70. Davies, *Doing a Successful Research Project*, 147; Denscombe, *The Good*

I discovered that there were three components necessary to maximize the chance that a new group of men would agree to take part. First, a recognized member of staff who had completed the project needed to introduce me and vouch for it. Second, the new group should contain no more than three people, and finally, that I explain the project to them personally. If any one of these components was missing the probability that the men would volunteer reduced significantly. For instance, towards the end of the fieldwork I approached the manager who had earlier agreed to the fieldwork being carried out on the site asking him if I could contact the staff in the main administrative/managerial block. He was happy for me to try to recruit from amongst the management, but suggested that he email all the managers on my behalf. As it was, only two out of a potential sixteen replied to indicate their willingness.

Thus, when one group finished the project they were usually able to introduce me to a new group who were often willing to volunteer and so over a ten month period seven groups completed the project. In only one instance did a group decline to take part, and that was because they were due to move site later that week. The first was a group of welders, the second utility men, the third were a group of engineers and the fourth a group of scaffolders. The fifth group comprised mainly mechanics, the sixth another small group of scaffolders and the seventh a group of managers. Each group typically comprised of a small team who lunched together in their own cabin/office. The only exception to this was the managers who, having individual offices, undertook the research alone at their desks. My youngest participant was aged twenty-two (John) and the oldest was sixty-two (Derek). The twenty men had differing levels of education and socio-economic backgrounds; however all were born in Britain and described themselves as "white British." None of them read the Bible, went to church or participated in any other religious activity on a regular basis. They either identified as having no religion or with the Christian faith. By the time the managers had completed the project it was clear that the same themes were reappearing in the data. I had reached saturation point and it was unlikely more data would add to the findings.[71]

These different groups followed the pattern set out earlier in this chapter. That is, having been introduced by another worker who had recently completed the project I presented it to them verbally and provided them with the Participant Information Sheet. A few days later I returned and answered any questions that had arisen, before inquiring if anyone

---

Research Guide, 17–18.

71. Davies, *Doing a Successful Research Project*, 149.

was willing to volunteer. Those who did then signed the Consent form and we arranged a schedule for completing the various questionnaires and Manuals. It usually took two weeks for the men to complete all of this before I then analyzed their data and arranged to meet them for a one-to-one semi-structured interview.

My description thus far does not do justice to the lived experience of undertaking this research; the reality was more convoluted and at times frustrating. Much in the same way as the researcher should identify themselves and their influence on the project, so too the difficulties and challenges must be acknowledged for they are also part of the research journey. Various issues cropped up throughout the fieldwork that resulted in it taking significantly longer than I anticipated. There was a week when the entire Plant closed down for essential maintenance and various holiday periods when the level of staff was reduced. At times the demands of work were such that the men were not able to meet at the hour they had indicated, and on other occasions some participants had periods of absence due to ill health. Sometimes when a group member was not present to complete the required research task they would offer to do so later that day or at home that evening. I agreed to this and it appeared to make no difference to the way they read the five texts. Unfortunately on two occasions I provided the wrong materials to two participants, thankfully the problem was resolved the following day when the issue came to light and I was able to give them the correct materials. Two participants withdrew from the project, one due to an accident that prevented him from returning to work, and the other out of choice. Therefore, an eighth group started but did not complete the project. In total the fieldwork lasted ten months.

Analysis

The data produced in the fieldwork required analyzing. Following Martyn Denscombe I viewed my data analysis and interpretation as one process,[72] and using a thematic approach I set out to "capture the dominant themes" present in the data.[73] Two main layers of analysis would take place. The first was at the individual level, for once a participant had engaged with all five texts and completed the associated questionnaires, I analyzed their data. This involved coding the various subjects, issues, ideas and comments that were raised and placing them in larger categories, which led to the identification of the main themes. This information allowed me

---

72. Denscombe, *The Good Research Guide*, 287–88.
73. Franzosi, "Content Analysis," 550.

to tailor the semi-structured interview to the participant's own readings. I undertook a subsequent wave of analysis once the interview had been transcribed, for only at this stage could the triangulation of the three data sources be done. Having completed this, I produced a one page summary of the participant's reading of the five texts.

The second layer of analysis was at the corporate level and took place once all the fieldwork was complete. It involved immersing myself for a series of weeks in all the data produced by the participants. During this time I reviewed each piece, once again coding, categorizing, and identifying the major themes. Having undertaken this first wave of corporate analysis a second wave followed, one focusing on the main themes identified and involved seeking further data related to them that affirmed, challenged or nuanced them. Finally, a third wave of analysis took place concentrating on any minor themes in the data or outlying categories to which I had not given due consideration. These layers and waves of analysis, reflect the attention to detail required by qualitative data analysis.[74] In total twenty interview transcripts (twenty-five to fifty minutes long), 140 questionnaires (one hundred related to the five texts and forty from the Entrance and Exit questionnaires) and sixty-nine annotated texts were analyzed from the fieldwork.

Conclusion

In this way I attempted to answer my research question, by designing and implementing a qualitative case study. This chapter has described the construction of my research tools and the undertaking of my fieldwork. I began by locating myself with reference to my work and noting some of the ways in which I influenced its shape. Particularly as a Christian, I had to demonstrate that my project was not evangelism in the guise of research. I did this by highlighting how I carried myself in the field, my construction of the research materials and the tone of this book. Having addressed this ethical issue, I returned to my research question and argued for the use of a mixed method approach comprising annotation, questionnaire, and interview. I then recounted how I used a pilot study to further refine the tools, before tracing the fieldwork I undertook. I noted the usefulness of George, my gatekeeper, and the snowball sampling technique that resulted in seven groups taking part. This chapter then concluded by outlining the various waves of analysis that took place, both for each individual participant and for the group as a whole.

---

74. Bazeley, *Qualitative Data Analysis*; Boulton and Hammersley, "Analysis of Unstructured Data," 250–56.

Therefore, in this first part I have traced the prompts, development, and refinement of my research question along with the construction of my research methods and implementing of the fieldwork. The second part now turns to consider the main findings from this case study. What follows reflects the thematic analysis that took place, for the findings are explored in a similar thematic fashion.

Part Two

Chapter 4

The Transactional Theory of Reading

IN THE SECOND HALF of this book I will argue that these readers' relationships with the five biblical texts shaped their readings of those texts. There are three strands to this argument and they make up the subsequent seven chapters. The first strand concerns the theoretical foundation that I build upon, and is addressed in this short chapter by unpacking Louise Rosenblatt's transactional theory of reading. In particular, two components of her relational view of reading are highlighted, for they most closely account for the findings from my case study. First, the reader and the text co-exist in a dynamic system indicating that they have a relationship of some kind prior to coming together in the act of reading. Second, all that the reader is in relation to the text shapes their reading of that text, with certain aspects of that relationship having a greater influence on the reading.

The second strand of my argument is made up of four examples which demonstrate the reality of the central claim theorized in the first strand. Each example explores a different aspect of the reader's relationship with the texts and its subsequent influence upon the readings. Accordingly, chapter 5 examines the impact of the reader's prior experiences of religion, chapter 6 the influence of the reader's sense of religious identity, chapter 7 the role of the reader's attitudes towards the Bible, and chapters 8 and 9 investigate the significance of the reader's beliefs about the Bible.

Chapter 10 continues to explore the relational nature of these readings, and here a series of unexpected readings are studied. These readings were shaped by, but did not conform to, the reader's relationship with the text. They form the third strand of my argument by demonstrating the capacity of a text to lead a reader into an atypical reading. In this way then the relational nature of these readings is argued, one involving both the reader and the text.

This present chapter begins by introducing Louise Rosenblatt's transactional theory of reading. I briefly describe the central tenets of her reader-response theory and in doing so highlight two particular ways in which this theory resonates with the findings of my own study. These are that the reader and the text exist within a dynamic system, and that the reader brings all that they are to a text with certain aspects of the reader informing the reading more than others. The transactional theory has its limitations and some of these are also presented, ultimately however I contend that this theory suitably correlates with, and expounds, the readings that took place at the Chemical Industrial Plant, something the remaining chapters will demonstrate.

Louise Rosenblatt and the Transactional Theory of Reading

Louise Rosenblatt (1904–2005) was an American educationalist and literary scholar, who is recognized as one of the early and significant voices within reader-response criticism.[1] Her transactional theory has been widely used by teachers in North America,[2] and has been applied to a variety of other interpretive contexts, including music,[3] advertising,[4] Bible reading practices,[5] and biblical interpretation.[6] It has been adapted to include a vocal and written component,[7] and merged with activity theory.[8] Wayne Booth in his foreword to the fifth edition of her work *Literature as Exploration* writes:

> Has she been influential? Immensely so: how many other critical works first published in the late thirties have extended themselves, like this one, to five editions, proving themselves relevant to decade after decade of critical and pedagogical revolution?[9]

While the main impact of her work has been in literary and pedagogical theory, in the area of biblical studies she is relatively unknown, for here reader-response critics like Stanley Fish and Wolfgang Iser are more commonly cited.[10] Indeed, as I indicated in chapter 1, there are many

---

1. Tompkins, *Reader-Response Criticism*, x; Roen and Karolides, "Louise Rosenblatt."
2. Sloan, "Reader Response in Perspective."
3. Cardany, "A Transactional Approach to 'Sing' by Raposo and Lichtenheld."
4. Begoray et al., "Adolescent Reading/Viewing of Advertisements."
5. Jennings, "Word and Spirit"; Pike, "The Bible and the Reader's Response."
6. Davies, *Double Standards in Isaiah*.
7. Dugan, "Transactional Literature Discussions."
8. Beach, "Critical Issues."
9. Booth, "Foreword," vii.
10. Barton, "Thinking about Reader-Response Criticism"; McKnight, "Reader-Response Criticism"; Moore, "Negative Hermeneutics, Insubstantial Texts"; Porter, "Why hasn't Reader-Response Criticism Caught on in New Testament Studies?"; Resseguie,

reader-response theories that have been used to explore the act of reading. In my case, it was only having undertaken the fieldwork and analyzed the data that I was drawn to the transactional theory of reading, for of the theories I considered it most clearly explained and described the reading phenomenon I observed. First, it understands that readers and texts co-exist in the same matrix, their previous encounters and associations will influence their subsequent coming together. Second, texts (and images) have a degree of agency, therefore a reader is able to vicariously participate in a time and place unknown to them through the act of reading, this is the power of a text. Third, unlike some theories that emphasize the reader's personality,[11] or interpretive community,[12] the transactional theory assumes a more holistic perspective understanding all that a reader is has the potential to shape the reading. Fourth, even though readers are understood in this broad way, when it comes to the act of reading certain readerly aspects rise to the surface influencing the reading whilst others fall into the background. Fifth, as part of this engagement with a text, every reader places himself or herself somewhere on an efferent-aesthetic spectrum as they read.

The convergence of my data with the transactional theory can be seen in these five points. However, in this chapter I principally focus on the two most significant points for my case study in general, other points will be engaged with more directly in subsequent chapters. The two that I will shortly address are that readers and texts co-exist in the same matrix and that certain readerly aspects will rise to the surface influencing the reader whilst others will fall into the background.

The transactional theory of reading is a reader centered theory and explores the act of reading from an anthropocentric perspective. This sits comfortably with the social scientific tools and methodology I adopted. At the beginning of *The Reader, the Text, the Poem: The Transactional Theory of the Literary Work* Rosenblatt notes that historically the focus of scholars has been upon the author or the text, and "the reader has tended to remain in shadow."[13] This is not a unique observation and is one which George Aichele and others have sought to address with reference to the Bible.[14] In Rosenblatt's case, she reflected on how actual readers (students) engaged with texts, theorizing the relationship that occurs between the reader and the text in the act of reading, something she calls the transactional theory of reading. By

---

"Reader-Response Criticism and the Synoptic Gospels"; Schwáb, "Mind the Gap."

11. Francis, "Ordinary Readers and Reader Perspectives on Sacred Texts."
12. Fish, *Is There a Text in This Class?*
13. Rosenblatt, *The Reader, the Text, the Poem*, 1.
14. Aichele et al., *The Postmodern Bible*.

focusing on the reader/text transaction, she brings the reader out from the shadow to assume their place alongside the author and the text.

The Interconnectedness of Reading

Rosenblatt builds on the idea of "transaction" promoted by John Dewey and Arthur Bentley in *Knowing and the Known*, where they argue there is no definitive divide between the knower, the knowing and the known, rather they are all interconnected. They were challenging the positivist paradigm that the subject and object were distinct and separate, positing in its place that both are part of the same matrix and so influence each other. This view is commonly held by social scientists,[15] and is an integral part of disciplines such as ethnography where the researcher and the researched are not viewed as separate entities but part of the same research matrix.[16] Ecology is another discipline where the inter-relatedness of the subject and object is indispensable, here animal, plant, and sea life are all understood to be part of one dynamic system.[17]

By applying this idea to reading, Rosenblatt argues that the reader and the text are not unconnected entities that come together in the reading of a text and then move on potentially unaffected by the reading (much like two snooker balls bouncing off each other).[18] Rather, reading is a relational activity involving two parties, the reader and the text, who have a reciprocal relationship, existing within the same matrix and influencing each other as they come together, much as a river and a river bank do.[19] Therefore, with regards to Bible reading, the following chapters will show that each of my participants had a pre-existing relationship with the biblical texts. These men were part of a dynamic system, a matrix, within which the five texts also existed and as they were brought together the nature and contours of the relationship became clear. This relationship was not a direct one because none of the men indicated that they were familiar with the texts. It was indirect for the five texts were associated with the Bible and wider Christianity, subjects which the participants had a direct relationship with, having previously encountered both.[20]

15. Gray, *Doing Research in the Real World*, 498–99.
16. Rosenblatt, *Making Meaning with Texts*, 47.
17. Ibid., xvii
18. Ibid., 40.
19. Dillard, *Living by Fiction*, 15.
20. Strictly speaking, no one ever encounters Christianity but they do meet Christians, attend Christian services and are exposed to traditions, rituals, and festivals

This relational view of reading is further developed by Rosenblatt, who posits, that in the act of reading both parties continue to influence each other:

> Reading is a constructive, selective process over time in a particular context. The relation between reader and signs on the page proceeds in a to-and-fro spiral, in which each is continually being affected by what the other has contributed. [. . .] As the text unrolls before the reader's eyes, the meaning made of the early words influences what comes to mind and is selective for the succeeding signs. But if these do not fit in with the meaning developed thus far, the reader may revise it to assimilate the new words or may start all over again with different expectations.[21]

According to Rosenblatt then, reading is not made up of the text asserting its meaning upon the reader, nor the reader extracting or creating a meaning out of the text. Instead, meaning emerges from the toing-and-froing that occurs in the reader/text relationship. It is a "two-way, reciprocal relation,"[22] and so "meaning is not 'in' the text or 'in' the reader. Both reader and text are essential to the transactional process of making meaning."[23]

Readers and Texts

By "reader," Rosenblatt does not focus upon one particular part of an individual, such as their psychological profile, personality, ideological stance, or a named social location. Instead, she highlights a multitude of things that make up an individual, such as their attitudes, experiences, beliefs, assumptions, feelings, personality and expectations. These the reader brings to the text, along with "many other elements in a never-to-be-duplicated combination [which] determine his inter-fusion with the peculiar contribution of the text."[24]

I would further add that for Rosenblatt there are three elements which she notes as shaping the reader and so the reading. First, there is the reader's personal association or connection with the text, which would include their attitudes, expectations and memories related to the text. Second, there are wider aspects of the reader that also contribute to the reader/

---

associated with the Christian faith.

21. Rosenblatt, *Literature as Exploration*, 26–27.
22. Ibid., 27.
23. Ibid., 27.
24. Rosenblatt, *Making Meaning with Texts*, 30.

text relationship, such as the reader's personality, temperament or present preoccupation. Third, the socio-physical context of the reading is also understood to play a role within this relationship, shaping the reading that takes place.[25] This plethora of influences shapes the reader's approach to the text and the reading act itself. In this way, Rosenblatt's transactional theory contends that the reader brings all that they are to the text, in a particular socio-physical context, all of which shapes the reading.

In my case however, I use the term "the reader's relationship with a text" to specifically refer to the reader's direct associations with the text, this would include their attitudes, experiences, beliefs, memories, and assumptions with reference to the text. This is because the readings that took place at the Chemical Plant revealed the significant influence of these readerly associations upon the readings. This limited definition of a reader's relationship with a text is also seen in Andrew Village's work:

> A person's relationship to a sacred text such as the Bible encompasses a number of different aspects. Among these are their attitude towards the Bible, their beliefs about the Bible and their use of the Bible. It would not be surprising if these were related to each other: people who have negative attitudes towards the Bible are unlikely to believe that it has any divinely ordained authority, and probably read it seldom if ever. Those who believe it to be the word of god will presumably have a positive attitude to it and will be more likely to read it. This broad generalization hides a more complex picture in which attitudes, beliefs and practices are distinct aspects of a holistic relationship to scripture.[26]

Rosenblatt understands a "text" to be "a set of marks or squiggles on a page, these become a sequence of *signs* as they meet the eyes of a reader,"[27] (emphasis in original); signs which can be interpreted. The transactional theory contends that the text can play two particular roles in any reading. First, it can act to stir-up,[28] evoke,[29] and stimulate the reader.[30] In other words, it provides something specific to which the reader responds.

---

25. Rosenblatt, *Literature as Exploration*, 30; Rosenblatt, *The Reader, the Text, the Poem*, 81.
26. Village, *The Bible and Lay People*, 29.
27. Rosenblatt, *Making Meaning with Texts*, x.
28. Ibid., xxv.
29. Ibid., 9.
30. Rosenblatt, *Literature as Exploration*, 31.

However, it is not limited to the role of stimulus, for it also has the potential to guide,[31] regulate, and lead the reader in the construction of meaning.[32]

Selective Attention

The transactional theory argues that as the reader comes to a text "some expectation, some tentative feeling, idea, or purpose, no matter how vague at first, starts the reading process."[33] Using William James's concept of "selective attention,"[34] Rosenblatt argues that particular associations, such as thoughts, feelings or experiences, will be pushed into the center of the reader's attention, whilst others fall into the background.[35] These initial responses are chosen from a multitude of others because the reader understands them to be the most relevant for this particular act of reading.[36] In other words, certain aspects of the reader's relationship with the text will be considered more significant to the reading than others, and so will play a more dominant role in the reading which takes place. In particular, Rosenblatt contends that every reader places herself somewhere on an efferent/aesthetic spectrum as she anticipates reading a text. If the reader understands that the text should be read for information, as one would a train ticket, then she reads from the efferent end of the spectrum. Whereas, if she believes it should be read with reference to the feelings, images, and thoughts that it stirs up, as one would a poem, then she would read from the aesthetic end of the spectrum.[37] Such a broad view of the reader and all that she brings to the text is foundational to the transactional theory and my use of it.

Once someone has begun to read, he and the text "are involved in a complex, nonlinear, recursive, self-correcting transaction,"[38] as they to and fro, acting and being acted upon. Rosenblatt is not as prescriptive as Wolfgang Iser, who describes the reader as following the "flow" of a text, anticipating the subsequent sentences, and filling in the gaps where that flow is interrupted.[39] Her broad view of a reader understands that he brings all that he is to the text and in the unique dynamic interchange

31. Ibid., 265.
32. Rosenblatt, *The Reader, the Text, the Poem*, 11.
33. Rosenblatt, *Making Meaning with Texts*, 8.
34. James, *Principles of Psychology*.
35. Rosenblatt, *Making Meaning with Texts*, xxiv.
36. Ibid., 6.
37. Ibid., 10–14.
38. Ibid., 9.
39. Iser, *The Implied Reader*, 280.

that takes place meaning emerges. In Iser's case, the textual gaps act as a stimulus and by filling in those gaps the text takes on greater significance for the reader.[40] Rosenblatt also understands that the text acts as a stimulus but this is not limited to textual gaps rather every sign on the page is a stimulus. In this way, the reader and the text's toing and froing produces meaning and significance.

Limitations of the Transactional Theory

The transactional theory is not without its limitations or critics.[41] For instance, it acknowledges the influence of other factors in any reading, including the context or "socio-physical" reading site. However, unlike contextual Bible reading approaches, such as CBS, it does not major on this influence, something highlighted by Richard Beach who responds by incorporating activity theory into the transactional model.[42] In doing so, he suggests that every reader's transaction with a text is situated within a wider socio-physical context, and it is this context which influences the reader's motivation, sense of identity, and interest in the text.

David Bleich argues against the transactional theory's assumption that texts have agency,[43] in that they can lead a reader, and the resulting limitation of meaning that ensues. This is one of the distinctions between Rosenblatt's theory and that of Stanley Fish, who proposes that there is no pre-existing text rather all texts are constructed in the mind of the reader. He argues that the reason two or more readers can reach a similar conclusion on the same text is because they belong to the same interpretive community, sharing the same interpretive strategy, which also means that any interpretation is limited by the same interpretive community.[44] Rosenblatt acknowledges that any meaning is possible, but argues that the text rather than the interpretive community limits the validity of meaning. In her theory there is a place for the reading community in correcting or nuancing the meaning that has been proposed (the example she gives is of a college class).[45] However, her focus is on the text and its role in restricting the range of possible meanings, not the interpretive community. In line

---

40. Iser, *Prospecting*, 33–34.

41. Connell, "The Emergence of Pragmatic Philosophy's Influence on Literary Theory."

42. Beach, "Critical Issues."

43. Bleich, "Epistemological Assumptions in the Study of Response."

44. Fish, *Is There a Text in This Class?*; Fish, "Interpreting the 'Variorum.'"

45. Rosenblatt, *Making Meaning with Texts*, 28.

with Gadamer and Iser she also argues that the text provides the potential for the reading transaction to produce new understandings outside of the reader's interpretive community.[46]

Similarly where a historical-critical approach to biblical interpretation would concentrate on the authorial intent and *Sitz im Leben* of the text, Rosenblatt acknowledges the role of the probable authorial intent and background to the text in guiding the reader's understanding,[47] but does not major on this either. The lack of attention to these historical aspects results in a theory that falls short of what some consider a balanced model of interpretation.[48] However, Rosenblatt is writing aware of a historical legacy that has prioritized the author and the text over the reader and sought to redress this imbalance by focusing on the reader.[49] Further, as an educationalist her purpose was to provide a theoretical foundation for the teaching of literacy not the construction of an interpretive model, which is, I suspect, another reason for her focus on the reader/text relationship.

This focus corresponds to my research enquiry as to how men would read five biblical texts. My interpretation of the data indicated that my readers were bringing to the texts a plethora of different experiences, identities, attitudes and beliefs. All of these associations were interlinked, often reinforcing each other, but at other times pulling the reader in different directions. In accord with the transactional theory of reading, ultimately certain aspects of the reader's relationship with the biblical texts played a more significant role than others and these are the subject of the proceeding chapters.

In doing so, I will present these aspects as individual findings from my case study. However, such an approach does stand against the tone of the transactional theory, for Rosenblatt's emphasis is on the interconnectedness of all the components that make up a reader's relationship with a text. Reading is a "complex network or circuit of interrelationships, with reciprocal interplay," she writes.[50] She does believe individual elements that make up the reader/text relationship can be identified,[51] but her emphasis is on the holistic nature of the relationship.

---

46. Rosenblatt, *Literature as Exploration*, 25.

47. Rosenblatt, *Making Meaning with Texts*, xxiii.

48. Gorman, *Elements of Biblical Exegesis*; Osborne, *The Hermeneutical Spiral*; Tate, *Biblical Interpretation*.

49. Rosenblatt, *The Reader, the Text, the Poem*, 1–5.

50. Rosenblatt, *Making Meaning with Texts*, 43.

51. Ibid., 42.

Mike Jennings adheres to this interconnected view of reading when presenting the findings from his doctoral research.[52] He charts the way one reader's (Simon) anxiety about the legitimacy of their Christian faith and the restorationist theology they adhered to intertwine shaping their subsequent Bible engagement.[53] However, in doing this Jennings only focused upon one reader out of his group of nine participants, the other eight played a minor role in his thesis. In my case, in order to demonstrate the impact of different readerly influences upon a reading I focus upon four different aspects, using at least two participants to illustrate each. This approach provides depth, clarity and allows for the exploration of various readers and readings but at the cost of not fully addressing the inter-related nature of these readings.

Conclusion

This chapter has provided the foundation and first strand of my central argument. I unpacked Rosenblatt's transactional theory of reading highlighting its view of the reader and the text as members of one dynamic system. In my case, I will go onto demonstrate that my participants already had some sort of relationship with the texts, one mediated through their connection with the Bible and Christianity. Moreover, because a reader's relationship with a text shapes their reading of it, the exact nature and flavor of that relationship would become clear as they read the five texts. The transactional theory also posits that a reader brings all that they are to a text, with certain elements of the reader informing the reading more than others. This will be seen in the following chapters as I demonstrate the influence of four different readerly aspects upon the readings that took place. Chapter 5 will consider the first of these, the role of my participants' experiences of religion in shaping their reading of the five biblical texts.

---

52. Jennings, "Word and Spirit."
53. Ibid., 157.

Chapter 5

Reader-shaped Readings—Experience

IN THIS CHAPTER I present the first example of the way in which my readers' relationships with the five biblical texts shaped their reading. Two men are considered whose readings are marked by their prior experiences of religion. Dave is a forty-four-year-old welder who grew up attending church with his family although he now identifies as "not at all religious." In his case, painful childhood experiences related to church would result in a "bitter" reading of the texts. Something similar happened when members of the public annotated a Bible in Glasgow's Gallery of Modern Art, and the parallels between these two cases are explored in light of insights from social psychology. Gary is a forty-eight-year-old utility technician who also identified as "not at all religious," and like Dave he also found that his prior experiences of religion significantly informed his reading of the five texts. In his case, it resulted in a lack of engagement, which is explored in light of Matthew Engelke's ethnography of the Friday Masowe weChishanu Christians in Zimbabwe who reject the Bible. The chapter concludes by reflecting upon the readings made by Dave and Gary in light of the transactional theory.

Dave's "Bitter" Readings

Dave is the leader of a small group of welders at the Chemical Plant and someone of whom other staff spoke highly. I once heard a manager comment that Dave "could build anything out of metal." For his part, Dave did not particularly enjoy his job, but he did appear to enjoy the banter and camaraderie with the rest of the welders. It had been years since Dave had read a Bible or heard one being read. He had no interest in religion and identified as "not at all religious." During his childhood however Dave, along with the rest of his family, regularly attended a number of evangelical churches. In Dave's case, the hypocrisy that he encountered resulted in his rejection of Christianity. He describes it in this way:

> Around fifteen, sixteen, I became aware of a hell of a lot of hypocrisy, because as I was turning into an adult I was seeing these people for what they really were. One face was what they were on a Sunday and the other face was what I could see they were behind closed doors and away from the church. And I didn't like, without, without exception it was everybody that was involved in that religion.

When asked to read the five biblical texts, Dave read them skeptically. By this I mean, having read an entire text, he focused on aspects of it with which he disagreed. A skeptical reader may agree with large sections of a text, however when asked about the text in general, they principally express their disagreement with it, providing evidence from the sections they object to. In this way they concentrate on the parts they reject and downplay those they accept. As chapter 9 will demonstrate, the specific content which the reader disagrees with varies according to the reader and the text, but they include a texts absolutist or bullying tone, its ethics, its lack of workability, its irrelevance, its contradictions, or its inaccuracies. With reference to Dave, his comments, annotations, and reflections nearly always revolved around ways in which the texts were wrong, immoral, unworkable, or intolerant. To read in this way contrasts an accepting reading. This is where the reader focuses on parts of the text with which they agree making little or no comment on anything they disagree (as is seen in Anthony's engagement with these texts which is explored in chapter 6). Thus, the terms "skeptical" and "accepting" are descriptive not evaluative, they are my attempt to detail and capture the reading phenomena that took place not a judgment as to whether the reading was correct or not.

None of the participants claimed to be reading "skeptically" or "acceptingly." I chose these terms and in doing so disregarded others that are employed within academia. Philip Davies for instance, uses the terms "confessional" and "non-confessional," to argue for a non-confessional reading of the Bible within biblical studies. A confessional reading, he posits, is one whereby the reader is more likely to dominate the biblical text, whereas a non-confessional reader "tries not to force her or his own expectations on the meaning of the text, is prepared to disagree, be shocked, and perplexed."[1] According to Davies, confessional readings are not wrong, but should be kept in the church. In a secular biblical studies department, the Bible student/academic should assume an etic position (that is an outsider's perspective) engaging with the Bible non-confessionally.[2] What is of primary

---

1. Davies, *Whose Bible is it Anyway?* 49.
2. Ibid., 50.

significance to my case study is the binary framework Davies assumes, that of "confessional" and "non-confessional" Bible reading, and this is a framework others have used.[3]

I also considered using a label such as "suspicion" or a "hermeneutics of suspicion." However, this term, once used positively by Paul Ricoeur concerning human knowledge,[4] has been presented as something in opposition to religious faith by others, for instance David Jasper refers to "hermeneutics of faith" and "hermeneutics of suspicion,"[5] and Miroslav Volf uses the pairing "hermeneutics of respect or suspicion."[6] Contrasting Davies, Volf argues that a hermeneutics of respect is preferable, lending itself to "the possibility of genuine disclosure" rather than a hermeneutics of suspicion which he suggests "is not a method of interpretation, it is a strategy for 'debunking.'"[7]

However, these and other terms such as "reading against the grain" or "resisting readers" do not fully describe the reading phenomenon I observed and tend to emphasize the reader rather than the reading event. Due to this and the diversity noted above I decided to make use of a pairing which, to the best of my knowledge, has not been used in the context of Bible reading before. This enables me to use and define the terms that I believed best describe what took place.

Dave's annotations on Proverbs 10:1–11 are a good example of a skeptical reading (see Figure 1).

---

3. Lewis, *Deaf Liberation Theology*; Milne, "Toward Feminist Companionship"; Moore, *Introducing Feminist Perspectives on Pastoral Theology*; West, "The Bible in the Pew."

4. Ricoeur, *Hermeneutics and the Human Sciences*.

5. Jasper, *A Short Introduction to Hermeneutics*.

6. Volf, *Captive to the Word of God*.

7. Ibid., 34–35.

Figure 1: Dave's Annotations on Proverbs 10:1–11

> A wise child brings joy to a father;
>> a foolish child brings grief to a mother. *LOVE IT*
>
> Tainted wealth has no lasting value,
>> but right living can save your life. *WHAT ABOUT WEALTH of THE CHURCHES POVERTY of BORN FROM OTHERS*
>
> The Lord will not let the godly go hungry,
>> but he refuses to satisfy the craving of the wicked. *RUBBISH*
>
> Lazy people are soon poor;
>> hard workers get rich. *WRONG*
>
> A wise youth harvests in the summer,
>> but one who sleeps during harvest is a disgrace.
>
> The godly are showered with blessings;
>> the words of the wicked conceal violent intentions.
>
> We have happy memories of the godly,
>> but the name of a wicked person rots away.
>
> The wise are glad to be instructed,
>> but babbling fools fall flat on their faces. *Still*
>
> People with integrity walk safely,
>> but those who follow crooked paths will slip and fall. *PEOPLE WITH HIGH VIS VESTS WALK SAFER*
>
> People who wink at wrong cause trouble,
>> but a bold reproof promotes peace.
>
> The words of the godly are a life-giving fountain;
>> the words of the wicked conceal violent intentions

His six comments all focus on parts of the text with which he disagrees. At times this is expressed directly, for example describing as "wrong" the proverb: "Lazy people are soon poor; hard workers get rich"; and at other times it is expressed indirectly, using humor or a more mocking tone, for example writing "love it" beside the first proverb. All of Dave's subsequent annotations on the other texts would also focus exclusively on aspects of the text with which he disagreed.

In the related questionnaires a similar pattern was seen, for again Dave's comments singularly concerned aspects of the texts he found objectionable. For example, the introductory question asked: What, if anything, "jumped out at you" as you read through the passage?

- For Proverbs 10:1–11, Dave wrote: "Some out of date and go completely against modern capitalist views."
- For 2 Samuel 5:17–25, he wrote: "How their God encouraged violence."
- For Matthew 18:21–35, he wrote: "Constant use of violent behaviour from God."
- For Psalm 88, he wrote: "Cruel and violent God. Tortures people if he doesn't get his own way."
- And for 2 John, he wrote: "This is John actively telling his Christian friends to behave antisemitic ."

This pattern continued in our interview, for once again Dave spoke about the texts disparagingly. His comparison of 2 Samuel 5:17–25 with "a Brothers Grimm book" illustrates and summarizes his skeptical engagement and subsequent reject of these five texts.

> When it's [Grimm's fairy tales] on about wolves biting babies heads off and, and in a way the Bible's the same. It's not, it's not real and it's lost its shock value now because of television and modern. At one point if you'd have read that [2 Sam 5:17–25], I don't know, not so much to me, but probably 100 years ago, if you'd have read that to a child six, seven years old you'd actually put the bejesus up them. You'd scare the hell out of them, and it would be a God of impending doom, "if you don't do as you are told and everything else." It would you know, it's a fantasy world isn't it.

Dave was one of the few participants to use emotional language when writing or talking about the texts. During our interview I asked him if any one text stood out, and he replied:

> Dave: Yeah, the last one, the last one negatively, it riles me [referring to 2 John].
>
> David: Aye ok, you'd described, you said you felt "angry," was one of your comments about it [quoting Dave's response to the questionnaire question: What if anything

was your gut reaction to this passage? i.e., how did it make you feel?].

Dave: Because it's like, it's like starting a religion based on declaring war on another religion. And I don't get it.

I asked Dave if he had any thoughts as to why he had read all the texts so skeptically and he directly linked his reading of these texts to his past experiences:

> Probably because I, of what I've, the people I've met, my upbringing, and the journey of my life. Religion is attached to a lot of negativity, because of the people, not because of the Bible or . . . . It makes, it just makes you look on the bad side of things really, I mean I could read it and pick out deliberately nice pieces but generally speaking, everybody I've ever known has used the Bible as an instrument to get their message across. And it's not the Bible's message, it is an interpretation of the Bible to get their message, and that's what I don't like.

Dave's direct linking of his childhood experiences of religion with his skeptical reading of the five texts is very helpful because it is not easily seen in the annotations or textual comments themselves, for he did not explicitly connect certain texts or ideas to certain experiences. Dave would go on to describe himself as feeling "bitter" towards religion, a sentiment he again linked both to his childhood and his reading of the five biblical texts. The Bible is the sacred text of Christianity, and so it and the Christian faith are intertwined. It is therefore no surprise that Dave would treat the five extracts from the Bible with antagonism in light of his feelings towards wider Christianity. The weight of his bitterness or negativity is emphasized by the fact that these painful experiences occurred at least thirty years ago and yet shaped these recent readings.

Dave's negative experiences of Christianity resulted in him identifying as "not at all religious," and expressing the hurt that he felt through the way he read the texts. His readings primarily concentrated on aspects of the texts with which he disagreed, something that is understandable in light of his experiences and is not unique. In different ways, Bob, Stuart, Matty, Andy G, Derek, and Gary all linked their prior experiences of religion to their readings of the texts.

Profaning a Bible at the Gallery of Modern Art (GOMA)

Outside of this case study others have noted such a phenomenon as well. For example, in 2009, the Gallery of Modern Art in Glasgow staged an exhibition *Sh[out]: Contemporary Art and Human Rights*. This was a major exhibition on the theme of Lesbian, Gay, Bisexual, Transgender, and Intersex human rights.[8] Jane Clarke the minister of the Metropolitan Community Church in Glasgow presented a Bible at it and an open invitation: "If you feel you have been excluded from the Bible, please write your way back into it."[9]

Yvonne Sherwood recounts how the content of the annotations that followed caused a public outcry, eventually leading to the Bible being placed in a Perspex box, preventing the public from further annotation.[10] Some of the annotations had a comical element, and Sherwood writes how "the prophet Obadiah gained the jolly supplement 'Obladee, Obladah.'"[11] Other comments though appear to echo something of the hurt and bitterness that Dave expressed: "Please burn after reading. Preferably before"; "I wish this book didn't exist"; "I am bi, female, and proud, I want no God who is disappointed in this"; and "Holy figures hide behind their religion to hide who they are. Once you have been raped by a priest, maybe you understand, as I have."[12]

In this public setting, the British public were taking the opportunity to comment on the Bible. They were not reading any specific text and responding to it as my participants were, but they were using a sanctioned setting to express some of their beliefs about and attitudes towards the Bible and wider Christianity. Such a setting disinhibited them, facilitating the responses above, some of which were expressions of hurt due to certain experiences connected to Christianity. This mirrors Dave's approach, for he too used the opportunity of a sanctioned setting to express his bitterness.

Sherwood's own interest in the GOMA exhibition was less on the reading events that took place and those who annotated the Bible and more on the Bible as an object and its subsequent profaning. She went on to consider in more depth the public outcry and media response to these events, suggesting that:

---

8. Sandell et el., "An Evaluation of Sh[out]."

9. Sherwood, *Biblical Blaspheming*, 9–10.

10. Ibid., 9–72. The public were then given access to a blank book where they could write their comments.

11. Ibid., 13.

12. Ibid., 10–12.

In a quasi-Christological passion scene, the Bible became a fellow empathetic sufferer. It was seen as suffering a double violation; an offence against its own rights (as a quasi-subject and a stand-in for all Christian subjects) and an affront against its role as a founding document of rights.[13]

My research is more concerned with the reader and the reading transaction, and less on the Bible as an object. However, what should be noted is that in this case and that of Dave, typically the readers dominated the texts. They used their opportunity to annotate, or comment on the Bible, as a vehicle through which to express hurt. Dave's readings of the five texts were particular to him, but the relationship between a reader's painful experiences and the readings that they shaped is not.

The field of social psychology sheds light on both Dave's reading of the five texts and to a lesser degree on the GOMA exhibition. In turning to this field, I am not claiming that Dave's readings can be wholly explained by it, but social psychology has been helpful in theorizing how people respond to different situations, and I am bringing those insights to bear upon Dave's Bible readings. This conforms to the broader sociological approach I have adopted and follows the example of others who have incorporated insights from social theory and social psychology into their studies of Bible reading practices or religious performance.[14]

"Bitter" Reading from a Social Psychology Perspective

There are at least two concepts found in social psychology that shed light on Dave's reading of the five texts. The first is disinhibition, which usually refers to "a reduction in the usual social forces that operate to restrain us from acting antisocially, illegally or immorally."[15] For example, Leon Mann investigated the role which deindividuation (a form of disinhibition) played on crowds who were goading individuals to commit suicide (by jumping off a building). He found that being part of a large crowd, standing at a distance from the victim and the darkness of night, disinhibited people resulting in a greater likelihood that they would bait and jeer the victim.[16] Disinhibition need not always result in antisocial speech or behavior. In his study on online disinhibition John Suler uses the phrase

13. Ibid., 24–25.

14. Camery-Hoggatt, *Reading the Good Book Well*; Esler, *New Testament Theology*; Herriot, *Religious Fundamentalism and Social Identity*.

15. Hogg and Vaughan, *Social Psychology*, 470.

16. Mann, "The Baiting Crowd in Episodes of Threatened Suicide."

"benign disinhibition" to describe "unusual acts of kindness or generosity" towards others in an online setting.[17]

In my case, the way in which I designed the research disinhibited my participants. They were given assurances of confidentiality and anonymity, and more specifically I requested their own thoughts and comments on the texts. The prior knowledge that any reading would be viewed as legitimate and valuable would have resulted in some men feeling free from certain inhibitions that may normally surround Bible reading.

There are two particular inhibitions worth noting, the first concerns tolerance and the second respect. First, as Sherwood points out, tolerance is viewed as a cornerstone of western democratic existence, and so in the West there is an implicit expectation that the Bible should be treated tolerantly rather than contemptuously.[18] Second, as the sacred text of Christianity, Britain's present and historically dominant religion, it is a text imbued with religious and moral significance. It may not be read very often by many, nor indeed thought of as relevant to modern life any more,[19] but as James Crossley argues, as part of Britain's heritage it "retains its symbolic and nostalgic power."[20] This reflects Robert Detweiler's suggestion that even non-believers would respect a sacred text from their own social tradition.[21] As such, it is therefore a book that many in Britain will feel should be treated with qualified appreciation rather than disdain. Such inhibitions however were lessened by the research setting, making it easier for Dave to read skeptically.

Catharsis is another concept that sheds light on Dave's readings. Popularly catharsis is understood as "letting off steam," and it is underpinned by the theory that expressing emotion, typically towards an inanimate object, is a way of releasing those emotions in a safe environment. For example, Patricia Middlebrook recounts that in Japan "several companies provide a special room where workers can take out their aggressions on a toy replica of their boss to relieve their tensions."[22] Cathartic theory is at odds with some research that suggests cathartic acts can result in an increased sense of anger or frustration rather than the alleviation of those emotions.[23] For

17. Suler, "The Online Disinhibition Effect," 321.
18. Sherwood, *Biblical Blaspheming*, 31.
19. Field, "Is the Bible Becoming a Closed Book?"
20. Crossley, "Biblical Literacy and the English King James Liberal Bible," 209.
21. Detweiler, "What is a Sacred Text?" 225.
22. Middlebrook, *Social Psychology and Modern Life*, 297.
23. Bushman, "Does Venting Anger Feed or Extinguish the Flame?"; Krahé, "Aggression."

example, research exploring the effects of viewing violent acts, or taking part in aggressive sports, has shown they can increase the level of aggression in the viewer/participant.[24] However, in a counseling or therapy setting the expression of pain, anger, sadness, and other negative emotions has been found to aid in the restoration of the person concerned.[25] For this reason scholars have advocated the use of a text (for example the Psalms) as a stimulus for the expression of emotion within a therapy, counseling, or pastoral setting.[26]

In Dave's case, his reading and annotating of the Bible was a cathartic act, something that cannot be known about those who annotated the GOMA Bible. Dave expressed his hurt and subsequent rejection of religion through reading the five texts skeptically. Having done so, his attitude towards the Bible seemed to change. In the Exit Questionnaire he was less critical of the Bible than in the Entrance Questionnaire. He was no longer as categorical in his Exit Questionnaire that the Bible was full of myths and legends or that it was untrue, and where in the Entrance Questionnaire he indicated that the Bible was irrelevant and out of date, this was not the case in the Exit Questionnaire. One possible reason for this is that having taken the opportunity to express his bitterness through reading skeptically, and understanding that those readings were accepted and valued, he felt less bitter.

This is the first example of the way in which some readers' experiences of religion significantly influenced their reading of the texts. In Dave's case, he used this sanctioned setting to express his bitterness towards religion by engaging skeptically with these texts. This demonstrates the influence that past experiences have in the life of the reader, and their relationship with the text. However, not all men's experiences of religion lead them to read as Dave did, in Gary's case they lead him to read the texts indifferently and skeptically.

---

24. Wann et al., "Belief in Symbolic Catharsis."

25. Hankle, "The Therapeutic Implications of the Imprecatory Psalms in the Christian Counseling Setting." Jemmer, "Abreaction—Catharsis."

26. Meyerstein and Ruskin, "Spiritual Tools for Enhancing the Pastoral Visit to Hospitalized Patients"; Owens, "The Psalms, 'a therapy of words'"; Ritblatt and Ter Louw, "The Bible as a Biblio-Source for Poetry Therapy"; Sawyer, "Towards a Pastoral Psychotherapeutic Context for Poetry Therapy."

Gary's Detached Readings

Gary is forty-eight-years old and is one of the utility technicians who kept the many boilers and tanks running in the Plant. He and his colleague Zadok were friendly, always offering me a cup a tea whenever I met them. Gary described himself as a "lover not a fighter" and that seemed an apt description of his approach to life. He did not attend church regularly but did speak fondly of the religious services which he took part in whilst at school.

Dave and Gary are similar in a number of ways: they are in their forties, work in a Chemical Industrial Plant, identify as "not at all religious," and both have had painful experiences of religion in the past resulting in their skeptical reading of the texts. In Gary's case, these experiences would shape his reading in two ways. First, those experiences would lead him to reject Christianity and so the Bible and these texts, viewing them as something personally insignificant. Second, he would directly link some of those experiences to the texts that he read.

Gary's skeptical readings were not as emotionally charged as Dave's. Instead, they were marked by a distinct indifference towards the texts, as became apparent by his lack of annotation on most of the texts. This contrasts with Dave who also rejected Christianity but annotated all five texts. Gary annotated the first two texts, but the rest were left blank. This seemed unusual so I raised this subject in our interview and he said:

> I read it and I re-read it, I have a general opinion of this, which isn't a strong opinion, because of the fact that I don't believe [. . .] You know, and if nothing stood out, ok nothing stood out. I tried to make, tried to see at the beginning, because I wanted it to be detailed for you, but then I thought well, but that's not how I feel and I realized after the second time that you know, that what you want is for me to give you my opinion, not to give you as much detail as, you know, as maybe could be given by somebody else.

Gary had annotated the first two texts because he felt a need to provide me with details and comments. Thankfully he realized that all I wanted was his opinion and that an unannotated text was just as valuable as one covered in notes. To that end he found that he had no comments to make on the final three texts and would probably have left the first two blank had he grasped this earlier. As our conversation developed we spoke about the value of an unannotated text and he said:

> Generally, nothing generally stood out because. And I believe that the reason for that, I don't believe in that [indicating the five

biblical texts]. So it's like, it's of no importance to me [. . .] I have a belief system or a non-belief system, I know what I know and I believe what I know, so I'm just stuck in my ways [he laughs].

In Gary's case his lack of annotation was a reflection of the unimportance and disbelief which he placed upon the texts, something he linked to a wider "non-belief system." In the corresponding questionnaires Gary typically highlighted areas that he disagreed with in the texts, indicating that four texts contained nothing worth remembering and all five were irrelevant to today's world. In our interview, Gary spoke about each text often emphasizing how unbelievable he found them or how unrealistic they seemed. For instance, when I passed him a copy of Psalm 88 and asked, "What did you make of that one?" He replied:

> Oh right, been there, been in trouble. Wow there you go, that's the same thing really, but putting his faith in the Lord and I think it's a big thing. What you need to do and if you don't believe, saying that anger has overwhelmed him, the terrors have paralyzed him, darkness is his closest friend, yeh, blaming the Lord for driving his friends away. I just thought, well that's somebody who's depressed to me, that's all that was, and they've obviously decided to blame the Lord which obviously I wouldn't do but . . . again it's just an unbelievable situation for me personally.

Gary had earlier indicated that his decision not to believe in God had been made in part due to two painful experiences. He recounted how the Roman Catholic Church of which his fiancée was a member had stated that, if they were to marry there, he had to agree that any children they had would be brought up within the Roman Catholic tradition:

> But I thought what a thing to say to somebody "you can't get married in my church unless you agree to my faith" and I just thought. That was a big thing to me at the time, because I didn't hold things that important faith wise.

He then went on to speak about the pressure that his wife and her grandmother put him under to attend church.

> Then it was, "oh we'd like you to come to church," "no I don't want to come to church," "well you should," "no I'm not going to." So in the end that was ok, but I just distanced myself from it all after that. [. . .] Anyway as I got older I just developed a decision based on everything else. I decided that I don't believe in God, don't believe in religion and that was the way I decided to go with it.

The condition which the church placed upon conducting their wedding, and the pressure Gary's wife and her "God fearing" grandmother put on him to attend church directly encouraged Gary to distance himself from Christianity. This in turn would result in his viewing the biblical texts as unbelievable and unimportant, all of which resulted in unannotated texts. Phil Zuckerman in *Faith No More: Why People Reject Religion*, notes this link between disbelief of the Bible and prior painful experiences. One of his participants was David, a former Jehovah Witness, and Zuckerman writes:

> Today he [David] can debunk the story of Noah's ark as being so implausible as to be nothing more than a fairy tale, and yet he believed in this "fairy tale" for more than half his life. Something happened to change his perspective. Something happened to tighten the screws and change the wiring of his internal credulity meter. What happened was this: his life didn't work out so well. His wife cheated on him, then divorced him, and he found himself stuck in a series of dead-end jobs, with little money to pay for even basic utilities. Thus, it wasn't really the manifest absurdity of the story of Noah's ark that caused him to view Christian beliefs with a skeptical eye. Rather, it was misfortune.[27]

Here what Zuckerman labels "misfortune" I have described as "prior painful experiences." "De-conversion" is assumed to be a multifactorial transition away from a faith community,[28] however, often people can recall an incident or context which they identify as the beginning of this transition.[29] In Dave's case, he directly linked his painful experiences to the skeptical readings he undertook. With Gary, his painful experiences resulted in his disenchantment with Christianity and the establishing of his "non-belief system." From such a position the Bible was then viewed with incredulity, treated with little importance and read skeptically.

The Masowe weChishanu's Rejection of the Bible

In my case with Gary, or Zuckerman's case with David, the Bible was rejected as these men moved away from a sense of religious affiliation. This rejection of the Bible has been noted in those who de-convert,[30] or distance

---

27. Zuckerman, *Faith No More*, 52–53.
28. Barbour, *Versions of Deconversion*; Streib, "Deconversion."
29. Zuckerman, *Faith No More*.
30. Wright et al., "Explaining Deconversion from Christianity."

themselves from organized Christianity.³¹ Matthew Engelke carried out one of the most detailed explorations of the rejection of the Bible by a group of people.³² He spent eighteen months (spread over a seven-year period) researching the Masowe weChishanu Church in Zimbabwe. As a group, they call themselves "the Christians who don't read the Bible,"³³ making this one of their defining features. They identify with the ministry of Johane Masowe (John of the Wilderness), a self-designated prophet who taught that people could receive the Word of God directly from the Holy Spirit and so did not need the Bible. Masowe's view changed and towards the end of his ministry he accepted the Bible as the Word of God, a contentious and divisive decision for his followers.³⁴ Nevertheless, the Masowe weChishanu Church continues not to use the Bible.

Engelke's context is different to mine, he is exploring the lack of Bible engagement within a church in Zimbabwe whilst I am exploring Bible reading by those outside the church in England. However, by choosing Engelke's study as a central conversation partner with Gary's readings two similarities are noted. First, the Bible is viewed as a tainted text by the Masowe weChishanus. It is a text linked to white missionaries and so to the colonial powers who subjugated their land, as Engelke writes: "In postcolonial Africa the Bible carries an indelible essence of white might."³⁵ From this perspective the Bible is inseparable from, and a tool of, both missionaries and colonizers. Engelke describes Masowe's childhood as one in which he was probably aware of missionary infighting and discord, suggesting that it "may be that these instabilities disabused him of the notion [. . .] that the Bible was significant or powerful as missionaries were claiming."³⁶ However, the more consistent emphasis that he presents is that of the Bible identifying with foreign oppressors and so being rejected. Masowe is said to have described the Bible as coming from "men with black hearts,"³⁷ and is quoted as saying you "should burn the religious books of the European as our forefathers did not have books."³⁸

Gary never described the Bible as a tainted text, but the way he read the five texts indicates he viewed it in this way, for he linked certain texts

31. Jamieson, *A Churchless Faith*, 86, 169.
32. Engelke, *A Problem of Presence*.
33. Ibid., 2.
34. Ibid., 102.
35. Ibid., 245.
36. Ibid., 86.
37. Ibid., 5.
38. Ibid., 94.

to specific painful experiences in his past. For example, Gary not only described his wife's grandmother as "God fearing" but he would go on to describe 2 John as being "written to get people to have a faith and believe in this faith, and there you go that is the punishment if you don't. God fearing, it's a God fearing text." This was a text that, like his wife's grandmother, was threatening and coercive, and he summarized it in this way:

> [What it is] saying is if you don't believe in God, well then that makes you an evil person. "Everyone who encourages such people becomes a partner in their evil work," what evil work is that then? Not believing in God? That's, I just thought well, I don't believe that I'm evil I've got very good intentions and got a lot of time for people and I wouldn't tell people they shouldn't believe in God, but equally people shouldn't tell me that I should believe in God.

Echoing his wife's and her grandmother's attempts to get him to church he would also suggest that 2 Samuel 5:17–25 and Psalm 88 were designed to convince people to believe in God. Most poignant however were his comments regarding Matthew 18:21–35 and the theme of forgiveness. Gary and his wife divorced and something of that experience informed his reading of this text:

> I know you can't do that [forgive] all the time, you can't expect everybody to forgive every single thing, but I think people should be looking to try and do that, for their own peace. But I can't say that I've been brought up, I can't say that it's the church that has taught me that. I would say that it is my family that has taught me that. [. . .] Getting divorced was a very difficult situation for me to deal with, em. But in the end I couldn't forgive what happened. I tried to see it and I still try to see it sometimes, but I don't get hung up on it anymore, because I can be happier and I am happier and I can be happier still by moving on.

Gary's linking of the texts to particular painful experiences in the past, the pressure he was put under to attend church or divorcing his wife, demonstrates the way these texts were tainted for him and the direct way in which these painful experiences shaped his reading.

For the Masowe weChishanu and Gary the Bible was a tainted text and so rejected. In the case of Johane Masowe and his followers it was because of the corporate painful experiences derived from the link between the Bible and the colonizers. In Gary's case this tainting was due to personal painful experiences, often involving religious people. In both cases, these experiences resulted in a detachment from the biblical text.

Second, for the Masowe weChishanu the Bible was "stale" and "out of date," irrelevant to their lives and the contexts they were living in.[39] They believed that the Holy Spirit would speak God's word directly to them, addressing contemporary issues and specific situations. In Gary's case, he viewed it as a text containing ancient wisdom which is either common to all of humanity or has now been superseded. He described the purpose and place of the Bible in this way:

> Back then [. . .] in general people weren't as educated as we are today. It was a way of explaining certain things in a different way or getting them to believe in certain things in a different way. Whereas today everybody's adults and most people are educated certainly within the Western World, I don't think it fits, I just don't think it fits.

This sense of irrelevance along with the accompanying tainted nature of the Bible was part of the reason both Gary and the Masowe weChishanu distanced themselves from the Bible.[40] Such a view of the Bible contrasts other Christians who have also experienced the effects of colonialization and yet understand it to be a liberating force.[41] For example, as Engelke points out,[42] the South African Desmond Tutu argues that the Bible is an authority other than the missionaries, one which challenges the social injustices and inequalities connected to colonizing.[43]

As someone who has a "non-belief system" and has "moved on," Gary's comments were not angry nor did they contain the level of emotion which Dave showed. Gary expressed a level of detachment towards Christianity and that was evidenced by his lack of annotation and the associated lack of significance that he placed in the five texts. In some way these texts were part of a previous stage in Gary's life, a painful one, but one that he had moved on from and these two factors significantly shaped his reading of the five biblical texts.

---

39. Ibid., 6.

40. Engelke notes two further reasons the Masowe weChishanu reject the Bible. Its materiality was considered evidence of its lack of authority, for it can fall apart or be used as toilet paper. Second, if the Bible is viewed as the Word of God then it can be used to challenge the authority of a church leader, so by rejecting the Bible this threat was also eliminated. See: *A Problem of Presence*, 245.

41. Mesters, *Defenseless Flower*.

42. Engelke, *A Problem of Presence*, 71–74.

43. Tutu, *The Rainbow People of God*.

Readers' Experiences and the Transactional Theory of Reading

Gary read all five texts in a very similar way, as did Dave. This suggests that it was not the content of the individual texts that activated certain memories, although Gary did link certain texts to particular experiences, rather the anticipation itself of reading a biblical text brought to mind particular past experiences that then informed their subsequent readings. Rosenblatt writes, "the text is the stimulus that focuses the reader's attention so that elements of past experience—concepts linked with verbal symbols—are activated."[44] These experiences would include previous readings of the same text or prior experiences that shape the reader's attitudes to or beliefs about the text. For Dave, Gary and at least six other participants, their prior relationship to Christianity was found to inform their reading of these texts. This relationship, with all its thoughts and feelings, was brought to mind as they were preparing to take part and became a dominant factor as they read each of the five texts.

It is worth noting that the memories which were stimulated in Dave and Gary, were not personal experiences of reading the Bible rather they concerned the actions of certain Christians. Dave's and Gary's readings of the five biblical texts demonstrate a link between the actions of certain Christians and the Christian faith and so the Bible. This resulted in the five texts which I gave them being associated with those experiences which occurred up to thirty years earlier. This web of association demonstrates the importance of viewing the reader and their subsequent reading not through one narrow preselected lens, such as personality or gender, but with an awareness of the myriad of factors within each reader which have the potential to impact the reading.

Furthermore, although in this chapter I have highlighted the role that Dave and Gary's experiences of religion played in their readings, there were other contributing factors, including their beliefs about the Bible and sense of religious identity. The subsequent chapters will touch on this, but there remains the need for further research into the multi-factorial and interwoven nature of reading transactions.

Rosenblatt posits that there is not one correct meaning, nor is any reader ever able to claim complete and absolute understanding of a text. Nonetheless, an appropriate (or responsible) reading can be claimed, with the possibility of equally valid interpretations existing, based on agreed criteria

---

44. Rosenblatt, *The Reader, the Text, the Poem*, 11.

for interpretation.[45] In arguing this, Rosenblatt builds on John Dewey's idea of "warranted assertibility,"[46] which contends that whilst absolute knowledge or truth cannot be claimed, one could speak of truth and knowledge in a qualified way, aware that new evidence may arise or different criteria used to interpret the context. The three criteria that Rosenblatt suggests should be used to measure the appropriateness of any reading are:

1. That the context and purpose of the reading event, or the total transaction, be considered.

2. That the interpretation not be contradicted by, or not fail to cover, the full text, the signs on the page.

3. That the interpretation not project meanings which cannot be related to signs on the page.[47]

In light of these three criteria, I would argue that Dave and Gary did not read the texts fully. Their experiences were so significant that they dominated the readings, resulting in each reader singularly focusing on aspects with which they disagreed and ignoring other large sections of text. A selective reading such as this produces an interpretation unsupported by the text.[48] The transactional theory assumes that in the toing and froing between the text and the reader, if the first conclusion reached is wrong the reader may evaluate their interpretation and there is the possibility that the "text itself leads the reader toward this self-corrective process."[49] Dave and Gary did not allow the text to correct their interpretation and accompanying rejection. They were unable or unwilling to suspend the dominant influence their past experiences were having upon the reading transaction. For this reason, their interpretation of the texts reflected their relationship with Christianity (in this instance their painful experiences at the hands of Christians) more than the signs on the page. This does not invalidate the readings that occurred, but it does suggest that the interpretations and responses to the texts were not fully supported by the texts.[50] Rosenblatt notes that a reader's:

> past experience and present preoccupations may actively condition his primary spontaneous response [to the text]. In some

---

45. Rosenblatt, *The Reader, the Text, the Poem*, 183.
46. Dewey, *Logic*; Dewey, "Propositions, Warranted Assertibility, and Truth."
47. Rosenblatt, *Making Meaning with Texts*, 23–24.
48. Ibid., 75–77.
49. Rosenblatt, *The Reader, the Text, the Poem*, 11.
50. Rosenblatt, *Literature as Exploration*, 77.

cases, these things will conduce to a full and balanced reaction to the work. In other cases, they will limit or distort.[51]

Conclusion

This chapter has demonstrated one of the ways in which a reader's relationship with a text shapes their reading of that text, in particular I have explored the influence of the reader's prior experiences. In Dave's case, his painful experiences of Christianity resulted in him reading the texts skeptically, focusing on aspects that he disagreed with, at times in emotionally charged ways. The parallels between his engagement with the five texts and the annotations on the Bible placed in the *Sh[out]* exhibition, demonstrated that his engagement was not unique. Gary's readings were then considered, and here the influence of his prior experiences was seen in the distance at which he held the text, the disbelief that dominated his readings and the direct links he made between certain texts and his experiences. In his case two parallels were noted between his engagement with the texts and the Masowe WeChishanu's rejection of the Bible as a tainted and irrelevant text.

In demonstrating the way in which these two reader's prior experiences shaped their reading of the five biblical texts, I have been arguing that a series of reading transactions took place. In particular, that Dave and Gary's readings can be explained by the transactional theory which allows for the experiences of the reader to inform their reading of a text, as was the case with these two men. The relational nature of reading is open to a plethora of readerly influences shaping the reading, and I now turn to explore a second such influence, the men's sense of religious identity.

---

51. Ibid., 75.

Chapter 6

Reader-shaped Readings—Identity

UNDERPINNING THE ASSERTION THAT my participants' relationships with the five biblical texts shaped their readings of those texts is an understanding that both my participants and the texts are part of the same dynamic system. They had an existing relationship before I brought them together, mediated through the reader's contact with the Bible and Christianity. The subsequent reading transaction that followed then clarified the tone of that pre-existing relationship. In this chapter, I will now consider the influence of the reader's sense of religious identity upon their readings. In particular I consider the readings of John, who identifies as an atheist, and Anthony, a Christian, highlighting how their different sense of religious identity resulted in very different readings. These readings are explored in light of two insights from social psychology which help to provide further lenses through which these men's responses to the texts can be understood. Having done this, a link between the participant's identity and the accompanying skeptical or accepting reading is suggested.

Case studies, such as this one, can produce insights that complicate commonly held assumptions, because by focusing upon one case in greater depth new insights can emerge which challenge pre-existing theories.[1] To that end, the chapter troubles contextual Bible reading theories which assume that the geographical setting in which the Bible reading takes place significantly influences that reading.[2] It does this by showing the major role that the reader's religious identity played in the readings rather than their workplace identity or setting.

---

1. Flyvbjerg, "Case Study"; Gerring, *Case Study Research,* 37–63.
2. Peden, "Contextual Bible Study at Cornton Vale Women's Prison, Stirling"; Riches, *What is Contextual Bible Study?*

Contextual Bible Reading

The Contextual Bible Study method (CBS) is one example of an approach to Bible reading that values the reader and their context, understanding that both will inform the reading which takes place. Readers are not encouraged to detach themselves from their social setting or their personal preoccupations, rather these are brought to the text so that there may be a meaningful connection between the reader, their context, and the text.[3] Susannah Cornwall describes it in this way:

> As might be expected from its name, CBS is deeply committed to context, and to recognizing particular social, economic, cultural and class settings as legitimate sites of God's revelation.[4]

In particular CBS understands that a reader's geographical location will inform their reading. John Riches writes:

> Contextual Bible Study is in an important sense "local." When you join a CBS group, you will almost certainly be joining with people who come from your own area, or who have some shared experience. CBS groups are set up to help people discuss the issues that are closest to home, whether those are the things that are happening in their daily lives, or important things that are going on in the community that surrounds them.[5]

For example, Alison Peden facilitated CBS sessions at a women's prison in Stirling and noted that the prison setting, and the inmates' experiences of arrest and imprisonment, informed how the Bible was read. The thoroughness of the prisoners' close reading of the passages caused her to wonder "whether their facility of noting words and sense comes from their experiences of endlessly poring over legal documents relating to their case, prison reports and so on."[6] The types of questions that were asked of the texts and ensuing discussion often related to the prison context and experience as well. For instance asking, "how long did Jesus get when he was arrested?" or was he "angry when he was arrested"?[7] Even though the women also linked their previous life experiences and female identity to the texts, Peden concludes that:

---

3. Riches, *What is Contextual Bible Study?* 15.
4. Cornwall, "Contextual Bible Study," 15.
5. Riches, *What is Contextual Bible Study?* 23–24.
6. Peden, "Contextual Bible Study at Cornton Vale Women's Prison, Stirling," 16.
7. Ibid., 15–16.

> CBS provided a wonderful way for women to make some sense of imprisonment and to give a language to their experience. [...] Their readiness to align text and their own context brought new insights and frames of reference to the Bible.[8]

The influence of the reading context is similarly affirmed by Louise Lawrence who undertook CBS in a city, a rural village and a fishing village and argues that CBS is a useful tool to help people recover a sense of place.[9]

Accordingly, it could be presumed that the Chemical Industrial setting of my own project would inform the Bible readings that took place there. Indeed, the transactional theory of reading also assumes that the setting contributes to the reading that takes place.[10] However, as this chapter will go on to illustrate, it was not the participants' work setting which significantly informed their readings but rather it was their sense of religious identity. In particular, I will consider John and Anthony who represent a group within the study, including Andy G, Mick, Matty, Derek, Ethan, Richie and Tony, whose religious identity played a direct role in their readings. John worked as a manager at the Plant and as an atheist identified as "not at all religious." This sense of atheist identity would shape and be reaffirmed by his skeptical readings. Anthony is another manager but identified as a Christian, and so "moderately religious." In his case, his Christian identity would go on to shape his readings of the five texts and as a result of having read them he would indicate a re-strengthening of his desire to read the Bible. Once again, John and Anthony's examples demonstrate the way in which a reader's relationship with a text shapes their reading of that text.

John's "Atheist" Readings

John is the youngest participant in my research, aged twenty-two, and he had worked as a manager at the Chemical Plant since graduating from University. John grew up in a Roman Catholic home and attended Catholic schools, but did not get Confirmed because by the age of thirteen he realized that he did not believe in God. John identified as an "atheist" and "not at all religious." He was not outwardly antagonistic towards Christianity, his parents identified as Catholic as did his girlfriend who attended church on a regular basis. Indeed, he felt that the Bible was good for teaching morals and

---

8. Ibid., 18.

9. She also facilitated CBS sessions with a deaf community and a group of clergy, showing that CBS is not interested in the geographical context but other social locations as well. See: Lawrence, *The Word in Place*.

10. Rosenblatt, *The Reader, the Text, the Poem*, 81.

those that studied it "will probably turn out as better people, than people who haven't." Nonetheless, John read four of the five texts skeptically: Proverbs 10:1–11, 2 Samuel 5:17–25, Matthew 18:21–35 and 2 John. As I will demonstrate this was a skeptical reading which was shaped by his atheist identity and which strengthened that same sense of identity. Figure 2 is a copy of his annotations on 2 Samuel 5:17–25.

Figure 2: John's Annotations on 2 Samuel 5:17–25

When the Philistines heard that David had been anointed king of Israel, they mobilized all their forces to capture him. But David was told they were coming, so he went into the stronghold. The Philistines arrived and spread out across the valley of Rephaim. So David asked the Lord, "Should I go out to fight the Philistines? Will you hand them over to me?" The Lord replied to David, "Yes, go ahead. <u>I will certainly hand them over to you." So David went to Baal-perazim and defeated the Philistines there.</u> "The Lord did it!" David exclaimed. "He burst through my enemies like a raging flood!" So he named that place Baal-perazim (which means "the Lord who bursts through"). The Philistines had abandoned their idols there, so David and his men confiscated them. But after a while the Philistines returned and again spread out across the valley of Rephaim. And again David asked the Lord what to do. "<u>Do not attack them straight on,</u>" the Lord replied. "<u>Instead, circle around behind and attack them near the poplar trees. When you hear a sound like marching feet in the tops of the poplar trees, be on the alert! That will be the signal that the Lord is moving ahead of you to strike down the Philistine army.</u>" So David did what the Lord commanded, and he struck down the Philistines all the way from Gibeon to Gezer.

[Handwritten annotations:]
If David had to go out and defeat the enemy himself, it's not 'the Lord' who has defeated them.

does not sound like anything 'the Lord' would say. Sounds more like he's deluded and hearing his own thoughts in his head.

John's skeptical reading is evidenced in his annotations on this passage where he twice argues that David did not hear the voice of "the Lord" and he defeated the Philistines without "the Lord's" help. In the accompanying questionnaire these criticisms were repeated. When asked: What, if anything "jumped out at you" as you read through the passage? John wrote: "David just seems to be mistaking his own tactics with something 'the lord' is saying to him." He would go on to describe this text as irrelevant and express frustration "that stories like this are believed."

During the semi-structured interview, as was my practice, I passed him a copy of 2 Samuel 5:17–25 and asked "what did you make of this one?" He replied:

> Ok, I mean this one especially, that this is in the Bible is just. I mean, this guy who's saying, "help me defeat these enemies, bla, bla, bla," and he was saying like, you know, how it was God who defeated them. But it wasn't, it was just this guy had some tactics on how to defeat them and then heard a little voice in his head say, "yeah, that's a good plan" and then he did it. And, and it just implies why would God chose one side over another? And you know, what makes this guy so special that you chose his side? And why would you even endorse conflict in the first place? It is just so counter-intuitive to what the Bible teaches.

John's skeptical reading of this passage can be seen in this multi-layered critique, rejecting the text not only on ethical and historical grounds, but also suggesting that it contradicts the general teachings of the Bible. John's reading of this text resembles his reading of Proverbs 10:1–11, Matthew 18:21–35, and 2 John, for with those texts he also singularly focused upon sections he disagreed with, resulting in their rejection.

In our interview, John would directly link his skeptical reading of these texts to his atheist identity. When I asked him if he had any general comments about the five texts, he said: "my gut feeling, you know, my attitude towards religion and stuff like that, from an atheist standpoint, that was sort of reinforced." He went on to suggest that my choice of texts "were a bit obscure, so if you were on the fence you would probably lean more towards not believing in God." Later when I brought to his attention the skeptical nature of his readings he responded saying:

> Reading all of those [the five biblical texts], just sort of affirmed to me that, yes, I am an atheist and I can't quite believe everything that's written in the Bible. Because at the end of the day it was a human, it was humans who wrote it; it wasn't any, you know, it wasn't, God didn't write this Bible.

At the end I asked him if the texts had been what he expected, and he replied:

> I guess because I've not looked at any passages from the Bible since I was [. . .] thirteen or something. I guess now I can, I'm more critical of it, I mean I can spot the errors in it a lot more, em. So I don't know, it's just reaffirmed that I am an atheist.

Contrasting the skeptical readings of the other four texts, John read Psalm 88 in a more accepting way. Nonetheless, his atheist identity would continue to shape his reading of this psalm, understanding it to uphold his sense of identity and belief system. He did not annotate this text, but when asked in the questionnaire, what, if anything, was your "gut reaction" to this passage, he wrote:

> Pleased that there is something in the Bible that suggests God doesn't exist and gives an accurate depiction of the lack of response that would be received when praying or searching for God.

Of all the texts, this was the only one he suggested was worth remembering "because it would help to come to the realization that God doesn't exist or doesn't care enough to respond, without wasting your whole life trying to get a response." These sentiments were repeated in the interview where John said:

> As they [the Psalmist] are reaching towards the end of their life they are thinking about dying and they still haven't had this connection with God and it's just like well, why have you continued, you know, believing in him?

John's readings show that once again the reader's relationship with the five biblical texts, on this occasion his sense of religious identity, shaped his reading of these texts. In particular, not only did John's atheist identity shape his readings but also he found that the readings strengthened that identity. Every reader's sense of identity will influence how they interpret a text, but in John's case it significantly overshadowed his reading. Much like Dave and Gary's readings, this was a transaction between the reader and the text dominated by the reader.

John responded to all the texts in a very similar way suggesting that it was not the content of the texts that produced the strong reaction rather it was the fact they were biblical texts. Rosenblatt does not refer to a reader's sense of identity shaping their reading, however she does note that "a personal preoccupation or an automatic association with a minor phrase or an attitude toward the general theme will lead to a strong reaction that has very little to do with the work."[11] I would argue that for John there was an "automatic association,"[12] between the five texts and the Bible, he read these five texts acutely aware of their biblical identity. They represented the wider Bible, a book viewed as the Word of God by the Roman Catholic Church, a church John had rejected. Thus, his atheist identity emerged as one of the most salient aspects of his relationship with these texts and resulted in him reading skeptically.

"Atheist" Reading from a Social Psychology Perspective

The subject of identity and Bible reading has been explored from a sociological perspective. For example, Liam Murphy notes the way in which the Bible is used to inform the identity and actions of charismatic Christians in Northern Ireland;[13] Akesha Baron highlights the role which the Bible plays in gender identity in a Mexican context;[14] and James Bielo builds on David Hess's concept of "dialogical,"[15] to explore the way a group of Lutheran Church-Missouri Synod (LCMS) women use a Bible study setting to mark out the distinctions between their denominational identity and that of others.[16] Common to all of these examples is the way the Bible, or biblical tropes, are engaged with by a particular individual or community and used to shape or reaffirm a socially constructed identity. Echoing these works and following the example set in chapter 5, I will explore John's readings in light of two concepts found in social psychology: social identity theory and schema theory. Having done so, I suggest that John's readings were more of an automatic, rather than intentional, response to a biblical text.

First, social identity theory understands that people have a sense of identity derived from their membership of a particular group, for example: their sports team, profession, ethnicity or religion.[17] Therefore, any one person has multiple identities as they are part of many social groups. The social

---

11. Rosenblatt, *Making Meaning with Texts*, 75.

12. Ibid.

13. Murphy, "The Trouble with Good News."

14. Baron, "'The Man is the Head.'"

15. Hess argues that his interpretations "are not only influenced by social contingencies but also situated in an arena of debate and dialogue with my Others," something he describes as "dialogical." See: Hess, *Science in the New Age*, 157.

16. Bielo, *Words Upon the Word*, 135–54.

17. Greil and Davidman, "Religion and Identity"; Hogg and Abrams, *Social Identifications*.

psychologist Henri Tajfel is usually credited as pioneering this theory and defined it in this way:

> Social identity will be understood as that *part* of an individual's self-concept which derives from his knowledge of his membership of a social group (or groups) together with the value and emotional significance attached to that membership.[18] (emphasis in original)

Biblical scholars,[19] and sociologists of religion,[20] have used the concept of social identity in their analysis of various religious and nonreligious communities. Some, like the contributors to *Social Identities: Between the Sacred and the Secular*,[21] use it as a label to refer to socially constructed individual and group identities, but take it no further. Others, like psychologist Peter Herriot, consider in greater depth various aspects of social identity theory with reference to particular cases: the Anglican controversy over gay clergy, and Mohammed Atta the leader of the twin towers attacks.[22] As I have shown, John understood that his atheist identity was the most salient identity when it came to reading the five biblical texts rather than his ethnicity (English) or job title (Process Manager). With reference to religious social identity, Jeffery Seul concludes, "religion frequently serves the identity impulse more powerfully and comprehensively than other repositories of cultural meaning can or do."[23] It is therefore no surprise that John referred directly to his atheist identity five times in our interview, but never mentioned his ethnicity or job title, even though I directly enquired about his work, training and future career.

Michael Hogg and Graham Vaughan go on to note that "people also think, feel, believe and behave in terms of the relevant prototype."[24] In other words, in a situation where a person feels their atheist identity is the most appropriate for that setting, the accompanying thoughts, feelings, beliefs, and actions will be informed by their expectation of what an atheist would think, feel, believe, and do. Furthermore, scholars have also found that people typically accentuate their response to something that challenges their social identity, enlarging the differences between themselves and an oppos-

18. Tajfel, *Differentiating between Social Groups*, 63.
19. Esler, *New Testament Theology*; Lau, *Identity and Ethnics in the Book of Ruth*; Tucker and Baker, *T. & T. Clark Handbook to Social Identity in the New Testament*.
20. Greil and Davidman, "Religion and Identity."
21. Day et al., *Social Identities*.
22. Herriot, *Religious Fundamentalism and Social Identity*.
23. Seul, "'Ours is the Way of God,'" 567.
24. Hogg and Vaughan, *Social Psychology*, 127.

ing group.²⁵ In other words, according to social identity theory someone who identifies as an atheist will probably have an enhanced response when asked to engage with a religious icon such as the Bible or a biblical passage, as seen in John's skeptical readings.

Second, social psychologists also use the phrase "self-schema" to describe the way an individual perceives her- or himself in relation to a particular context.²⁶ Self-schema theory and social identity theory overlap, for both presuppose that people have multiple identities and that an individual's sense of identity shapes how he or she responds to a setting. However, self-schema theory also includes character traits or a personality profile that may be thought of as part of a personal rather than social identity.

Schema theory, of which self-schema is a subset, is principally concerned with how humans respond to and make sense of everyday life. Louise Pendry describes a schema as a "cognitive shortcut,"²⁷ because it is a way of interpreting and responding to situations without the need to think about them, it is an automatic process we are unaware of. Part of the purpose of a schema is to provide a person with coherence and stability in potentially highly complex and uncertain situations, and it is therefore a powerful thing. Schema theory has influenced educational practices, especially with reference to reading, for it understands that each reader's schema informs how she or he reads.²⁸ The theory is applied directly to biblical exegesis by Jerry Camery-Hoggatt who argues, "the mind organizes experience into schemas and then taps those as it needs to in order to fill in the gaps in the language of the text."²⁹ Mary Crawford and Roger Chaffin also use schema theory when reflecting on the difference between male and female readers in their study. They suggest that the readers' sense of gender, as part of their schema, shaped the readings that occurred, resulting in a difference between the genders.³⁰

According to self-schema theory, "our sense of who we are is dramatically shaped by the current situation, but also influences our interpretation of it."³¹ In John's case, it was his sense of atheist identity that he felt was most appropriate for reading the five biblical texts, and it was this identity

---

25. Eiser, "Accentuation Revisited"; Lyons, "Social Psychology 1."

26. Lyons, "Social Psychology 1."

27. Pendry, "Social Cognition," 94.

28. Wharton-McDonald and Swiger, "Developing Higher Order Comprehension in the Middle Grades,"; Pearson, "The Roots of Reading Comprehension Instruction."

29. Camery-Hoggatt, *Reading the Good Book Well*, 97.

30. Crawford and Chaffin, "The Reader's Construction of Meaning."

31. Morf and Koole, "The Self," 135.

that shaped that reading. A self-schema not only enables a person to engage with information easily, but it often results in a response that affirms the schema;[32] schemas are very resistant to change and "people are resistant to schema-disconfirming information."[33] In other words, normally the information is processed in such a way that the schema is maintained and the person's sense of stability and coherence remains. In John's case, his atheist identity (self-schema) influenced his reading of the biblical texts in such a way that that same identity would be re-affirmed.

These concepts from social psychology are automatic mechanisms all humans use to navigate life, and accordingly they should be understood as spontaneous responses to a stimulus. Not only do they explain some of reasons why John's atheist identity was the salient factor in shaping his readings, but they also indicate that this was an instinctive response. In many ways, he could not help but read the texts in that way. Such a reading, dominated by the participant's sense of religious identity, was seen in other men as well and Anthony provides a good comparison.

Anthony's Christian Readings

Anthony is a fifty-nine-year-old manager at the Plant and was looking forward to retirement. He keeps active, playing tennis regularly, golf on occasion, and had bought a kayak the previous summer. Anthony grew up going to a local Church of England and continued to attend church on and off throughout his life. At present he does not regularly attend, but his wife does. He identified as a Christian and someone who is "moderately religious," describing God as "somebody who's prepared to listen, and you can sort of have a conversation with and I'm not always very good at doing that." His view of the Bible was informed by his Christian faith, understanding it to be God's message to humanity. Due to the strength of his religious identity, I did not imagine Anthony being the type of participant who would take part in my project. However, he fulfilled the entrance requirement in that he did not regularly attend church or read the Bible, so he was included.

Anthony read the five texts in an accepting way, concentrating on parts that he agreed with. Anthony's annotations on 2 Samuel 5:17–25 are presented in Figure 3.

---

32. Lyons, "Social Psychology 1," 332.
33. Hogg and Vaughan, *Social Psychology*, 60.

Figure 3: Anthony's Annotations on 2 Samuel 5:17–25

> When the Philistines heard that David had been anointed king of Israel, they mobilized all their forces to capture him. But David was told they were coming, so he went into the stronghold. The Philistines arrived and spread out across the valley of Rephaim. So David asked the Lord, "Should I go out to fight the Philistines? Will you hand them over to me?" The Lord replied to David, "Yes, go ahead. I will certainly hand them over to you." So David went to Baal-perazim and defeated the Philistines there. "The Lord did it!" David exclaimed. "He burst through my enemies like a raging flood!" So he named that place Baal-perazim (which means "the Lord who bursts through"). The Philistines had abandoned their idols there, so David and his men confiscated them. But after a while the Philistines returned and again spread out across the valley of Rephaim. And again David asked the Lord what to do. "Do not attack them straight on," the Lord replied. "Instead, circle around behind and attack them near the poplar trees. When you hear a sound like marching feet in the tops of the poplar trees, be on the alert! That will be the signal that the Lord is moving ahead of you to strike down the Philistine army." So David did what the Lord commanded, and he struck down the Philistines all the way from Gibeon to Gezer.

Annotations:
- belief that God was on his side.
- belief that what is promised happens.
- Was this expected behaviour? Were they weaker without idols to worship?
- obedience
- ?

Anthony focuses on David's belief in, and obedience to, God. He read this as an accurate historical account, not questioning its ethics or the idea that God communicated with David and the questions Anthony posed concerned the significance and motivation behind David's actions in confiscating the Philistine's idols. In the related questionnaire Anthony summed up this passage with the phrase "communication and obedience" indicating this was its key lesson and was one worth remembering.

In our interview, Anthony spoke briefly about this text, saying

> David seems to have great faith in God and God seemed to help him a lot, and didn't seem to eh. But as, it almost gave the impression as long as David did what God said then God will deliver.

Here again the concepts of communication and obedience are seen along with "faith." Anthony contrasts John, raising none of the latter's questions or critiques. Anthony read all the texts in a very similar way, drawing out what he understood to be their central message in an accepting way. He would go on to describe all the texts as worth remembering and relevant to today's world.

In the same vein as John, however, his sense of religious identity shaped his reading of, and response to, the five texts, but in his case it was a Christian identity. Anthony did not directly link his readings to his religious identity, but when asked why, unlike many of the other men he had read these texts acceptingly, he replied "I think I approached the passages in a positive way, I was looking for there to be a positive message in them."

Anthony identified as a Christian and viewed the Bible as a divinely inspired book, a book which contained "positive messages." To that end when he read through the five texts, he did so "looking for there to be a positive message in them," he read them acceptingly. Much like John, it was his religious identity and associated beliefs that informed his reading of the texts rather than his workplace identity. As social identity and self-schema theory anticipate, his Christian identity was instinctively assumed to be the most salient for this setting, and it then shaped his reading of the texts.

Unlike John, he did not explicitly state that reading the texts had reinforced his religious identity and beliefs. Instead, Anthony expressed the sentiment that reading these texts had been a positive experience and had encouraged him to read the Bible more, stating:

> I would be quite happy to read the Bible, but I don't always find the time. It's not my bedside book and I wouldn't know where to start you know, maybe you should just open it and read something and hope.

He would repeat this sentiment later, saying:

> Sometimes reading the Bible and being asked to think about what you've read gives people the, people who want to, the time to maybe reflect a little bit on how that relates to them and what they are up to. And that's where reading the Bible is a good thing. Sometimes, I wish I did it more often.

A few weeks after finishing the project I passed Anthony's office and we spoke briefly. He told me that he had accepted an invitation from a man at his wife's church to take part in a Bible reading course. In accord with social identity and self-schema theory, Anthony's attitude towards the Bible was strengthened as he expressed and acted upon a desire to read the Bible more.

Furthermore, in much the same way that John's readings were overshadowed by his atheist identity, Anthony's were overshadowed by his Christian identity. For instance, even though Psalm 88 is one where God does not respond to the Psalmist's cry for help and scholars such as Artur Weiser have described it as "unrelieved by a single ray of comfort or hope,"[34] Anthony interpreted it as if it claimed that God would intervene. Where John believed that Psalm 88 questioned God's existence and directly affirmed his atheist belief, Anthony suggested it demonstrated that "God is always there, even if it's not clear what he is doing or whether he is listening." He went on to say that this was a psalm designed to "strengthen our faith" and "test our faith." Such a reading echoes Robert Detweiler's description of a "faithful reader" being one who:

> Approaches the text aggressively, determined to believe it, and hence she "fills in" the indeterminacies in an attitude of acceptance, adopting a position she would not take with any other kind of text.[35]

Anthony was able to find a positive message in the most hopeless of texts.

Identity and Bible Reading: A Link

Other participants mirrored the difference noted between John and Anthony's readings as well, for it was their sense of religious identity that most closely correlated with how skeptically or acceptingly the texts were read. Most of the men who read skeptically identified as "not at all religious" (Dave, Sam, Ethan, John, Matty, Andy K, Gary, Peter, Mick, Zadok and Stuart), and the four men who read acceptingly (Andy G, Tony, Derek and Anthony) all had some sense of religious identity. A skeptical or accepting binary could be suggested, with the existence of a link between these readers' sense of religious identity and their subsequent reading.

At times this link was a direct one, and the men's sense of religious identity dominated their readings, as was the case with John, Anthony, and a group of seven others. However, more often it was indirect, as was seen in the case of Dave and Gary, where their experiences of religion informed their readings and also resulted in them identifying as "not at all religious." Whatever the case, the reader's religious identity often corresponded to their reading of the texts.[36] The significance of this is especially

---

34. Weiser, *The Psalms*, 586.
35. Detweiler, "What Is a Sacred Text?" 224–25.
36. In my analysis of the data no significant difference was noted when the age,

notable when other influences are considered. For example, out of over two hundred annotations, only two directly linked part of a text to the Chemical Industrial context, see Figures 4 and 5.

Figure 4: Dave's Annotation on Proverb 10:9

| People with integrity walk safely, but those who follow crooked paths will slip and fall. | PEOPLE WITH HIGH VIS VESTS WALK SAFER |

Figure 5: Bob's Annotation on Proverbs 10:8

| The wise are glad to be instructed, but babbling fools fall flat on their faces. | As an engineer, I live by this. All of our knowledge is limited and can be extended |

None of the questionnaire responses linked the workplace to the texts and none of the participants directly link the work setting to any of the Bible passages at interview. The only other occasion in which someone connected the Bible to the workplace happened when Derek, a sixty-two-year old welder, was illustrating the usefulness of the Bible. Derek identified as a "non-practicing Catholic," having grown up attending church. However, he "moved on" from the religious upbringing of his youth, married a Protestant and sent his children to a Protestant school. Nonetheless, he had not lost his Catholic identity and for that reason identified as "moderately religious."

With regards to reading and studying the Bible, Derek said: "If you had the teaching and the learning and the ability to recall what you've read years ago, you, I think you'd be a far better person." He then went on to give an example from his workplace to illustrate this point.

> Somebody says: "Have you seen that spanner?" I'd go "have I seen that spanner? No, but I saw a spanner, it might be yours over there." And you ask some of the young lads nowadays: "Have you seen that spanner?" "No". "You've not seen it? You know the one I was carrying and what I was talking to you and tapping on my knee?" "No, not seen it." And then possibly

---

educational background, or profession of the participants was specifically considered.

twenty minutes later you walk past where he's been working and the spanner is on the floor.

The two annotations and Derek's comment, were the only instances where a connection was made between the Bible and the Chemical Industrial context. This minimal linking of the reading site to the readings which took place does not reject the presupposed contextual nature of any reading event, but suggests that the influence of certain contexts may not be quite what some have assumed. In this case study, the workplace setting and identity played a minor role in the reading event compared with the readers' religious identity.

There are two ways in which this lack of workplace influence should be qualified. First, the participants were primed by being told that this research focused on men who do not regularly read the Bible.[37] This was more likely to stimulate the men's sense of religious identity rather than their workplace identity. The weight given to this priming influence is difficult to gauge. What would be required is a comparable study where the participants are invited to read through a series of texts having been told that the influence of the reading site was being explored.

Second, as I will show in chapter 8, there is the potential that the workplace context encouraged a particular type of reading, even if it did not result in the participants directly linking the texts to their immediate working environment. That chapter demonstrates how most of these men read the texts as one would an instruction manual or guidebook. One reason for this could be the reading environment, for the other literature in their offices and portacabins were work related handbooks and protocols. Once again though the influence of this environmental factor is hard to gauge, and my conclusion in chapter 8 is that it may have contributed to the way the texts were read, but there were more significant factors such as the men's belief that the Bible is a moral guide.

In the context of a woman's prison, Alison Peden found that her female readers asked questions of the text which were informed by their context, such as "how long did Jesus get when he was arrested?"[38] and were readily able to make links between the prison setting and the Bible. However, on only three occasions did my participants directly link their workplace context to their readings or the Bible in general. While acknowledging the two qualifications above, I would contend that this case study troubles the assumption that a reader's geographical setting has a

---

37. My thanks to Paul Rodway and Astrid Schepman for alerting me to this.
38. Peden, "Contextual Bible Study at Cornton Vale Women's Prison, Stirling," 15.

significant bearing on the reading which takes place, as some contextual Bible approaches suggest.[39]

Rajeswari Rajan makes a similar observation when reflecting on her own geographical location in India, for she notes that her affiliations rather than her geographical location shape her engagement with the world. She writes: "Location, however, is not simply an address. One's affiliations are multiple, contingent and frequently contradictory."[40] In her case, she is struggling to unpick her Indian postcolonial feminist identity from her academic one. The former is typically viewed as a peripheral position rooted in a particular life setting, whist the latter is one with status and linked to the western academy. The theologian Nema McCallum (this is a pseudonym) also notes the diversity of influences upon an individual and their response to the world (or a text). In her case, it is her experiences of being in psychiatric care as a young person rather than her gender that predominantly inform her work, even though she assumes the label "feminist theologian." She writes:

> [My] experience of psychiatry, not my identity as a woman, is far more potent in affecting my sense of justice, style of theology, understanding of other people and thinking about God.[41]

In the case of John, Anthony, and many of the men in this case study, it was their sense of religious identity and related affiliations which would dominate their readings, rather than the Chemical Industrial reading site.

Conclusion

John's and Anthony's readings are further examples of a reader's relationship with the five texts shaping their reading of those texts, in their case it was their sense of religious identity, for John, an atheist, read skeptically, whilst Anthony, a Christian, read acceptingly. The concepts of social identity and self-schema theory were used to explore why these men responded in this way. Indeed, this identity not only shaped their readings but was also reaffirmed in those readings. John and Anthony however were not alone and a correlation was noted between most of the men's sense of religious identity and their reading of the five texts.

These readers elevated their sense of religious identity over and against other socially constructed identities, such as their profession. This,

---

39. Lawrence, *The Word in Place*; Riches, *What is Contextual Bible Study?*
40. Rajan, *Real & Imagined Women*, 8.
41. McCallum, "Anonymity Desirable, Bibliography Not Required," 51.

along with the lack of any significant linking between the reading site (a Chemical Industrial Plant) and the texts themselves challenges contextual Bible reading theory. It would expect the geographical context of the reading to play a meaningful role in the reading that takes place, and in my case study it did not.

However, the link between the men's religious identity and the associated skeptical or accepting reading that I have been arguing for must be nuanced, for there were exceptions. As I will now go on to explore there were men whose religious identity did not correspond to the expected skeptical or accepting reading.

Chapter 7

Reader-shaped Readings—Attitude

Up until this point I have made use of a "skeptical or accepting" couplet to describe these men's readings. My use of this pairing is similar to other binary frameworks used, such as "confessional or non-confessional,"[1] and "hermeneutics of respect or suspicion."[2] What follows will nuance this idea. Two readers are presented, Victor and Paul, whose religious identity did not correspond with their reading of the texts. In their case their attitude towards the texts had a greater bearing on their reading than their sense of religious identity. Victor identified as "not at all religious" and had an open attitude: he was keen to "be fair" to the texts. This resulted in him being one of only two participants who read the texts both skeptically and acceptingly, breaking the binary framework. Paul identified as "moderately religious" but had a doubting attitude that led him to focus on things he disagreed with in the texts, overall he read skeptically. Demonstrating that the link between a reader's religious identity and their reading is not always present. His skeptical reading however was not as all encompassing as some men's, for on occasion he referred to certain texts positively. These two examples do not result in the rejection of the link between a reader's religious identity and their reading of the texts, rather it suggests that a spectrum is preferred to a binary framework, and cautions against the assumption that all (non) religious men will read the Bible in a certain way.

What follows, is the third example of the relational nature of reading and again is one where the reader assumes a controlling position in the reader/text relationship, on this occasion it is the reader's attitudes that dominate. Leslie Francis defines an attitude as:

> A relatively permanent and enduring evaluative predisposition to a positive or negative response of an affective nature which is based upon and reflects to some extent evaluative concepts or

1. Davies, *Whose Bible Is It Anyway?*
2. Volf, *Captive to the Word of God.*

beliefs learnt about the characteristics of a referent or group of referents.[3]

This definition corresponds well to other multi-dimensional ones,[4] and Francis has applied it to the study of religion.[5] Attitudes play significant roles in how any individual navigates life, and so it should be of no surprise that they shaped the Bible readings.

Most of the men directly expressed a particular attitude, or set of attitudes, towards the biblical texts, the Bible, Christianity more broadly or religion in general, which was seen to inform their readings. However, what follows will deal with two men in particular, both of whom were unsure what to believe about the Bible and in different ways described themselves as "sitting on the fence" in relation to it. However, their attitudes towards the five biblical texts were very different.

Victor's "Fair" Readings

Victor is a thirty-one-year-old scaffolder, who had previously worked for thirteen years as a delivery driver. He identified as "not at all religious," having never regularly gone to church nor read the Bible. Like most of my participants he indicated that school was the main context where he was exposed to the Bible. However, unlike many of the men, Victor did have a Bible at home. It belonged to his one-year-old son who received it at his Christening.

In the Entrance Questionnaire I tried to gauge the participant's attitudes to and beliefs about the Bible by giving them twenty-two statements about it. Victor indicated that he did not hold any strong opinions on the Bible: for thirteen of the statements he indicated "neither agree nor disagree," and he was "unsure" about a further five. This corresponded with his view of God, for he described himself as being "half and half, I'm in the middle," neither believing nor disbelieving. Nonetheless, in light of the link which I noted earlier between the reader's sense of religious identity and their reading of the texts, I expected Victor to read the texts skeptically as most of the other men had, but he did not; he read them both skeptically and acceptingly. He did not concentrate solely on parts of the text with which he disagreed, instead he commented on the text in general, agreeing with some parts and disagreeing with others. For example, 2 John is a text

---

3. Francis, "Monitoring the Christian Development of the Child," 4–5.

4. Coolican, *Research Methods and Statistics in Psychology*; Summers, "Introduction."

5. Francis and Kay, "Attitude towards Religion."

that Victor did not annotate because "nothing jumped out." In the related questionnaire and at interview he summed it up in a very similar way: "This passage to me is all about how love is real and that how they believe in the love of God." Victor went on to note things he agreed and disagreed with in this text. This was a text about "love," and this was something he valued, writing, "I agree that love is good." However, he then went on to qualify that statement by adding that "I don't believe that just because you love someone it means that the love is from god." Victor concluded that this passage was not that relevant to today's world because "I think you love people for you and not because god is with us." By highlighting areas and concepts in the text with which he agreed and others with which he disagreed, Victor's reading of this text was one which contained both skeptical and accepting elements; he broke the binary.

Of the other four texts, Victor read two slightly more skeptically, Proverbs 10:1–11 and 2 Samuel, and two slightly more acceptingly, Matthew 18:21–35 and Psalm 88. That is to say, his readings of the former had a few more comments pointing out problems he had with the text, whilst his readings of latter had more comments highlighting aspects he agreed with in the text. For example, his annotation of Matthew 18:21–35 comprised of the short statement shown in Figure 6.

Figure 6: Victor's Annotations on Matthew 18:21–35

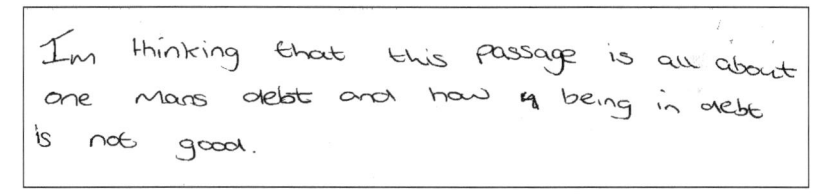

> Im thinking that this passage is all about one mans debt and how being in debt is not good.

Victor summarizes the passage as being "about one mans debt" before implying that it emphasizes "how being in debt is not good." This comment does not indicate whether he agrees or disagrees with the text, but in the accompanying questionnaire he described the passage as one worth remembering because "debt is a bad thing." During our interview I passed Victor a copy of this text and asked him what he made of it, and he said:

> It was more about, that he was kind of in debt and that [. . .] he thought he'd got away with it and, kind of, was forgiven. And then obviously at the end it, kind of, came back to him. I put: "it always catches up with you."

Victor had read this text differently to most of the other nonreligious men. He had not concentrated on aspects of it with which he disagreed rather he focused on what he understood to be its main point, "that debt catches up with you." Contrasting his opinion on 2 John, he thought Matthew 18:21–35 was a text worth remembering because it warned against getting into debt, a warning he agreed with. Victor's interpretation of this parable contrasts most scholars, who suggest that forgiveness is its central theme, in light of its opening question "Lord, how often should I forgive someone who sins against me?"[6] I enquired if there were any reasons, such as a past experience, why he had focused on avoidance of debt rather than the merits of forgiveness in this parable, but Victor indicated that there were none; it was just how he had read the passage.

During our semi-structured interview I pointed out to Victor that the way he read these texts was different to the skeptical readings undertaken by most of the other nonreligious men. He replied:

Victor: I think, probably I, I think when I read it I gave it a chance, I just didn't think, "oh this is about the Bible, it's going to be rubbish." I read it and thought about it.

David: Was that a conscious decision "I'm going to give this?" Or is that just your kind of personality?

Victor: Yeh, because I wasn't, I was going to be fair, I wasn't going to read it and think well, "this is rubbish," "I don't understand it," and write down any old, "I don't understand," "I don't agree."

Victor, proactively decided to give "it a chance." He was "going to be fair." Victor was aware of the skepticism that I have identified with a nonreligious reading of these texts but he chose to suspend it and assume an open attitude. This did not lead to a consistent accepting reading of the texts, but to a skeptical and accepting one. In this way then a further aspect of a reader's relationship with a text is seen to shape their reading, in this case it was their attitude towards the text.

Victor's decision to assume an open attitude was not unique to this occasion. Victor and his wife had their son Christened and gave him Godparents, because "it's just the normal thing what people do." These Godparents gave their son a children's Bible at the Christening and, in line with the open attitude Victor demonstrated in my project, he and his wife have read it to their son. He said: "I mean it's not that routine to be honest. Bedtime routines, but at first we were reading him, like bath and then book and then

---

6. Keener, *A Commentary on the Gospel of Matthew,* 456–61; Nolland, *The Gospel of Matthew,* 751–62.

bed. So we were reading him a part of it." Victor's attitude towards the Bible was evidenced prior to his encounter with the five texts I gave him, as seen in his decision to read his son bedtime Bible stories.

Rosenblatt notes that a degree of self-awareness and an appreciation of the influence of our prejudices is desirable in a reading transaction. She writes of the reader:

> His first need is to understand his own emotional response to the person or situation [Rosenblatt infers text as well]. He realizes that preoccupations and prejudices may have led him to exaggerate some things and ignore others. He has to bring his basic moral or psychological assumptions out into the open to test the validity of their application to this new situation.[7]

Rosenblatt is arguing that if a reader found their preoccupations and prejudices to have resulted in a misunderstanding of a text, they should be able to disassociate themselves from those preoccupations and prejudices to some degree. The result of this should be a more appropriate reading, for a "good" reader is one who "submits himself to the guidance of the text."[8]

In Victor's case, even prior to reading the first text he had made a decision to try not to prejudge them or read them as many other nonreligious men had. He was aware of the potential that every reader's preoccupations and assumptions have to shape the reading and he sought to acknowledge and ignore them as best he could. Victor's reading echoes Wolfgang Iser's description of a reading experience as one where "we must suspend the ideas and attitudes that shape our own personality before we can experience the unfamiliar world of the literary text."[9] Victor did not suspend his attitudes, but did limit the degree of skepticism with which he engaged the texts, in this way he was able to consider that which was foreign to him in a more hospitable way. Similarly, Hans-Georg Gadamer who pointed out the impossibility of a reader's prejudices not informing their reading, describes a reader as one who is willing to "remain open to the meaning of the other person or of the text."[10] In doing so he anticipates that ultimately "the text may present itself in all its newness and thus be able to assert its own truth against one's own fore-meaning."[11]

Victor decided to give the texts "a chance" as he was "going to be fair." He was the only participant to express a sense of having chosen to adopt an open attitude. In turn, his reading of the texts was then shaped by that

---

7. Rosenblatt, *Making Meaning with Texts,* 215.
8. Ibid., 265.
9. Iser, "The Reading Process," 65.
10. Gadamer, *Truth and Method,* 238.
11. Ibid., 238.

attitude. Perhaps because of this decision, Victor was the only participant who noted that in 2 Samuel 5:17–25 the Philistines were the aggressors. Most of the men referred to this text as if King David and the Israelites were the aggressors. His example challenges the skeptical/accepting binary framework developed in the previous chapter and acts as note of caution against assuming that all nonreligious men will read the Bible skeptically. In his case, an open attitude resulted in a skeptical and accepting reading that did not correspond to his religious identity. This does not result in the rejection of this link rather it highlights the need for caution regarding the assumption that all men who identify as nonreligious will read the Bible skeptically.

Paul's Doubting Readings

Paul is another example of someone whose attitude towards the five biblical texts would significantly shape their reading of those texts and who also troubles the earlier binary framework. Paul is a thirty-six-year-old scaffolder, who identified as "moderately religious" describing himself as a "non-practicing" Catholic. He attended a local Roman Catholic Church as a boy, only stopping when his family moved away from the church parish. Much like Victor, he is married and also has a young son, whom he plans to send to church when older. Paul was also unsure about the Bible. Of the twenty-two statements about the Bible in the Entrance Questionnaire, he indicated "neither agree nor disagree" nineteen times. It was therefore no surprise when he later described himself as "sitting on the fence." On the three occasions when he did not indicate "neither agree nor disagree" he responded as might be expected from a moderately religious man. For instance, indicating that the Bible was not full of myths and legends and that he imagines he will read the Bible in the future. Therefore, I thought he would read the texts acceptingly, but he did not.

Paul read three of the texts skeptically (Prov 10:1–11, 2 Sam 5:17–25 and 2 John), tending to concentrate on the parts he disagreed with. For instance, Paul, like Victor, did not annotate 2 John; he said "nothing stood out," and so left the text blank. However, in both the questionnaire and interview he focuses on two problems he had with the text. First, he said it claimed "if you don't, sort of, follow the beliefs, or this, then you'd be, sort of, cast aside." Second, that it contradicts itself in that God "commanded that you love one another, but he's also given orders that people battle against one another [. . .] it's like singing off one hymn sheet and singing off another isn't it?" This was a text that he considered to be of no relevance to today's society and bordered on the "bullying" as it taught "get on side or face being cast aside." Accordingly, God's rule "looks more like a dictatorship," which contrasts with the idea that "everyone is supposed to be free aren't they? But in that [2 John] they are not."

Nonetheless, Paul did not read all the texts skeptically; Psalm 88 and Matthew 18:21–35 were texts he read skeptically and acceptingly. His annotations of Matthew 18:21–35 are seen in Figure 7.

Figure 7: Paul's Annotations on Matthew 18:21–35

> Then Peter came to him and asked, "Lord, how often should I forgive someone who sins against me? Seven times?" "No, not seven times," Jesus replied, "but seventy times seven! "Therefore, the Kingdom of Heaven can be compared to a king who decided to bring his accounts up to date with servants who had borrowed money from him. In the process, one of his debtors was brought in who owed him millions of dollars. He couldn't pay, so his master ordered that he be sold—along with his wife, his children, and everything he owned—to pay the debt. "But the man fell down before his master and begged him, 'Please, be patient with me, and I will pay it all.' Then his master was filled with pity for him, and he released him and forgave his debt. "But when the man left the king, he went to a fellow servant who owed him a few thousand dollars. He grabbed him by the throat and demanded instant payment. "His fellow servant fell down before him and begged for a little more time. 'Be patient with me, and I will pay it,' he pleaded. But his creditor wouldn't wait. He had the man arrested and put in prison until the debt could be paid in full. "When some of the other servants saw this, they were very upset. They went to the king and told him everything that had happened. Then the king called in the man he had forgiven and said, 'You evil servant! I forgave you that tremendous debt because you pleaded with me. Shouldn't you have mercy on your fellow servant, just as I had mercy on you?' Then the angry king sent the man to prison to be tortured until he had paid his entire debt. "That's what my heavenly Father will do to you if you refuse to forgive your brothers and sisters from your heart."

Annotations (handwritten): "DOLLARS?", "Thought that sounded dodgy", "of money does not exist", "A lot to let go"

Paul's two statements do not reveal an overly skeptical or accepting reading. However, in the accompanying questionnaire he indicated that concepts like "mercy and compassion" were at the heart of this text and these virtues were worth remembering and relevant to today's world. In his interview however he was less positive about this passage. He began by speaking about forgiveness, saying: "yeah, the first one lets him off, which is out of the kindness of his heart, it's great." However, he then goes on to concentrate on the punishment the King orders:

> I'm just unsure about the punishment that he got because, you know, because he, because he let him off [. . .] it just seems to, well, he's tried to get his money back and then, we don't know the reasoning and that's why I'm a bit, I don't know.

This reading reflects Victor's skeptical and accepting reading in that Paul notes parts of the text with which he agrees and parts with which he disagrees. In light of Paul's readings we discussed his attitude towards the Bible in our interview:

> Paul: I'm still quite on the fence with some of the things, even though, like I say, I'd like to believe. I'm also, well, I don't know. You know, I do have it in my head that I do, I do believe in Christ and stuff, but I'm still open-minded to, you know, when you say the example, the hungry will, the poor will, what is it? The poor will? [referring to Prov 10:3]
>
> David: The Lord will not let the hungry, the godly.
>
> Paul: The godly go hungry. And it's when you hear stuff like that and you think, they do. And I think sometimes folk, that's. I'm not. That's why I'd rather sit on the fence, but I'm not. That's why I'd rather sit on the fence instead of saying I agree or disagree.

At the end of every interview, as Tom Wengraf indicates, it is considered good practice to ensure that your participants are given the opportunity to add a further comment or ask any questions.[12] Paul wanted to know if there were other Catholics who also found that the Bible's content did not match their life experience, asking:

> I mean I'm talking in the sort of, I can't remember, what do you call them? The Catholic family, did they ever go "well these

---

12. Wengraf, *Qualitative Research Interviewing*, 205.

things aren't exactly, these things aren't happening." [Referring to the proverb "the godly will not go hungry."] So, yes, ask the question: "Why?" to themselves. And I'm just wondering did they ever ask themselves those sort of questions?

Paul was struggling to relate his life experience with the implications of his religious affiliation. He is not alone in asking questions about the significance of the Bible in the modern world. James Bielo noted something similar in an evangelical men's Bible study group in Michigan, USA. He observed that at times the men's life experience contradicted some of what they were reading in the Bible:

> Throughout their study of Proverbs the LCMS [Lutheran Church-Missouri Synod] men devoted at least one discussion in every meeting to whether or not a particular text should be read as a "promise from God": a timeless certainty unbound by circumstance.[13]

When faced with this challenge, most of the LCMS group opposed interpreting proverbs as promises but rather concentrated on their practical outworking.

Paul's engagement with the texts contrasts Anthony's. Both these men identified as "moderately religious," spoke positively about their church experiences, and expressed a desire to re-engage with the Bible, however Anthony read acceptingly and Paul skeptically. This difference reflects a much larger diversity of Bible-reading strategies used by Christians. Some read miraculous accounts as being literally true and others do not;[14] some strive to resolve ambiguities and others warn against it;[15] some focus on the relevance of the text,[16] and others use a "Jesus hermeneutic";[17] some choose to read selectively,[18] others do not read it at all,[19] and yet others describe Bible reading in terms of daily nourishment.[20] There is a diversity found in how Christians read the Bible, one reflected in the plethora of Christian identities, and Paul and Anthony are part of that.

---

13. Bielo, *Words upon the Word*, 54.
14. Village, *The Bible and Lay People*, 57–76.
15. Beal, *The Rise and Fall of the Bible*.
16. Malley, *How the Bible Works*.
17. Rogers, *Congregational Hermeneutics*.
18. Llewellyn, *Reading, Feminism, and Spirituality*.
19. Engelke, *A Problem of Presence*.
20. Strhan, *Aliens and Strangers*, 109–36.

In the case of Paul and Victor, however, they were both unsure about the Bible, but one of the main differences between their readings was their attitude towards the five biblical texts. Where Victor indicated that he had never actively read the Bible and so had not formed a concrete opinion on it, Paul had. However, the Christian beliefs that informed his childhood were now seen to be faulty in light of his life-experience. Doubt would mark Paul's readings of these texts, resulting in a skeptical reading. This once again challenges the link between a reader's religious identity and their reading of the texts. In Paul's case, his doubting attitude was a greater influence than his moderate religious identity.

Identity and Bible Reading: A Spectrum

When Paul's readings are compared with Dave or Gary's what is noticeable is that not all men who read skeptically did so to the same degree. Indeed, when these twenty men's readings were analyzed, rather than a skeptical/accepting binary, a spectrum was seen, as presented in Table 1.

The six men who in most settings (annotation, questionnaire and interview) commented on most of the texts skeptically I labeled "Strongly Skeptical." Those who referred to most of the texts in most settings skeptically but on occasion acceptingly, I described as "Typically Skeptical." The final skeptical group, of whom Paul was part, I labeled "Somewhat Skeptical," for they engaged with these texts skeptically but inconsistently so, at times affirming texts or aspects of the texts as well.

The middle group of Bob and Victor typically read the texts skeptically and acceptingly. There were those who read the texts affirmingly in most settings but on occasion skeptically and so were labeled "Typically Accepting." Finally, the smallest group in the table has only one member, Anthony, who engaged affirmingly with most of the texts in most of the settings. This table shows that the link between the participant's religious identity and their reading of the texts remains, but the examples of Victor and Paul provide a note of caution by highlighting that other factors, such as a reader's attitude, can have a greater impact upon the readings.

Table 1: The Spectrum of Skeptical and Accepting Readings

	Not at all Religious Participants	Slightly Religious Participants	Moderately Religious Participants	Very Religious Participants
Strongly Skeptical Reader	Dave Sam Ethan John Matty	Phil	—	—
Typically Skeptical Reader	Andy K Gary Peter Mick	—	—	—
Somewhat Skeptical Reader	Zadok Stuart	Richie	Paul	—
Skeptical and Accepting Reader	Victor	Bob	—	—
Somewhat Accepting Reader	—	—	—	—
Typically Accepting Reader	—	Tony	Andy G Derek	—
Strongly Accepting Reader	—	—	Anthony	—

The spectrum I have presented above, and the various ways in which different aspects of the men's relationship with the texts shaped their readings, confirms that this cohort of men should not be thought of as one homogenous group. Lois Lee undertook ethnographic research amongst those who identify as "not religious," a label many of my participants used. She highlighted the diversity of positions this identity refers to. In particular, she noted five different ways in which this label was used: as a "synonym for another nonreligious identity" such as atheist or humanist; to "indicate a loose or general nonreligious position"; to express a rejection of religion but openness to alternative spirituality; by those who rejected religious/spiritual categorization in general; and to communicate a personal indifference towards religion.²¹ Callum Brown and Gordon Lynch also conclude, "people of no religion should not be regarded as a homogeneous group. They are extremely diverse in their outlook, philosophical position, and priorities."²²

Using very different language, a survey produced in 2007 by Tearfund entitled *Churchgoing in the UK*, subdivided the male population of the UK with reference to their attitudes towards churchgoing.²³ It indicated that along with 11% of the male population who attend church regularly, another 13% of men are either open to the idea of attending church or attend infrequently, 28% have attended church in the past but have no desire to attend again, and 38% have never attended church and do not plan to do so.²⁴ These three latter categories all refer to men outside the church, demonstrating again that they are not one homogenous group and my own findings are not anomalous.

Pairings such as "skeptical or accepting," "confessional or non-confessional," and "hermeneutics of suspicion or respect" should therefore be used with caution. Binary models like these imply that there are only two ways of reading the Bible and that all readings within each category are alike. However, readers like Paul and Victor and the breadth of readings noted in this case study challenge these assumptions.

Conclusion

This chapter has therefore troubled the skeptical/accepting binary the previous chapter proposed, for there was a spectrum of readings, reflecting the diversity of participants. There were those, like Victor, a nonreligious man, who read skeptically and acceptingly, and Paul, a moderately religious man, who read somewhat skeptically. Indeed, as a group a range of skeptical and/or accepting readings were seen. Moreover, the link made earlier between the men's religious identity and their reading of the texts was also challenged, for Victor and Paul's readings did not conform to this pattern. This does not result in the dismissal of this link, rather it warns against a naïve assumption that all men will read the texts according to their religious identity and

---

21. Lee, "Secular or Nonreligious?" 470–76.

22. Brown and Lynch, "Cultural Perspectives," 340, additionally Theos's *Post-Religious Britain?: The Faith of the Faithless*, similarly notes a variety of beliefs and practices amongst those who describe themselves as nonreligious.

23. In the USA similar research has been undertaken using the labels "Always Unchurched," "De-Churched," "Friendly Unchurched," and "Hostile Unchurched," see: Stetzer et al., *Lost and Found*.

24. The final 10% are accounted for as belonging to another religion or being unassigned.

highlights the diversity of readers. Ultimately though, it was Paul and Victor's attitudes towards the five biblical texts which this section explored, for although both described themselves as "sitting on the fence" with regards to the Bible their attitudes would result in very different readings.

Aware of the dangers in assuming that these men are one homogenous group, chapters 8 and 9 will now explore the way a reader's beliefs about the five biblical texts shaped their reading of those texts. This is the fourth example I am using to evidence my central claim. In doing so, I will not focus on two men in particular, as I have done with each example until now, rather I will deal with them as a single cohort, for there were two beliefs which shaped nearly every participant's reading.

Chapter 8

Reader-shaped Readings—Belief 1

THE PREVIOUS THREE CHAPTERS explored the influence of the reader's prior experiences of religion, religious identity, and attitudes towards the five biblical texts. In doing so, I presented Dave and Gary, John and Anthony, and Paul and Victor. These different couplets were used to demonstrate and unpack three different ways in which a reader's relationship with the five texts influenced their reading of those texts. Thus far I have concentrated on aspects of this relationship that heavily influenced some men's readings but not others. Rosenblatt argues that due to a process of "selective attention" certain experiences, feelings, ideas and thoughts will be pushed to the forefront of a reader's mind, shaping their reading more than others.[1] Thus, Dave connected his skeptical readings to his prior experiences of religion, but John connected his to his atheist identity. This does not mean that Dave's nonreligious identity did not play a role in his reading of the texts, nor that his experiences and identity were unconnected, rather it shows that for him his experiences were a more significant factor. Each of these three couplets (Dave and Gary, John and Anthony, and Paul and Victor) represented a theme to emerge from my data, one seen in other men as well, but not in the group as a whole.

The next two chapters now turn to consider a fourth aspect or theme: the impact of the reader's beliefs about the five biblical texts upon their reading of those texts. Contrasting the three earlier examples, this was evidenced in nearly all of the men's readings. Therefore, I will break from the pattern established in the previous three chapters by present data from a wide number of men to demonstrate the pervasiveness of this finding instead of focusing upon two particular readers.

I will focus on two beliefs about the Bible that are not always noted, but emerged as strong themes in my data. In this chapter I will first highlight the way these men typically read the texts for information, as one would a

---

1. Rosenblatt, *Making Meaning with Texts*, xxv.

manual or guidebook. Using multiple examples I demonstrate the nature of this reading and its prevalence. This reading style is then compared with different labels scholars have used to describe such a reading phenomenon, and I argue that the term "efferent" as used by Rosenblatt is the one that corresponds best. Three possible reasons are given for the widespread efferent reading of the texts: the research materials encouraged the reader to assume an efferent stance towards the texts; the reader's personality and gender resulted in them assuming such a standpoint; and the reader's belief that the Bible is a didactic text or guide led them to read it efferently. Ultimately I will contend that although all three played a part, it was the participants' belief about the Bible that was the most significant factor. In the follow chapter I will show that they also believed reading the Bible was potentially transformative. This was perceived as a threat by most of the men and they responded by "counter-reading." This is the term I use to describe the personal sense of threat felt by a reader that results in a skeptical reading of a text and so the invalidating of that text and the disarming of the threat. In providing these final examples, these two chapters complete the second strand of my argument.

Andrew Village describes beliefs as:

> Specific ideas or thoughts about something. In technical terms, belief occurs when an attribute is linked to an object: existence may be linked to God, trustworthiness to your vicar, or the presence of life to Mars.[2]

More often than not, when considering belief about the Bible, scholars have made use of a propositional and individualistic understanding of belief, focusing on issues of veracity, divine inspiration, and relevance.[3] Village's study, for instance, in part concerned:

> The extent to which the Bible might be literally versus symbolically true, the extent to which it might contain errors of fact, the degree to which its truths are exclusive to Christianity or available from other faiths, and the extent of biblical authority.[4]

This contrasts a practice-centered understanding that is linked to function and performance, or an institutional and society understanding connected

---

2. Village, *The Bible and Lay People*, 29.

3. For example see: Clines, *The Bible and the Modern World*; Field, "Is the Bible Becoming a Closed Book?"; Freathy, "Gender, Age, Attendance at a Place of Worship and Young People's Attitudes towards the Bible"; Harrison, *Attitudes to Bible, God, Church*; Walker, "The Religious Beliefs and Attitudes of Rural Anglican Churchgoers."

4. Village, *The Bible and Lay People*, 36.

with group affiliation.[5] In my research, because of its practical nature, I have assumed a propositional and practice-centered view of belief.

Reading the Texts as Textbooks

When examining the data produced by the readers, I noticed that most of the men read most of the texts for information that they then critiqued. That is to say, no matter the genre nearly all the passages were handled as if they were guidebooks or didactic texts (of questionable quality). For example, Mick, a thirty-year-old scaffolder who described himself as "not at all religious," having never regularly read the Bible or gone to church, referred to Proverbs 10:1–11 in this way:

> Yeah, this to me was more like instructions of the path maybe. That they expect you to take, or otherwise these foul things are going to happen to you. That's what I thought it was.

To read Proverbs 10:1–11 in this way is perhaps no surprise for this short list of aphorisms lends itself be to read as a compendium of wisdom or guidance. Indeed, the book as a whole has been described as:

> A course of study (a collection of wisdom teachings and saying)
>
> designed to foster wisdom (the development of discernment and character)
>
> using literary-rhetorical resources (juxtaposition and metaphor).[6]

In other words, the text itself (a didactic one) and the reading style (for information) correspond.

As a letter, 2 John could also be described as having an instructional element, and Andy G, a forty-nine-year-old mechanic who, as a Freemason, identified as "moderately religious," was not alone in picking up on that:

> Basically yeh it was eh, it was just eh a letter telling the followers of Christianity not to forget what it's all about and to keep on behaving in, as they should do towards others.

Andy G handled this letter as if it were a didactic text, distilling its message accordingly. His summary indicates that he read this passage in order to identify what he understood to be its central purpose.

However, both Matthew 18:21–35 and 2 Samuel 5:17–25 had a narrative component and may have encouraged a reading style which did not

---

5. Day, *Believing in Belonging*, 3–27.
6. Koptak, *Proverbs*, 23.

focus upon what was to be learned. Nonetheless, my participants consistently read these two texts for information as well (which they typically rejected). For example, Peter, a fifty-six-year-old electrician who identified as "not at all religious," read Matthew 18:21–35 and said:

> It's offering you pie in the sky. That is my biggest problem with it, you want the good things in life now and while you are living, what happens after you die is beside the point.

His critique of this text reflects a reading which believes the text to be a guide or manual, with the promise of "pie in the sky" when you die for those who follow it. Richie, a forty-six-year-old mechanic who identified as a "lapsed Catholic" and so "slightly religious," described 2 Samuel 5:17–25 as "nonsense." When asked to clarify this comment he said:

> Richie: A personal opinion, I mean I don't think it ever happened, no.
>
> David: Ok, that's really helpful. And you are not the only one to say that.
>
> Richie: That's someone going to an army and trying to give them a bit of belief that God is on their side, isn't it? What better way to say, "I actually spoke to him and he's told us what to do." People will follow that then won't they?

Richie's reflections on this passage focus on its historical reliability, and although he does not reject the battle account itself, he does reject the claim that God helped David. In the related questionnaire he would indicate that this was a text designed "to make the [present-day] people of Israel believe God is on their side." This again demonstrates a reading for information, understanding it to have a message for present-day Jews.

Literary theories, like the transactional theory of reading, suggest that poems and songs should not be read for facts, but rather for the images and ideas they convey and for their potential to transport a reader to a different world.[7] This is the case for biblical poetry as well,[8] of which Psalm 88 is one example. However, most of my participants also read this text for information, resulting in a disjunction between the text's genre (poetry) and the reading style (for information). For example, Sam is the twenty-four-year-old engineer who I presented in the introduction, and his reading of Psalm 88 typifies the way most of the men read it. Psalm 88 is a psalm of lament

---

7. Rosenblatt, *Making Meaning with Texts*, 11.
8. Miller, *Interpreting the Psalms*, 29–30; Westermann, *The Psalms*, 5–9.

and has been described as a song,[9] a prayer,[10] and a poem.[11] In the short descriptor I provided for the men, I described it as a song. Sam's annotations of this text can be seen in Figure 8.

Figure 8: Sam's Annotations on Psalm 88

> O Lord, God of my salvation, I cry out to you by day. I come to you at night. Now hear my prayer; listen to my cry. For my life is full of troubles, and death draws near. I am as good as dead, like a strong man with no strength left. They have left me among the dead, and I lie like a corpse in a grave. I am forgotten, cut off from your care. You have thrown me into the lowest pit, into the darkest depths. Your anger weighs me down; with wave after wave you have engulfed me.
>
> You have driven my friends away by making me repulsive to them. I am in a trap with no way of escape. My eyes are blinded by my tears. Each day I beg for your help, O Lord; I lift my hands to you for mercy. Are your wonderful deeds of any use to the dead? Do the dead rise up and praise you?
>
> Can those in the grave declare your unfailing love? Can they proclaim your faithfulness in the place of destruction? Can the darkness speak of your wonderful deeds? Can anyone in the land of forgetfulness talk about your righteousness? O Lord, I cry out to you. I will keep on pleading day by day. O Lord, why do you reject me? Why do you turn your face from me? I have been sick and close to death since my youth. I stand helpless and desperate before your terrors. Your fierce anger has overwhelmed me. Your terrors have paralyzed me. They swirl around me like floodwaters all day long. They have engulfed me completely. You have taken away my companions and loved ones. Darkness is my closest friend.

Annotations (handwritten):
- Overall a very negative 'song' of man pleading
- No chords in the song
- Passage shows that god can turn on people
- he must have done something wrong

---

9. Anderson, *The Book of Psalms*, 622.
10. Tate, *Psalms 51–100*, 393.
11. Hossfeld and Zenger, *Psalms 2*, 391.

Sam's annotations indicate that he read this text for information, which he analyzed and commented on. He critiqued the genre, describing it as a "very negative song" and noted that it had "no chorus." Before highlighting that it "shows that god can turn on people," a comment indicating he has read this text with an eye for what information or teachings the psalm is trying to communicate. His comments on this text at interview were similar:

> It seemed a bit long-winded to be a song, if you know what I mean. But I don't know, they might have had different songs back then. Em, no I, I thought this was quite negative really, showing how again, how God can be cruel and he can, if you don't do, if you don't follow him or do what he says, then he'll make your life miserable I suppose.

Sam's response to this psalm shows that it has been read in a didactic fashion. He analyzed this text as a song, finding it lacking in necessary format and style. Then, focusing on its content he surmised that it has a central instruction, or fact, which is: "if you don't do what he [God] says, then he'll make your life miserable." This was a teaching that Sam found unbelievable and personally irrelevant.

Tony is a fifty-five-year-old engineer who described himself as a "Catholic" and "moderately religious," attending church every five or six weeks. He read this psalm in a similar way, identifying a key teaching, or fact. Tony did not write a comment on the text, but his answers in the related questionnaire and during our interview showed that he believed it taught "you cannot turn to god only when you are in despair as you will not receive any comfort." This response demonstrates that he had read this poem for information. Unlike Sam however, Tony did not describe this as an unbelievable and distasteful teaching, because of his sense of religious identity he believed this psalm contained a warning for others, not him.

Derek is a sixty-two-year-old welder who identified as a non-practicing Catholic and so "moderately religious," but unlike Tony he had not been to church for years. In line with his religious identity, he read this psalm acceptingly, focusing on the parts with which he agreed. He did not annotate the text, but in the questionnaire he described this passage as promoting "the power of prayer." During our interview he suggested that this was a passage that encouraged perseverance in prayer:

> You pray every week to win the lottery. In a roundabout way, you are trying to find something to get you that little bit better, but if it doesn't happen, well what do you do? Go in your shell and mope around? No you've just got to get back up and do it again, and start all over again.

Once again this poem is being read for information, demonstrated by the identifying of a central teaching that Derek affirmed.

Bob is a sixty-one-year-old part-time manager, who identified as "slightly religious," because he was neither overtly religious nor anti-religious. Initially I thought he had read this psalm from a more imaginative and affective position. His annotations on this text were descriptive in nature often restating or summarizing sections of the poem and so did not clearly indicate how the poem had been read. However, in the accompanying questionnaire he wrote that "the fears in the passage are with us all to some degree," and "we all worry about our ultimate fate at the time of death/after death." These two comments raised the possibility that he had entered into the world of the poem, identifying with the psalmist and finding that it resonated with his own fears. However, when he spoke about this text in our interview he was very matter-of-fact, saying:

> This is a person who perceives themself as a weak person who's sort of trying to plead his case with God, em, "Your terrors have paralysed me, they swirl around like flood waters," "darkness is my closest friend." So this is somebody in despair, they need some CBT counseling or something.

He did not suggest that this text had a "message" or instruction, but nonetheless, in this setting he read it factually, for information, distilling the poem into key elements that he responded to in a slightly mocking way.

The examples above give a flavor of the way in which most of the men read most of the texts, for information. As Figures 9, 10 and 11 show, when analyzing the data I found that 83% of the annotations, 91% of the questionnaire responses and 75% of the texts discussed at interview indicated that the reader had attempted to read the text for information.

READER-SHAPED READINGS—BELIEF 1　　　　　155

Figure 9: Annotation Content

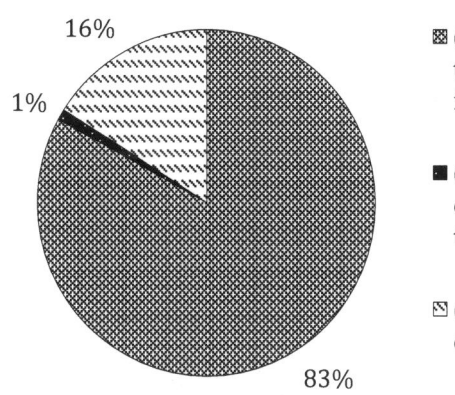

- 16% Comments indicate text read for information
- 1% Comments mainly express confusion at text
- 83% Comments principally descriptive in nature

Figure 10: Questionnaire Content

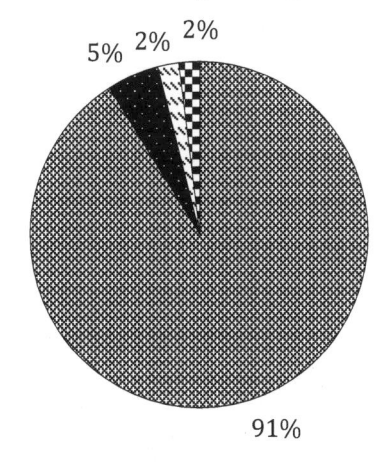

- 5% Answers indicate text read for information
- 2% Answers mainly express confusion at text
- 2% Answers were principally descriptive comments
- 91% Other

Figure 11: Interview Content

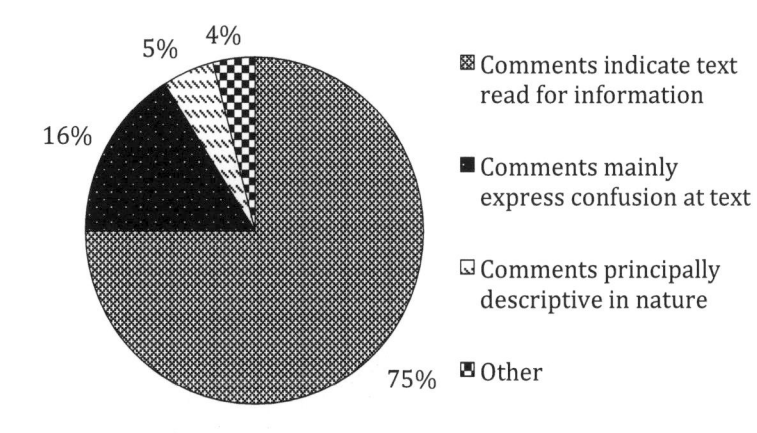

- 5% Comments indicate text read for information
- 4% Comments mainly express confusion at text
- 16% Comments principally descriptive in nature
- 75% Other

The comments, or answers, which did not indicate that the text was being read for information were typically descriptive in nature, with the participant restating or summarizing part of the text, or were expressions of confusion towards the text. For instance, Andy K is a twenty-six-year-old welder who identified as "not at all religious," having never regularly read the Bible or attended church. When reading the texts he consistently expressed a sense of confusion towards them. Andy K did not annotate any text and in the five accompanying questionnaires confusion was explicitly expressed twenty-one times. For instance, when asked to write a one-line summary of Proverbs 10:1–11, he wrote: "Out of my depth"; when asked what his "gut reaction" was to 2 Samuel 5:17–25, he wrote: "very confused. If I had read the whole Bible I could give a better answer, that's how I feel"; and when asked if there was anything worth remembering about Psalm 88 he indicated "no," because he did "not fully understand what was going on."

At interview he again expressed a sense of confusion towards all five texts. I was concerned that perhaps literacy was an issue and that even though I had chosen a Bible translation with a low reading level, Andy K may have struggled to read the texts. Thus, I tentatively asked if he had difficulty reading other literature. He indicated that he did at times, but in this instance he understood the content of the passages, his problem was that he could not place them within a wider framework so as to make sense of them.

I wonder if Andy K was not only struggling to place these texts within a wider biblical context, but did not know how to read them. Other participants described themselves as being unaware of a biblical framework or grand narrative (such as Mick, Victor, Peter, Sam, Zadok, Matty, and John), but they did not express the same level of confusion as Andy K. It is possible that unlike them, he had not learnt how to read the Bible. The result of which was when asked about the texts he was able to describe their content to some degree, but found them all confusing.[12] Andy K was an exception however in general most of these men read most of the texts as if they were didactic texts. Reading in such a way that they focused on the content, facts,

---

12. In the Entrance Questionnaire, when asked to respond to twenty-two statements concerning the Bible, he ticked "do not know" on eight occasions and for the other fourteen statements he generally indicated a mild, if qualified, acceptance of the Bible. However, his response to the same statements in the Exit Questionnaire shows a clear shift towards a general disregarding of the Bible. I brought this to Andy K's attention during our interview, and asked if he had any suggestions why this had occurred. He said: "Don't know, I might just have started, I don't know. I might just have got a different view after reading it." This implies that as a consequence of finding he could not make sense of the five texts Andy K assumed a more skeptical view of the Bible.

or teaching of each passage, critiquing and usually rejecting them as irrelevant, unworkable, unethical, or unbelievable.

Rosenblatt's Efferent/Aesthetic Spectrum

Certain literary theories resonate with this type of reading. For example, George Steiner's description of a reader as a "critic,"[13] has been applied to Bible reading,[14] and is one that has certain similarities with my participants' readings. Both they and Steiner's "critic" are concerned with analyzing a text and forming a judgment about it, one they verbally expressed to others. However, there are two reasons why Steiner's "critic" and his accompanying critic/reader model do not fit with the readings produced at the Plant. First, Steiner's "critic" distances him- or herself from the text in order to gain a better appreciation of it. He writes:

> The motion of criticism is one of "stepping back from" in exactly the sense in which one steps back from a painting on a wall in order to perceive it better. But a good critic makes this motion conscious to himself and his public.[15]

This was not commonly seen in the readings at the Plant and those men who did step back, such as Gary, did so out of indifference rather than a desire to see the text more clearly. Second, Steiner's "critic" is one who "makes the tenor of his arbitrariness transparent."[16] In other words, he is aware of his own biases and the influence this has upon his perception of the text, something he publicly discloses.[17] Some of my participants, such as Dave and Victor, were aware of their own partiality and verbally acknowledged it. Others however, like Sam, were not. As the Introduction shows, it was only when presented with his readings that Sam realized the influence of his preconceptions upon them. Therefore, although Steiner's description of a reader as a "critic" has certain overlaps with some of my own participants' readings, it does not fully describe them.

Another theory can be found in Paul Ricoeur's writings, for he describes the process of interpretation as a dialectic of "explanation" and "understanding."[18] By "explanation" he means the analytical work of reading

13. Steiner, "'Critic'/'Reader.'"
14. Fowler, "Who is 'the Reader' in Reader Response Criticism?"
15. Steiner, "'Critic'/'Reader,'" 423.
16. Ibid., 427.
17. Ibid., 428–29.
18. Ricoeur, *A Ricoeur Reader*, 43–64.

a text holding it at arms-length. This differs from "understanding" where the distance between the text and the reader is closed and meaning is personally appropriated. The Catholic feminist biblical scholar Sandra Schneiders builds on Ricoeur by suggesting that the Bible can be read for "information" or for "transformation." By this she means "to be intellectually enlightened or to be personally converted."[19] At first glance, the labels "explanation" or "information" appear to correlate with my participants' readings for they too focused on the content of the text. However, these concepts, as used by Ricoeur and Schneiders, assume that the reader will learn through the reading of the text. Many of my participants, however, did not view their readings as learning experiences. When asked if there was anything worth remembering about the text, the fourteen men who read skeptically said "no" on sixty-three out of seventy occasions (90%).[20]

These theories are not exhaustive and others also have a degree of overlap with my own findings.[21] In my case though, the terms that most accurately describe this aspect of the readings are Rosenblatt's "efferent" and "aesthetic" labels.[22] As I have recounted, Rosenblatt's transactional theory posits that as readers approach a text they prepare themselves to read it guided by cues from the text, the wider context, and their relationship with the text. In particular, she describes an efferent/aesthetic spectrum that all readers situate themselves on as they prepare to read a text and remain on during the toing and froing of the reading transaction itself. This spectrum is one that educationalists have used when exploring reading.[23]

Where the readers places themselves on the spectrum shapes the way they read the text, and because it is the readers who position themselves on the spectrum, the same text can be read in different ways.[24] At one end of the spectrum is an "efferent reading stance," which Rosenblatt describes as being "involved primarily with analyzing, abstracting, and

---

19. Schneider, *The Revelatory Text*, 13.

20. The two men who read skeptically and acceptingly said "no" on four out of ten occasions (40%) and the four men who read acceptingly said "no" on four out of twenty occasions (20%).

21. For example, see: Britton, *Language and Learning*; Langer, *Envisioning Knowledge*; Leland et al., "Reading from Different Interpretive Stances"; Pike, *From Personal to Spiritual Transaction*.

22. Rosenblatt, *The Reader, the Text, the Poem*, 23–25.

23. For example see: Harvey and Goudvis, *Strategies that Work*; Karolides, "The Transactional Theory of Literature"; Kesler, "Evoking the World of Poetic Nonfiction Picture Books."

24. Rosenblatt, *The Reader, the Text, the Poem*, 23–25.

accumulating what will be retained after the reading."[25] This reading stance is one which pays more attention to the "cognitive, the referential, the factual, the analytic, the logical, the quantitative aspects of meaning."[26] She gives the example of a mother, who, having found her child on the floor with an open bottle of pills, snatches the bottle away from the child and scans its label to see if the contents are harmful. The mother is reading efferently, her attention is focused on accumulating the appropriate information that will inform her subsequent actions.[27] Other examples of texts that would be read from an efferent standpoint include a train ticket, DIY manual, menu, newspaper, or guidebook. This was the stance which my participants adopted when they came to read the five biblical texts, as the examples at the start of this chapter demonstrate.

At the opposite end of the spectrum is an "aesthetic reading stance" which is "focused primarily on experiencing what is being evoked, lived through, during the reading."[28] This stance is focused on the present, on the reading event itself.[29] For instance, the mother, who earlier snatched the bottle of pills from her child, may find herself curled up on the sofa lost in the latest novel. She is not reading to accumulate information that will inform her subsequent actions, rather she is reading for pleasure.[30] Rosenblatt writes:

> The aesthetic reader pays attention to-savors-the qualities of the feelings, ideas, situations, scenes, personalities, and emotions that are called forth and participates in the tensions, conflicts, and resolutions of the images, ideas, and scenes as they unfold.[31]

Rosenblatt's use of "aesthetic" to refer to a particular reading stance should not be confused with the appreciation or consideration of beauty or art. These definitions are not unconnected but they should be viewed as distinct. Examples of texts for which a reader would normally assume an aesthetic reading stance include a novel, poem, play, or song.

Therefore, according to Rosenblatt's transactional theory, a poem/song like Psalm 88 should be read aesthetically. However, it is the reader who chooses the reading stance and my participants did not read this poem/

---

25. Ibid., 184.
26. Rosenblatt, *Making Meaning with Texts*, 12.
27. Rosenblatt, *The Reader, the Text, the Poem*, 23–24.
28. Ibid., 184.
29. Ibid., 24.
30. Miller and Faircloth, "Motivation and Reading Comprehension," 309.
31. Rosenblatt, *Making Meaning with Texts*, 11.

song from an aesthetic standpoint, seeking to live through and in the reading experience. They typically read it from an efferent stance, paying close attention to its content and logically evaluating it.[32]

The adoption of an efferent reading stance by these men is a further example of the way in which a reader's relationship with the five biblical texts shaped their reading of those texts. As the transactional theory hypothesizes, and as I will show, it was the men's beliefs about the texts that resulted in their efferent engagement with these texts, in particular, the belief that the Bible is a moral guide.

Prior to examining the link between these men's beliefs and their readings, it should be noted that Rosenblatt's spectrum is not without its weaknesses. First, there is a discrepancy between Rosenblatt's theory and the reality of reading. She is careful to point out that the efferent/aesthetic spectrum is not a binary framework but a continuum and both aspects are found in every reading encounter.[33] Not only that, but in one line of a text the reader may move between both ends of the spectrum as their attention changes from one part of the text to another. Typically though most readers assume a position somewhere close to the middle of the spectrum.[34] However, the examples she provides are of an efferent or an aesthetic reading, there is no illustration of a reading from the middle ground or moving from one end of the spectrum to the other. In other words, the theory refers to a spectrum, but the examples given by her suggest a binary. My case study mirrors her choice of examples but stands against her theory, in that my participants did not tend to locate themselves in the middle of the spectrum nor was there any obvious movement between the two ends of the spectrum. Their readings were predominantly efferent in nature.

There are also certain genres or reading events that do not conform to, and are not suitably described by her efferent/aesthetic spectrum. For example, Eric Paulson and Sonya Armstrong argue that reading a piece of course work with the purpose of giving feedback to the student, is not suitably described by Rosenblatt's spectrum.[35] They propose a three-dimensional one, which takes into account the reader's and writer's stances. Cynthia Lewis

---

32. Psalm 88 was read from an aesthetic stance by one participant, Stuart, as is explored in chapter 10.

33. Rosenblatt, *The Reader, the Text, the Poem*, 184.

34. Ibid., 37.

35. Paulson and Armstrong, "Situating Reader Stance within and beyond the Efferent-Aesthetic Continuum."

modifies the spectrum by expanding its aesthetic component,[36] and others have added a "critical stance,"[37] and an "expressive" one.[38]

In my own case, I would argue that parables are a form of indirect communication and although there are a wide variety of biblical parables typically they are understood to be stories or statements with two levels of meaning.[39] Therefore, they should be engaged with at the story or affective level and so require an aesthetic stance, but they are also read for information which may result in action, thus they should also be read from an efferent standpoint. I would contend that parables should be read fully aesthetically and fully efferently, an act that Rosenblatt's continuum does not allow. Of course, the actual readings which take place may not correspond to these theoretical assumptions, and in my case all of my participants principally read Matthew 18:21–35 efferently. However, my purpose is to explore a series of readings, facilitated by Rosenblatt's theory, not to remodel or develop that theory.[40] In light of the reading stance adopted by most of my participants and its correlation with Rosenblatt's "efferent" label, I will continue employing her efferent/aesthetic spectrum.

Three Antecedents to Reading Efferently

Being aware that a researcher and the research materials have the potential to "prime" a participant,[41] I reviewed the fieldwork concentrating on any ways in which the men may have been led to assume an efferent standpoint. I also attempted to identify other influences that would have encouraged the adoption of such a stance. Three main factors were identified: the research materials guided the participants to assume such a stance; the readers' personalities and gender resulted in their reading the texts in this way; and the men's belief that the Bible was some sort of textbook or guide, resulted in them adopting an efferent stance. Ultimately I will argue that this third factor principally resulted in the assumption of an efferent stance towards these texts, although the first two contributed to it as well.

36. Lewis, "Limits of identification."
37. McLaughlin and DeVoogd, "Critical Literacy as Comprehension."
38. Soter, et al., "Deconstructing 'Aesthetic Response' in Small-Group Discussions about Literature."
39. Parker, *Painfully Clear,* 28–48; Snodgrass, *Stories with Intent,* 8; Stein, "The Genre of the Parables," 48.
40. Potential therefore exists to explore and remodel Rosenblatt's efferent/aesthetic spectrum, especially in light of genres or contexts that do not conform easily to it.
41. Baron and Byrne, *Social Psychology,* 88.

The Influence of the Research Materials

Reflexivity involves "recognizing the extent to which your thoughts, actions and decisions shape how you research and what you see."[42] One aspect of this is the way in which the research tools influence the data that emerges. Therefore, I reviewed my materials for evidence that they encouraged the men to assume an efferent reading stance and identified four things. First, the research material that contained the biblical texts was described as a "Manual." "Manual 1" contained Proverbs 10:1–11, "Manual 2" contained 2 Samuel 5:17–25, and so on. Second, four out of the five texts in some way lent themselves to an efferent reading stance (Prov 10:1–11, 2 Sam 5:17–25, Matt 18:21–35 and 2 John), and the first text any participant encountered was Proverbs 10:1–11. Third, in the questionnaire which accompanied each text, three of the questions could only be answered if an efferent stance was adopted, for example "What, if anything did you agree with in the passage?" Finally, in asking people to engage with these texts as part of a research project, they may have assumed an analytical posture.

However, even though the annotation and questionnaire was called a "Manual," verbally I referred to that component of the research as "the annotating part" and "the questionnaire part," and of the five texts, three lent themselves to an aesthetic reading stance (2 Sam 5:17–25, Matt 18:21–35, and Ps 88). In the questionnaire, of the fourteen questions asked eleven could be answered from an efferent or aesthetic standpoint, and during the interview the main question which I asked about the texts ("What did you make of that text?") was open to an efferent or aesthetic reading. Finally, although the participants were invited to take part in a research project, I tried to present the reading task in as open language as possible. Typically, before the participants were about to read a new text I would say:

> Please remember, there are no right or wrong answers, I'm just interested in your take on all of this. Your opinions, thoughts, insights, feelings, ideas, memories, whatever, is what I'm interested in. And, an unannotated text is just as valuable as one full of comments. It's your response, whatever that is, that I'm interested in.

In this way I attempted to provide a setting where the men could engage with these texts in whatever way they wanted, something the front sheet of each "Manual" emphasized.

Therefore, the research methods did encourage an efferent reading of these texts but they did not inevitably cause the adoption of an efferent

---

42. Mason, *Qualitative Researching*, 5.

standpoint. Overall the research materials slightly favored an efferent stance, but were open to both reading stances. More significant factors were the participants' personality and gender, and their beliefs about the Bible, as I will demonstrate.

The Influence of the Reader's Personality and Gender

Under the umbrella of contextual Bible reading, Leslie Francis and others have used Jungian personality theory to explore the influence of a reader's personality on their reading of the Bible.[43] This approach is one which:

> maintains that the reading and interpretation of text is shaped by individual preferences within the perceiving process (sensing and intuition) and within the evaluating process (thinking and feeling).[44]

Accordingly, a "thinker" is more likely to focus on "seeing what the text means in terms of evidence, moral principles or theology. They will be drawn to using rationality and logic to identify the ideas and truth-claims in a text."[45] A "feeler" is more likely to focus on "applying the human dimensions to present day issues of compassion, harmony and trust. They will be drawn to empathizing with the characters in a narrative, and will want to understand their thoughts, motives and emotions."[46] When it comes to this evaluating process of personality a gender difference is noted, for it has been found that women are more likely to be "feelers" and men are more likely to be "thinkers."[47]

Other scholars have found similar reading differences between men and women,[48] and boys and girls,[49] although they have not rooted this dif-

---

43. Francis, "Ordinary Readers and Reader Perspectives on Sacred texts"; Village and Francis, "The Relationship of Psychological Type Preferences to Biblical Interpretation." This theory has also been applied to preachers and the preaching process, see: Francis and Village, *Preaching with all our Souls*.

44. Francis, "What Happened to the Fig Tree?" 873.

45. Francis, "Ordinary Readers and Reader Perspectives on Sacred Texts," 89.

46. Ibid, 88–89.

47. Kendall, *Myers-Briggs Type Indicator*; Myers and Myers, *Gifts Differing*; Robbins and Francis, "All are Called, but some Psychological Types are More Likely to Respond"; Sorensen and Robinson, "Gender and Psychological Type."

48. Bleich, "Gender Interests in Reading and Language"; Flynn, "Gender and Reading"; Hutchings, "E-Reading and the Christian Bible."

49. Logan and Johnston, "Investigating Gender Differences in Reading"; Rosen, "Gender Difference in Reading Performance on Documents Across Countries."

ference in personality theory. Özen Odağ reviews some of the quantitative and qualitative research in the area of reading and gender, concluding that men "claim to read much less emotionally, more rationally, and primarily for the purposes of broadening knowledge."[50] Women on the other hand are considered to be "more emotional readers, as readers who become deeply engrossed by characters' fates, and readers who retrieve a sense of pleasure and relaxation from reading."[51]

Odağ is keen to point out that there are inconsistencies and weaknesses in this research field, for example many of the surveys ignore contextual factors that may exacerbate any gender difference.[52] In turn, her work investigates how the type of text read (either experience type texts or action type texts) impacts the emotional engagement of men and women readers. Although some differences are noted she concludes "the emotional responses of males and females during reading are highly dependent on (con)textual cues."[53]

My purpose is not to explore any gender difference in reading and related socio-cultural factors which may contribute to this,[54] for my study was not a comparison between men and women. Instead, I wish to point out the similarities between Rosenblatt's "efferent," Francis's "thinker," and Odağ's "male reader," for all three terms describe a person who reads with a concern for information which is logically analyzed and judged. Correspondingly, the labels "aesthetic," "feeler" and "female reader" all describe a reader who is emotionally engaged with the text, concerned for the characters and the developing plot.[55]

This raises the possibility that the men in my study read the biblical texts from an efferent standpoint because of the influence of their personality and gender. This suggestion is further strengthened when taking into account these men's normal reading practices. When my participants discussed their own reading habits, it was typically with reference to nonfiction such as newspapers, historical accounts, or sports reports. For example,

50. Odağ, "Emotional Engagement during Literary Reception," 858.
51. Ibid., 858.
52. Ibid., 859.
53. Ibid., 856.

54. See Rhoda Unger's "Using the Master's Tools" for a broader discussion on this subject, or Mary Crawford and Roger Chaffin's "The Reader's Construction of Meaning" who link the difference between men and women readers to schema theory, suggesting that a reader's gender, as part of their schema, shaped the reading.

55. Importantly the work of Francis, Odağ, and Rosenblatt was all undertaken in a twentieth- and twenty-first-century Western context, the same context my participants find themselves in.

Andy G, said "I don't tend to read many storybooks; I'm more a reference book person. I like finding out how things work or what things are about, rather than stories." This preference for nonfiction fits the suggestion that men are more likely to read efferently and corresponds with other research indicating that men are more inclined to read nonfiction than women.[56] Furthermore, the typical reading material found in these men's offices and staff rooms were handbooks, manuals, protocols, and so on, which would also have reinforced the naturalness of an efferent stance. This mirrors Alison Peden's thought that the experience of close reading legal documents resulted in the women prisoners also undertaking a thorough close reading of the Bible passages during their CBS sessions.[57]

Therefore, my participants' adoption of an efferent stance could be due to their personality and gender, corresponding with their choice of nonfictional literature and reading context. However, there is a final and more compelling reason why the participants adopted an efferent stance, for the data shows that before being given the first text most of the men had decided what reading standpoint was required.

The Influence of the Reader's Beliefs

One of the preparatory tasks the participants had to complete was an Entrance Questionnaire containing the question: "In your own words, what is the Bible?" In their replies to this question, sixteen participants indicated that the Bible was a guide or textbook, in other words a text that should be read efferently. For instance:

- John wrote: "The Bible is a guide to Christians about how they should go about their lives."

- Sam referred to it as: "A book for Christians containing god's teachings and lessons."

- Derek, a non-practicing Catholic, wrote: "What you yourself base your life and your children's upbringing, in the scope of religion."

- And Phil, a forty-eight-year old electrician, who identified as "slightly religious," because he did not disbelieve in God, described it as "a book containing an organization's beliefs."

---

56. Hartley, *Reading Groups*, 25–71; Summers, "Adult Reading Habits and Preferences in Relation to Gender Differences."

57. Peden, "Contextual Bible Study at Cornton Vale Women's prison, Stirling."

Some men did refer to the Bible as a storybook, but one with a didactic purpose, for instance:

- Dave described it as "A collection of accounts and stories of times past, rearranged to suit religious groups."
- Peter, a fifty-six-year-old electrician who identified as "not at all religious" wrote: "A book of stories and interpretations of how we should behave."
- So too Tony, a fifty-five-year-old engineer and Catholic, referred to it as: "A collection of stories that have an ethical and moral message about how we should conduct ourselves in relation to our interactions with our fellow human beings."

There were four men (Gary, Zadok, Richie, and Mick) who responded by singularly suggesting that the Bible is a story, implying that it should be read from an aesthetic stance. For instance, Zadok, a fifty-nine-year-old utility technician who identified as "not at all religious," simply wrote: "A collection of stories." Mick, a thirty-year-old scaffolder who identified as "not at all religious" described it as "A storybook." However, no difference was noted between these four men's readings and the readings of the other sixteen men who described the Bible in efferent terms. One possible reason for this could be that by referring to the Bible as a story they understood it to be a story with a teaching or message. The data therefore is not overwhelming, however it does indicate that the majority of the men believed that the Bible was some sort of didactic text. This was their view prior to reading any of the five texts, and with that belief in place an efferent standpoint would be expected as they came to read the texts.

These findings tie in with other contemporary research. The 2012 Theos report *Post-Religious Britain? The Faith of the Faithless* found that the largest cohort of those sampled indicated that the Bible was "a useful book of guidance and advice for our lives but not the Word of God."[58] Alan Le Grys reached a similar conclusion:

> The empirical data gathered for this study from interviews and churches across the Medway region suggests that the Bible is overwhelmingly regarded as a moral and doctrinal handbook.[59]

This echoed earlier findings by Nick Spencer and Yvonne Richmond who analyzed sixty interviews of non-churchgoers discussing various subjects including the Bible. They found that the Bible was often viewed as an

---

58. Theos, *Post-Religious Britain?* 21.
59. Le Grys, *Shaped by God's Story,* 132.

advice or rulebook, albeit an unreliable one.[60] Matthew Engelke undertook ethnographic research with Bible Society and noted their desire for the Bible to be de-manualized. He describes Bible Society staff reflecting on the findings from some focus groups:

> One of these had been with young, unchurched parents, some of whom suggested that perhaps the Bible's moral guidelines could be used to help raise well-behaved children. Despite the good intentions, this kind of sentiment always worried members of the team. It stripped the Bible of its full meaning. It was a disembodiment and objectification of the very incarnation that defines the Christian message. "How do we get away from using the Bible as a manual?" Ann asked.[61]

All these examples demonstrate that my participants' belief that the Bible is a textbook resonates with the conclusions others have drawn.[62] For example, reflecting on his North American context Timothy Beal writes: "This idea of the Bible as a divine manual for finding happiness with God in this world and salvation in the next is so familiar to us today that we might assume it's been around forever."[63] Rosenblatt herself suggests that religious texts, such as the Bible, are "read mainly efferently."[64]

I would argue that this was the most significant reason why the men read the texts efferently. While other studies have shown gender to inform certain beliefs about the Bible, for example women are more likely to believe the Bible is true compared with men,[65] both Spencer,[66] and Le Grys,[67] quote male and female participants to evidence their findings. This implies that the gender of these participants did not play a role in forming this view

---

60. Spencer recounts how there were three common views of the Bible. First, that it is an advice or rulebook, second, that it is a biography or history book, and third, that it is a storybook, akin to a fairy tale. These views were often accompanied by the beliefs that the Bible was untrue and unreliable. See: Spencer, *Beyond the Fringe*, 143–45.

61. Engelke, *God's Agents*, 23.

62. This view of the Bible corresponds well to research amongst the British public which noted that Jesus is popularly viewed as a "moral/spiritual teacher" or "good man." For example, see: Barna, *Transforming Scotland*; Bissett, *Outside In*; Spencer, *Beyond the Fringe*.

63. Beal, *The Rise and Fall of the Bible*, 6. See also Smith, *The Bible Made Impossible*, 3–6.

64. Rosenblatt, *The Reader, the Text, the Poem,* 36. She adds that they could be experienced as works of art "under different conditions or by people with different urgencies," Ibid., 36.

65. Field, "Is the Bible Becoming a Closed Book?"

66. Spencer, *Beyond the Fringe*.

67. Le Grys, *Shaped by God's Story*.

of the Bible. So too, Engelke's comment suggests that there was no gender distinction. Of course, it could be that these researchers did not analyze their data with an eye to gender difference. However, with qualitative research (as Le Grys and Spencer undertook) the data produced guides the analysis, so if the data showed a gender distinction then the researcher has the opportunity to note it. The use of both male and female participants to evidence their arguments suggests that a gender distinction was not noted and so may not have existed.

Therefore, in the reading transactions that took place at the Chemical Plant, most of the men assumed an efferent stance as they prepared to read the five biblical texts, they did this principally because they believed that the Bible is a didactic text. Other factors such as personality, gender, or the research methods themselves would have corroborated this belief in as much as they worked with such a belief, and its related efferent readings stance, rather than against them.

Conclusion

This chapter has continued to argue that the reader's relationship with the five biblical texts shaped their reading of those texts. In particular, I considered the role of the reader's beliefs in informing the subsequent reading. Highlighting various readings, I showed that these texts were typically read for information, as one would a textbook. This may not be an issue for a passage like Proverbs 10:1–11, but is arguably less appropriate for a poem like Psalm 88. Nonetheless, even with this text most of the men tried to read it looking for facts or a teaching that they could extract and critique. I then proposed that the efferent/aesthetic spectrum, which is part of the transactional theory, explains this reading phenomenon. It posits that a reader decides upon a reading stance prior to engaging with a text and the stance then shapes the reading transaction that follows. Finally, I explored three possible reasons for the adoption of an efferent stance by these men, suggesting that the research materials influenced them in this direction and their personality and gender probably reaffirmed the appropriateness of an efferent stance. However, I argued that principally it was the reader's belief that the Bible, and so the five biblical texts, was some sort of guide or textbook which resulted in them assuming an efferent stance towards the texts and reading them for information. There was another belief however which also significantly shaped how these texts were read, and that concerned the potential agency of these texts.

Chapter 9

Reader-shaped Readings—Belief 2

THIS CHAPTER EXPLORES A second belief which would dominate these readings. That is, that the Bible had a transformative potential and any reader who engaged with it would expose themselves to this influence. By using the terms "transformative" and "transformative potential" I am describing a shift towards the Christian faith because this was the type of transformation many of my participants anticipated. Indeed, part of the reason many of my participants read the texts skeptically was because they believed the biblical texts might try to convert them. This sense of threat was further emphasized by the assumption that I, a "religious guy," was facilitating the process. Thus, I argue that these men counter-read the texts, that is, they responded to an assumed threat posed by the text's assumed transformative potential, which resulted in their skeptical reading of the texts. This act of reading reveals a belief in the biblical text's transformative potential which challenges those who argue that the Bible has lost its status in the West,[1] but also troubles its supposed transformative capacity as these men were able to disarm that perceived threat.

The Bible's Transformative Potential

In chapter 1, I made mention of liberation theology and in particular its connection to contextual Bible reading practices. Within this and other streams of Christian theology, Bible reading is viewed as a liberating and transformative act. For example, *Conversations*, a CBS guide produced by the Scottish Bible Society and The Contextual Bible Study Group, lists various principles that undergird CBS. The first is "belief in the liberating and transforming power of God's Word in the Scriptures and in people's

---

1. Aichele, *The Control of Biblical Meaning*; Vincent, "The Death and Resurrection of the Bible in Church and Society."

lives,"[2] and accordingly Louise Lawrence refers to CBS as a "transformative ritual."[3] Advocates of contextual Bible reading are well aware of its role in the oppression of people but understand that this need not be the case. Carlos Mesters reflecting on Bible reading amongst the poor in Brazil describes the use of the Bible as "the source of their freedom in the face of the abuses of power."[4]

The idea that the Bible is transformative is not only found in liberation theology, but throughout different expressions of the Christian church, for Christians view the Bible as, in some way, the Word of God. It is understood to be a privileged location where God can be encountered.[5] This in turn means that many Christians view the Bible as a transformative text, one they seek to reflect on and critically submit to.[6] Accompanying this belief in the Bible are stories recounting its agency-like qualities, for example, "falling open to a particular chapter and verse-to exactly what a given reader needs to hear."[7] This can be seen in the 2011 Bible-reading initiative *Biblefresh* that encouraged British Christians to consider the question, "How has the Bible changed your world?"[8]

Much of what has been noted above concerns the church's view of the Bible as a transformative text in the life of the Christian. However, a similar expectation can exist of those outside of the church. There is a popular opinion within Christianity that if a nonreligious person were to read the Bible they may find themselves positively changed by the experience. For example, Bible Society write: "All our efforts are driven by one conviction: **we believe that when people engage with the Bible, lives can change—for good**"[9] (emphasis in original). Robert Detweiler, perhaps reflecting on his experience in the USA noted:

> One can observe in evangelical Christianity sacred texts functioning simultaneously as directly and indirectly life-transforming. The New Testament, especially the gospels, is held to contain the

---

2. Scottish Bible Society and the Contextual Bible Study Group, *Conversations*, 11.

3. Lawrence, *The Word in Place*, 122–23.

4. Mesters, *Defenseless Flower*, viii.

5. Schneiders, *The Revelatory Text*; Schneiders, *Written That You May Believe*; Volf, *Captive to the Word of God*, 34.

6. Hoggarth, *The Seed and the Soil*; Rowland and Vincent, *Bible and Practice*; Smallbones, "Teaching the Bible for Transformation"; Wink, *The Bible in Human Transformation*.

7. Engelke, *God's Agents*, xv.

8. "The Bible Changed my Life."

9. Bible Society, "About Us," lines 8–9.

formula for redemption (consisting of, minimally, an expression of contrition for one's sins and of belief in a "personal" savior), but it also is sometimes treated as if it possesses near-magical properties: if only persons could be persuaded to read it, the very encounter with the words would change their lives.[10]

The organizers of a recent English biblical literacy project express a similar sentiment when they state that the "Bible can awaken faith and bring life."[11] This belief results in British churches and para-church organizations undertaking "Gospel drops," where they distribute copies of a Gospel (or the entire New Testament) to members of their wider community, in the hope that these people will read it and be changed. Entire organizations, such as the Gideons International, Bible Society, Biblica, Wycliffe Bible Translators and others exist to provide those who have not read the Bible with the opportunity to do so, in that hope that they will encounter God through reading it. Engelke sums up this sentiment when noting Bible Society's commitment to providing Bibles without note or comment. He writes:

> Certainly the early Victorian missionary age was characterized by a faith in the Bible's ability to speak for itself, to stand free from history and transmit universal meanings. This understanding of the Bible's agency is still central to the Bible Society movement's ideology of dissemination.[12]

This belief in the transformative potential of the Bible is reaffirmed by various testimonies of its impact upon people's lives. Organizations concerned with Bible translation (for instance Wycliffe Bible Translators) and distribution (such as Gideons International) regularly publish stories highlighting the significance of Bible reading in the lives of individuals and communities. For instance, one of the reports on the United Bible Society's website is entitled "*'God's Word changed my life,' says former street kid*," and concerns Groum Pale whose life story "is testament to the restorative and healing power of God's Word and the love shown towards him by Christians."[13]

In light of the demise of Christianity in the West, however, the Bible's lack of transformative power has also been noted. Fergus Macdonald for instance, reflecting on the difference between the southern and northern hemispheres, writes:

10. Detweiler, "What is a Sacred Text?" 221.
11. Wood, *Let the Bible Live*, 9.
12. Engelke, *God's Agents*, 4–5.
13. Smith, "'God's Word Changed My Life,' says Former Street Kid," lines 13–16.

> The Word of God, which for the writer to the Hebrews and today's Christians in the younger churches of the South is "alive and active," appears to be comatose and silent in the churches of the Western world.[14]

With reference to the Bible's place in western society and the significance of the concept of "canon" for biblical meaning, George Aichele writes:

> The biblical canon plays a significant diminished role in the contemporary world. It is arguable that the Bible no longer has any genuine canonical hold over anyone today, no matter how loudly some people might protest.[15]

This sentiment is also reflected by those who note the decline in the role of the Bible in British life.[16] None of the participants in my research regularly read the Bible, and most said they did not believe it was true or divinely inspired. However, as I will go on to highlight, they read the texts as if they had a transformative potential, but one they were able to neutralize.

Reading Skeptically

Of the twenty men, fourteen read most of the texts skeptically, and a variety of different approaches were undertaken in these readings. Some men focused on parts of the text which they viewed as inappropriately absolutist, for example:

- Mick described Proverbs 10:1–11 as: "Rules of how you should behave or this, or that, would happen to you. And for me that's, that's not for everyone, if you know what I mean. It's not, em. It shouldn't be taken as black and white things, you know what I mean? There's a lot of different, em, permutations about how things can pan out."

- Matty, a thirty-nine-year-old scaffolder who identified as "not at all religious," rejected 2 Samuel 5:17–25 on ethical grounds and because of the God presented in it: "If he's supposed to be a peaceful forgiving person, then striking people down in raging enemies in floods. It just, it just speaks anger, the words speak anger to me. And that sort of,

---

14. Macdonald, "Engaging the Scriptures," 193.
15. Aichele, *The Control of Biblical Meaning*, 221.
16. Field, "Is the Bible Becoming a Closed Book?"; Pietersen, *Reading the Bible After Christendom*; Vincent, "The Death and Resurrection of the Bible in Church and Society."

for what's supposed to be a loving helpful book, it just annoys, like. It looks like a war passage to me, for a tactical war."

- For Zadok the directive to forgive in Matthew 18:21–35 was unworkable. He said: "How often should you forgive someone? If they keep causing you grief, you just try and avoid them or whatever you do. You can't just sit there and keep forgiving them, can you?"

- Peter described Psalm 88 as a "bullying" text and went on to say: "You know, and that to me, I thought that was more, somebody who was to read that who was ill, terminally ill or something, I'd think that would be more frightening than anything else, and I didn't like it, I didn't like it at all."

- And Phil, a forty-eight-year-old "slightly religious" electrician noted that 2 John contradicted previous texts: "You know some passages will say 'help and protect your fellow man,' and then the next thing says 'well if he doesn't really agree with what you mean, or what we say leave him alone.'"

As the previous chapters have highlighted, many of these skeptical readings were not simply manifestations of the Bible having been rejected as something offensive or irrelevant, there was often a personal backstory to it. This was not always the case however, some of the men were unsure as to why they had read as they did. Zadok, for instance, said: "Whilst I'm reading, I don't know why I do it, I'm looking for faults in it. Now that's, now that's myself, why do I look for faults in it? I don't know."

Therefore, I also approached this subject indirectly asking why they thought I had difficulty getting men to participate in the project, citing the trouble I had establishing the pilot study. Such an approach is common amongst researchers examining a subject where the participants' may feel a degree of uncertainty or social pressure to conform to a certain view.[17] Mick's response was typical of most of the men: "Maybe, maybe they are just scared of religion or something. Or scared that it's going to be pushed, thrust in their face and, like, sort of be a little bit overbearing with it." The main reason given for people refusing to participate was "fear" that there would be an attempt to convert them. Another common answer given was that religion carried a "stigma" as did a religious icon like the Bible and by taking part they too would be stigmatized, phenomena that others have also noted.[18]

17. Oppenheim, *Questionnaire Design, Interviewing and Attitude Measurement*, 210.

18. Hay and Hunt, "Understanding the Spirituality of People Who Don't Go to Church," 24; Spencer, *Beyond Belief?*

However, the men indicated that although others may have felt that way and so refused to take part, they did not have any of those concerns. This though may reflect the participants' mind-sets at the end of the project rather than the start. On one occasion, a group of men closed the door to their office before they began to engage with the first text, I assume so that colleagues would be discouraged from walking in and seeing what was going on. By the time it came to reading the third text they no longer closed the door and it remained open for the rest of the project.[19] These actions may reflect the stigma attached to reading the Bible.

When analyzing the content of the interviews and the closing comments in the questionnaires I found that eleven of the fourteen the men who read skeptically indicated they believed that the text, or the wider project, would try to influence or convert them. For example, Matty is a thirty-six-year-old scaffolder who identified as "not at all religious." During our interview he asked if I had purposely chosen controversial texts and was surprised to hear that I had selected texts I considered not to be overly provocative. I went on to add that I had also chosen texts that were not concerned with proselytizing. He responded: "I was kind of surprised actually, because I expected more of that to be honest." Matty's comment shows that he assumed he would be evangelized and that the texts, and/or my project, would attempt to convert him. Ethan, a forty-year-old engineer, when asked if he had any extra comments he would like to make regarding 2 John, wrote: "At times the passage almost felt like it tried too hard to want people to believe." Gary described 2 John as being "written to get people to have a faith and believe in this faith, and there you go that is the punishment if you don't." Sam, suggested that the Bible's purpose was "getting people to behave" a certain way, "controlling people I suppose and guiding people." John believed that the Bible tried to convince people of God's existence. He said "I've not read the Bible cover to cover, but the general gist is it's always trying to force it down your throat: Jesus does exist; God does exist." Zadok was asked if the five biblical texts had reaffirmed any kind of pre-existing expectations? He said: "No I've not moved [. . .] I haven't moved one way or the other." His reply demonstrates that one of his expectations was that reading the texts would result in an attempt to "move" him in a certain direction. In other words, the texts' agenda was to lead him towards, I would suggest, a more accepting view of Christianity.

These comments resonate with both the central assertion that fear of conversion was the main reason people refused to take part and with the

---

19. For further discussion on the role of stigma and identity, see Major and O'Brien, "The Social Psychology of Stigma."

finding that most of the men viewed the Bible as a textbook or guide. This leads me to conclude that the skeptical nature of many of these readings is not only an expression of rejection of the Bible, but reflects an assumption that my research, and in particular the biblical texts, might try to influence them in some way or other. Even though most of the men indicated that they did not believe the Bible was true or divine, their responses show that they believed reading these texts, in this context, had the potential to be transformative.

The role of the researcher must also be considered in these skeptical readings. In chapter 3 I reflected in detail on my own position within this research and what follows is an account of the main occasion that my presence influenced the skeptical nature of these readings. Some of the participants assumed I was "religious." On one occasion, when I was introducing myself to a new group of men, one of them said "are you that religious guy that's doing research?" This implies there was probably a popular view in the Chemical Plant that a "religious guy" was undertaking research. Although it was my practice not to disclose my own religious views prior to or during the research, the assumption existed that I was "religious." However, there was a degree of uncertainty regarding my religious identity and motivation. I presented myself as a researcher involved in a secular, if unusual, piece of research. This was a University-based piece of work and part of a degree-awarding process. One participant even suggested that I might be an "atheist" and the question I was most often asked at the end of the interview concerned my own religious identity. So the assumption that I was "religious" was probably there, but it was a loose one. Of course, the participants were correct in labeling me "religious," so although I attempted to relate to them as a researcher my manner may have communicated something of this religious identity in a way I was unaware.

The label "religious," as the men pointed out, is one that carries a stigma and possibly the expectation that I was seeking to convert people to "religion." This in turn may well have contributed to the men reading the texts skeptically. Tony expressed this particularly clearly. When discussing why some men refused to take part in the project, he said:

> I think it is, there is an element of, I always dislike having, em, eh, the Jehovah's Witnesses coming to my door. So I think there's an element of fear. And, is this person going to try to turn me into something, or influence me?

Not only were the texts deemed to be a possible threat, but so was I and these two beliefs reinforced each other. Carl Tighe noted something similar when using the Bible in a creative writing class. His students were extremely nervous assuming that he was "trying to teach religion or to 'convert' them to something."[20] David Wood reported something similar when he was facilitating a biblical literacy project in Northern England, part of which attempted to engage those who did not attend church regularly with the Bible. He "often sensed a distrust, a feeling that there was a hidden agenda, that the project was really a form of covert evangelism, whose real aim was to bring people back to church!"[21] To this end, the most notable reaction I received at the Chemical Plant involved a worker who identified as a "militant atheist" and had heard that I was looking for volunteers for a Bible-reading project. As I walked into the staff room he and two other colleagues shared, he walked out indicating that he wanted nothing to do with the project.

In Tighe's case and in mine, this "fear" or nervousness passed. My growing friendship with the participants and lack of attempt to proselytize dispelled the perception that I and this project were attempting to coerce these men to convert. Tony went on to say:

> But when people meet you then, on a one-to-one basis, they realize there's nothing particularly sinister to this at all. And actually you are not asking for people to, you know, come to church.

This was also the case for the worker who described himself as a "militant atheist," although he never took part in the project we ended up establishing a good rapport and he would later facilitate my entry into another group of men.

It is worth noting that the degree of skepticism with which the texts were engaged did not decrease as my friendship with the participants increased. The last text was handled more skeptically than the first, even though by then my relationship with the participants was such that they were happy to vouch for me and the project as they introduced me to another possible group. If fear that I was undertaking covert evangelism was the principle reason for their skeptical readings then I would have expected the level of skepticism to decrease as the men got to know me. The fact that it did not suggests that the participants' belief in the transformative power of the texts was of greater significance than my religious presence.

Counter-reading

When considering the skeptical readings which took place in light of the participants' belief that the Bible may have an agenda to influence and/or convert them, a belief reinforced by my presence. I would argue that these

---

20. Hine et al., "Practicing Biblical Literacy," 191.
21. Wood, *Let the Bible Live*, 43.

men read the texts in such a way as to disempower the perceived transformative potential of the texts, something I describe as "counter-reading." This is a reading style emanating from a reader's personal response to an assumed threat that is posed by a text's assumed transformative potential. This response can be seen in a skeptical reading of a text and often in its accompanying rejection. By highlighting the errors, inconsistencies, contradictions, poor ethics, irrelevances, or unworkability a reader has demonstrated that the text and its claims are invalid. This results in the neutralizing of the threat possessed by the text's transformative potential.[22]

Counter-reading is similar to a "resisting reading,"[23] or "reading against the grain."[24] These also assume that the text has a particular ideology, worldview or agenda, which the reader is seeking to highlight, challenge and perhaps provide an alternative to. Such readings often identify with the phrase "hermeneutics of suspicion," to express a distrust of the biblical text.[25] Significantly though, the terms "resisting readers" and "reading against the grain" are not used to refer to the reader's personal defensive response but to a wider impersonal ideological engagement with the text. For example, Judith Fetterley's *The Resisting Reader: A Feminist Approach to American Fiction* considers eight texts through a feminist lens. In her introduction she explains the need for resisting readers and describes the foundation of her book in this way:

> It is based on the premise that we read and that what we read affects us-drenches us, to use Rich's language, in its assumptions, and that to avoid drowning in this drench of assumptions we must learn to re-read. Thus, I see my book as a self-defense survival manual for the woman reader lost in "the masculine wilderness of the American novel."[26]

Although this preface acknowledges the individual reader in the reading event, Fetterley goes on to undertake a broad impersonal feminist critique

---

22. This sense of threat and subsequent defensive response on the part of the reader are different to the defensive stage in Normand Holland's psychoanalytical literary theory DEFT (defense, expectation, fantasy and transformation). In Holland's case, the defensive response is connected to the reader's identity theme, something that developed in them from their earliest infancy, See: Holland, "Unit Identity Text Self."

23. Braun, "Resisting John"; Fetterley, *The Resisting Reader*; Harding, "In the Name of Love."

24. Clines, *Interested Parties*; Domeris, "Reading the Bible Against the Grain"; West, "Taming Texts of Terror."

25. Aichele et al., *The Postmodern Bible*, 272–308; Fiorenza, *Bread Not Stone*; Volf, *Captive to the Word of God*.

26. Fetterley, *The Resisting Reader*, viii.

of four short stories and four novels, rather than articulating the personal threat she hints at in the preface. In Fetterley's case, a resisting reader refers to an impersonal ideological reading of a text.

Likewise, David Clines in a chapter entitled "God in the Pentateuch: Reading against the Grain," notes that:

> Reading against the grain implies that there *is* a grain. It implies that texts have designs on their readers and wish to persuade them of something or other. It implies that there are ideologies inscribed in texts, and that the readers implied by texts share the texts' ideologies. But, as I have suggested earlier, readers are free to resist the ideologies of the texts.[27] (Emphasis in original)

In his case, reading against the grain is synonymous with ideological criticism.[28] He ignores the reader's personal sense of threat or distaste while reading and the resulting defensive response which that may elicit. Clines mirrors Fetterley by equating, in his case, reading against the grain with an impersonal ideological critical reading.[29]

Willi Braun comes close to incorporating a reader's personal sense of threat attached to a text or reading transaction, when he refers to a "defensive reader."[30] However, in his case he is referring to a reader's awareness of the negative impact which a text has had in other times and places, and to that end he refers to the "menace of the gospel text itself."[31] With reference to John's Gospel, he notes:

> The less than glorious historical effect of the Fourth Gospel's closed ideology, an effect that has turned victims of John's irony into real victims of Christian anti-Semitism and has fostered

---

27. Clines, *Interested Parties*, 206–7.

28. Clines disagrees that texts intrinsically have grains or ideologies, rather he argues the grain/ideology is the agreed meaning or practice of an interpretive community. Nonetheless, because people make reference to texts as having grains/ideologies he continues to use that language. See: *Interested Parties*, 207.

29. Some scholars such as: Alaghbary, "A Feminist Counter-Reading of 'Indian Women'"; Britt, "Male Jealousy and the Suspected Sotah"; and Wurst, "Dancing the Minefield," have used the term "counter-reading" synonymously with ideological criticism, reading against the grain or being a resisting reader. For example, Mieke Bal's edited collection *Anti-Covenant: Counter-Reading Women's Lives in the Hebrew Bible* could be described as a series of readings utilizing feminist criticism. What is missing is any significant focus on the nature of the personal response from each of the authors. This collection is an example of an impersonal ideological critique of various texts from the Hebrew Bible and is not an example of counter-reading as I am using the term.

30. Braun, "Resisting John."

31. Ibid., 63.

a hatred for "the world" as the inevitable shadow side of the gospel's justly celebrated promotion of love for members of the in-group.[32]

Although Braun is highlighting a reader's personal sense of displeasure, this is attached to the historical legacy of the text, rather than the sense of threat which that text poses to the immediate reader. He is not alone in this critique, for it is one that feminist and post-colonial critics have also made. For instance, part of the interpretive method adopted by Elisabeth Schüssler Fiorenza and other contributors to *Searching the Scriptures* is one that identifies the crime of "patriarchal murder and oppression" by "carefully tracing its clues and imprints in the texts in order to prevent further hurt and violations."[33]

Finally, my readers were not undertaking a form of deconstructive criticism either. Although they often sought to demonstrate that the five texts lacked validity and credibility, their skeptical readings were often multifaceted and resulted in a holistic rejection of a text. Deconstruction criticism on the other hand involves the narrower task of demonstrating the way in which a text undermines itself. For example, David Clines notes that the book of Job argues against the dual claims that righteousness is always equated with a good life and unrighteousness with suffering. However, in the final chapter, Job who has acted righteously throughout his sufferings is rescued from them and re-installed with greater wealth than he had at the start of the book. This final act of restoration is therefore at odds with the central arguments built up through the book.[34] A deconstructive reading such as this not only lacks the personal threat my participants felt, but also does not reflect the breadth of skeptical engagement undertaken by my participants.

By using the term "counter-reading" I am capturing a reading style emanating from a reader's personal response to an assumed threat, which is posed by a text's assumed transformative potential. The act of counter-reading demonstrates that these readers viewed the reading event as potentially transformative, something they opposed. This belief that the Bible has a transformative potential and that reading the biblical texts could change a person, appears to contradict most of my participants' view that the Bible is neither divinely inspired nor true. Rosenblatt writes, "our attitudes may be clarified either by a violent reaction against what we have read or by

---

32. Ibid., 63.
33. Fiorenza, *Searching the Scriptures*, 11.
34. Clines, *What Does Eve do to Help?* 106–23.

assimilation of it."[35] In my case, the participants' beliefs about the Bible were brought to the surface as they came to read the texts.

There are three reasons why these men had an underlying belief in the Bible's transformative potential and so too the five biblical texts. First, the participants' assumption that I was a "religious guy" and that I too was involved in this attempt to convert them to religion would have reinforced the belief that these readings had the potential to change them. Second, as Robert Detweiler points out, even a nonbeliever would treat a sacred text from their heritage with respect, and such texts are viewed as transformative with a response expected from the reader.[36] The Bible is still viewed as a sacred text by Christians, the largest religious group in Britain,[37] and historically it was a source of authority influencing much of Britain's past and present culture. The echoes of that legacy are seen in present-day British society, where biblical images or tropes are used widely within our culture,[38] for instance Katie Edwards traces the use and portrayal of Eve in contemporary advertising (2012).[39] My participants' counter-readings are another example of this legacy. Third, if something is read efferently the reader expects him- or herself to be informed and led by the text. These men assumed that the Bible, as a guidebook or manual, would inform and lead them, something they sought to resist by counter-reading.

There was a small group of four men who read the texts in a more accepting fashion, tending to focus on aspects of the texts with which they agreed. These men, along with Bob who identified as "slightly religious" and read both skeptically and acceptingly, had similar beliefs to the skeptical readers regarding the transformative potential of the texts. However, the belief that these texts were seeking to convert or direct them to live in a certain way was not perceived as a threat. They already viewed themselves as "religious," to some degree. So although they were not regular churchgoers and did not read the texts uncritically, ultimately they made the same assumptions as the other participants but identified with the texts rather than against them. One of exceptions to this was Victor, the scaffolder whom I considered in the previous chapter. He identified as "not at all religious" and yet his responses to the texts contained no sense of threat, expectation of coercion, or attempt to counter-read. I wonder if his decision to give "it a

---

35. Rosenblatt, *Literature as Exploration,* 41.

36. Detweiler, "What is a Sacred Text?"

37. In the 2011 Census of England and Wales 59% identified as Christian, 25% as having "no religion," 7% did not state their religion, 5% identified as Muslim and 4% identified with other religions (Office of National Statistics, 2012).

38. Crossley, *Harnessing Chaos*; Edwards, *Rethinking Biblical Literacy.*

39. Edwards, *Admen and Eve.*

chance" resulted in an openness to the Bible's status as a sacred text. Victor would sum up his readings of the five biblical texts with the phrase: "I don't know if it's true or not, or w[h]at to believe." This was not an expression of confusion or frustration, rather having attempted to read the texts fairly, he had not reached a conclusion regarding his view of the Bible.

Therefore, as most of these participants approached these texts, they focused on a particular belief about the Bible that would shape the subsequent reading transactions. They believed there was the possibility that reading the Bible would impact them and many of them felt unsafe because of this. This sense of threat was reinforced by the assumption that I had a similar agenda, and so the majority responded to this by counter-reading.

This troubles the opinion expressed by George Aichele,[40] and Ray Vincent,[41] that the Bible is no longer treated as a book with authority in western societies, a conclusion easily reached in light of the decline in belief in, and use of, the Bible. Although none of these men read the Bible regularly and most of them indicated that they did not believe it to be true or divinely inspired, when it came to reading it, they read it as if it were a sacred text, one capable of transforming them. This suggests that they, to some degree, believe in the agency-like qualities of the Bible to which Christianity adheres.

However, the act of counter-reading also troubles the assumption that Bible reading is always a transformative experience for in this case these readers were able to disarm the transformative potential which they sensed. With the exception of Dave's cathartic reading experience and Stuart's reading of Psalm 88 (which is explored in chapter 10) none of the men who identified as "not at all religious" indicated that their readings had been transformative. I compared their responses to the twenty-two statements about the Bible in the Entrance and Exit Questionnaires, and asked them directly in the Exit Questionnaire if they had been affected positively and/or negatively by reading the five passages? In the interviews I also considered this, but assuming a more indirect approach, asking if they had been surprised by the texts? There was very little difference between their Entrance and Exit responses to the twenty-two statements, and in the Exit Questionnaire and interview the men typically suggested that their views on religion or the Bible remained unchanged. Gary, when asked if these readings had affected him, said "I am set in my ways." In other words, he had not changed. Zadok reflected on his readings and wrote, "I don't think I've been swayed one way or the other." Bob too remained unchanged, "it's been good to have

---

40. Aichele, *The Control of Biblical Meaning*, 221.
41. Vincent, "The Death and Resurrection of the Bible in Church and Society."

read these texts," he wrote, "but they do not change my views as the words of man are often attributed to God." Other participants indicated they had moved further away from belief in God or the Bible. For example, Matty would describe the effects of reading the five texts as having "pushed me more away from the Bible." So too John found that reading the texts had "reaffirmed" his atheist identity and beliefs.

Christian scholars have reflected on their belief in the agency-like qualities of the Bible, and yet the ability for people to read it and find that in doing so they are not drawn towards the Christian faith.[42] Miroslav Volf focuses upon the reader's personal resistance towards the Bible, suggesting:

> We are modern men and women, individuals standing on our own two feet, masters and mistresses of our own choices and destinies—or so we think. For others to insert us into their story and envision the proper end of our lives, define for us the source and substance of human flourishing, and tell us what we should or should not desire, is for them to violate us as self-standing individuals. The Bible as a sacred text, however, does just that.[43]

Similarly, Nick Spencer concludes that people tend to resist the Bible by treating it as irrelevant, untrue, and full of contradictions, because "a deconstructed Bible, which allowed me to pick and choose and made fewer (or preferably no) demands on me, was an acceptable Bible."[44] This idea that an "acceptable Bible" is one that places minimal demands upon a reader is echoed in David Clines's *The Bible and the Modern World*. He recounts undertaking a keyword search of "Bible" in a prominent British newspaper (*The Guardian*) for the six months between April and September 1992. One of his observations is that the Bible was considered a foundation of moral values as long as they coincide "with contemporary values."[45] Correspondingly in my case study, the text that was read least skeptically was the parable of forgiveness (Matt 18:21–35); most of my participants agreed that the general concept of forgiveness was a good one.[46]

---

42. There are, of course, examples of Christians resisting the Bible or finding it lacking in transformative potential, (see: Hoggarth, *The Seed and the Soil*, 13–25; Thiselton, *New Horizons in Hermeneutics*, 36) and also of non-Christians reading the Bible and describing it as a positive experience, but not transformative (in the way my participants believed), such as occurs in Scriptural Reasoning groups (see: Ford, "An Interfaith Wisdom").

43. Volf, *Captive to the Word of God*, 32–33.

44. Spencer, *Beyond the Fringe*, 149–50.

45. Clines, *The Bible and the Modern World*, 77.

46. There was a difference in the degree of skeptical reading noted between the five passages. Placed in order of how skeptically they were read, they are: 2 Sam 5:17–25,

Spencer also suggests that in Britain:

> Actual knowledge of Christianity is very limited but it is mistaken for genuine knowledge, causing people to become automatically resistant to the Gospel on the premise that they "already know what it is all about." We think we have studied religious texts (when really we did some RE at school and have a Bible somewhere at home), and so when we reject Christian claims we think we do so on the basis of informed consideration.[47]

He describes this limited exposure to Christianity (and the Bible) that British people grow up with and the subsequent resistance they express at a later point in life as "inoculation." "They have had a low-grade version of the real thing in their minds for so long that they have become immune to the genuine article."[48]

Sandra Schneiders considers what transformative potential the Bible has for those outside of the church. She writes: "one cannot experience the Bible as scripture unless one can perceive in the text the very particular self-disclosure of God that is the content and form of Christian faith."[49] She goes on to suggest that "faith" is required when reading the Bible, implying that a person with no Christian faith would struggle to read it in a Christian transformative way. In the same way, Kevin Vanhoozer, building on Stanley Hauerwas,[50] and Francis Watson,[51] suggests that "the Bible is more likely to be misunderstood by an unbelieving and unaffiliated individual than by a believing and practicing member of the church."[52] Accordingly, the three participants who did suggest that the texts had impacted them in a transformative way (Anthony, Andy G, and Derek), all read the texts acceptingly and had some sense of religious identity. All three also indicated a desire to read the Bible more. For example, having read the five texts Derek indicated that he "should make time and read my Bible so I can understand more about the teachings of God."

---

2 John, Prov 10:1–11, Ps 88 and Matt 18:21–35. Even though Matt 18:21–35 was read least skeptically, this should not be understood as having been read acceptingly, it was typically read skeptically but in a more qualified way.

47. Spencer, *Beyond the Fringe*, 143.
48. Spencer, *Beyond Belief?* 4.
49. Schneiders, *The Revelatory Text*, 60–61.
50. Hauerwas, *Unleashing the Scripture*.
51. Watson, *Text, Church and World*.
52. Vanhoozer, *Is There a Meaning in This Text?* 378.

Conclusion

Ultimately though, this chapter has demonstrated another aspect of the relational nature of reading by further highlighting the influence of the reader's beliefs. I began by highlighting the way in which the participants acknowledged that "fear" was associated with Bible reading. Accompanying this was a sense that by reading these texts they might feel pressurized to change their lives or convert and the assumption that I was a "religious guy" added to this sense of threat. In light of this belief they responded by counter-reading the texts, reading them in such a way as to disarm their assumed threat. These actions show that although these men neither read the Bible regularly nor thought it to be true or divinely inspired, they were handling it as one would a sacred text. This phenomenon challenges those who suggest that the Bible is no longer viewed as a book of power in the West. Nonetheless, it also troubles the popular Christian assumption that reading the Bible is a transformative experience, for these men were able to defend themselves against it.

This then was my final example to evidence my central claim that these readers' relationships with the texts shaped their reading of them. These four examples presented throughout chapters 5, 6, 7, 8, and 9 make up the second strand of my argument, and chapter 10 now turns to consider the third and final strand. Up to this point most of these readings have been ones where the reader, in some way, has dominated the text. These were readings undertaken in a self-affirming way. The transactional theory posits that texts are not only able to stimulate readers but they are able to lead them.[53] Furthermore, it is in this toing and froing between the reader and the text that new understandings are produced.[54] To that end, my penultimate chapter reflects on how a reading may be shaped by, but not conform to, a reader's relationship with the text.

---

53. Rosenblatt, *The Reader, the Text, the Poem*, 11.
54. Rosenblatt, *Literature as Exploration*, 25.

Chapter 10

Text-shaped Readings

THE TRANSACTIONAL THEORY OF reading understands both the reader and the text to be entities capable of contributing to the reading. So far, however, what has been demonstrated are different ways in which the reader has dominated this relationship, for it was their experiences, identities, attitudes, and beliefs, which shaped the reading. This penultimate chapter will review this reading phenomenon, noting other contemporary research which highlights similar findings, and its affinity with the reader-response criticism of Stanley Fish.[1] Fish contends that texts are not able to lead or provoke a reader into an unexpected reading because the reading which takes place is shaped by the reader's interpretive community. In other words, the text contributes nothing to the reading, and the reader (molded by their interpretive community) contributes everything. Three final examples from my case study are then considered. These were occasions when the men read the texts in an unexpected way, one contrary to their preconceptions, expectations, or normal way of reading. Their views, preconceptions, or theories were not reaffirmed in their reading of the texts, but were challenged, resulting in an atypical reading. This suggests that the text is able to stimulate a reader into a reading outside of their assumptions. These examples form the third strand of my central argument, and serve not only to challenge Fish's theory, but to demonstrate a final way in which a reader's relationship with the five biblical texts shaped their reading of those texts.

The Influence of the Reader

I have been arguing that the relationships which the men had with the five biblical texts shaped their readings of those texts. This has been achieved in two ways. First, the transactional theory has been used to explain how a reader's relationship with a text may inform his or her reading of that

---

1. Fish, *Is There a Text in This Class?*

text. Second, I have evidenced four different ways in which these men's relationships with the five texts shaped their readings of those texts. Dave and Gary's readings were explored and I highlighted how their prior experiences of Christianity resulted in bitter and detached readings. John and Anthony's were then presented, and in their cases John's atheist and Anthony's Christian identity were seen to be defining factors in their readings. Victor and Paul followed, both men whose readings did not match their sense of religious identity. In their case, however, it was their attitude towards the biblical texts that shaped the readings, Victor deciding to give the texts "a chance" and Paul doubting their validity. Finally, I noted that these men's beliefs about the Bible, and so the five biblical texts, also molded their readings. First, believing the texts to be some sort of instruction manual, they read them from an efferent standpoint. Second, believing them to have a transformative potential, most of the men counter-read the texts, so as to disarm this threat. The few men who did not counter-read were typically those who had some sense of religious identity and so identified with the texts rather than against them. In all these cases, different aspects of the readers' relationship with the texts were seen to inform the subsequent reading of those texts.

In demonstrating the validity of this central claim, most of the examples given as evidence have been ones where the reader has had prime of place. In other words, it was the reader's experience, sense of identity, attitude or belief that played an overriding factor in the reading which occurred. For instance, Gary's detached reading concluded that the texts were all irrelevant, John found that the texts affirmed his atheist identity, Paul's doubting attitude resulted in a skeptical reading confirming his doubts, and believing the Bible to be an instruction manual the men read it from an efferent standpoint. Victor is the exception in that he attempted to limit the influence of his preconceptions; nonetheless that same attitude of fairness was seen to inform his readings.

Reader-shaped Readings

This dominant role which my readers assumed should not be thought of as unique to this group of men, for scholars have noted that those inside the church have often read the Bible in such a way as to "fit very neatly into a system of values already believed."[2] As Brian Malley writes:

2. Briggs, *Reading the Bible Wisely*, 130–31. It has been similarly noted that the image of Jesus claimed or promoted by a particular individual or group often reflects their own identity or concerns, see: Francis and Astley, "The Quest for the Psychological

> It is a truism that what a reader makes of a text turns heavily on the context the reader assigns to the text and to the sorts of hermeneutic assumptions the reader brings to bear on the text, and that these in turn bear the imprint of the social and historical context of the reader.[3]

Scot McKnight captures the essence of Malley's observation, when he, as a Christian, writes "every one of us adopts the Bible (and at the same time) adapts the Bible to our culture."[4]

This is something that Liam Murphy highlights when he contrasts the way the Bible is used and read by Orangemen and charismatics in Northern Ireland. He notes that the Orangemen focused on a number of Old Testament themes concerned with God's people feeling threatened, whilst other biblical images or texts were rarely mentioned:

> Saint Paul's focus on death and redemption is largely absent, as are the motifs of loving ones neighbours, turning the other cheek, humility in the face of power, and so on. In fact, with the exception of Revelation, the New Testament is generally neglected in Orange ritual. Instead we find stress placed on Pentateuch-orientated Judaism: a vengeful God who defends the righteous and abandons sinners to their well-deserved fate.[5]

He later writes that:

> Like Orangemen, charismatics frequently invoke reference to scripture in justification of their views and practices. The difference lies not in whether or not scripture occupies a privileged place in charismatic culture, but in their willingness to emphasize some books, chapters, and verses, some images and motifs over others.[6]

Jesus"; McKnight, *The Blue Parakeet*, 48–49; Nienhuis, "The Problem of Evangelical Biblical Illiteracy"; Pelikan, *Jesus through the Centuries*; Prothero, *American Jesus*. In the early 1900s Albert Schweitzer famously wrote: "each successive epoch of theology found its own thoughts in Jesus; that was, indeed, the only way in which it could make him live. But it was not only each epoch that found its reflection in Jesus; each individual created Jesus in accordance with his own character." See: *The Quest for the Historical Jesus*, 6.

3. Malley, *How the Bible Works*, 10.

4. McKnight, *The Blue Parakeet*, 13. See also Smith, *The Bible Made Impossible*, 75–78.

5. Murphy, "The Trouble with Good News," 15.

6. Ibid., 17.

Murphy is showing how these two groups of Christians read the Bible and use biblical images to uphold their different ideological and theological biases. This observation corresponds closely to that made by biblical scholars, postcolonial critics, and missionaries who have similarly noted the impact of a reader's social location upon their Bible reading (see chapter 1).

It is not only Christian lay people who have been seen to read the Bible in this way, the leaders and clergy have as well. In an experiment exploring how fifty lay people and fifty clergy read Mark 7:1–8 (a text concerning eating with unclean hands), Mark Powell found that the lay people identified with the disciples or the Pharisees, but the clergy tended to identify with Jesus.[7] Ian Dickson recounts the findings of *The Use of the Bible in Pastoral Practice*, a research project conducted by Cardiff University and Bible Society in 2002–3. This project considered how those in church leadership, and the wider Christian community, used the Bible. Dickson notes:

> The responses indicate a view of the Bible as a "product"; suitable for reinforcing particular pre-existing stances and ministries, making use essentially a pragmatic decision. What "worked" best in my/our interests? It was Bible use with a consumerist edge.[8]

Anthony Thiselton also describes this self-affirming, consumerist reading of the Bible:

> The nature of the reading process is governed by horizons of expectations already pre-formed by the community of readers or by the individual. Preachers often draw from texts what they had already decided to say; congregations sometimes look to biblical readings only to affirm the community-identity and life-style which they already enjoy.[9]

Even biblical scholars have been found to read the Bible in a way that conforms to their cultural or theological position. Gary Williams undertook a survey of commentaries on the book of Nehemiah, focusing on chapter 5. He found that commentators in the USA or Britain were less likely to reflect on present-day issues of poverty and debt than scholars in developing countries, even though these themes are central to Nehemiah 5.[10] Williams further notes how a scholar's theological view also shapes their reading. For instance, he highlights that one of Cyril Barber's ap-

---

7. Powell, *What Do They Hear?* 38–60.
8. Dickson, "The Bible in Pastoral Ministry," 109.
9. Thiselton, *New Horizons in Hermeneutics*, 8.
10. Williams, "Contextual Influences in Readings of Nehemiah 5."

plications of this text is that "Pastors face the same problem. It is always easy to allow oneself to be sidetracked by some worthy social cause."[11] Williams suggests that Barber's comment "flies in the face of the text's emphasis" and in part is a reaction to the social gospel.[12] Williams is yet again demonstrating the way in which a reader's ideological or theological assumptions are upheld in their reading of a text.

Judith Stack-Nelson, reflecting on her experience of teaching at various Bible seminaries in the USA argues that typically students are taught how to read the Bible in line with a particular theological position rather than how to read the Bible well. She writes:

> Our teaching often focuses on training pastors and church leaders to find what we think they *should* find in the biblical texts. We train them to find scholars and commentators who say the things that, through their seminary training, they know are approved of by their professors, things that are familiar, things they are already expecting to hear. We do not empower them to be better readers *themselves*.[13] (Emphasis in original)

Such a use of the Bible is found in wider culture and politics as well. James Crossley has traced the use of the Bible with particular reference to English popular culture and politics over the last forty to fifty years.[14] What he highlights is the way in which the presentation given of the Bible matches the particular agenda of the politician or artist. For example, he borrows Yvonne Sherwood's term "Liberal Bible,"[15] to describe an "understanding of the Bible as supportive of freedom of conscience, rights, law and consensus."[16] It is this Liberal Bible he and Sherwood argue was read and promoted by politicians such as George W. Bush, Margaret Thatcher, and Tony Blair. Crossley notes that such a view and reading of the Bible is a shift away from an earlier one he calls "the Absolute Monarchist's Bible, where decisions made by the monarch were to be seen as proof of divine power."[17]

In his provocatively entitled book *Abusing Scripture*, Manfred Brauch retells, from family experience, how many Christians in Germany aligned themselves with Hitler and Nazism. He then reflects on how the Bible was used to affirm this behavior, recounting:

11. Barber, *Nehemiah and the Dynamics of Effective Leadership*, 93.
12. Williams, "Contextual Influences in Readings of Nehemiah 5," 60.
13. Stack-Nelson, "Beyond Biblical Literacy," 294.
14. Crossley, *Harnessing Chaos*; Crossley, "What the Bible Really Means."
15. Sherwood, *A Biblical Text and its Afterlives*.
16. Crossley, "What the Bible Really Means," 24.
17. Ibid., 24.

> As a young teenager growing up in postwar Germany, I asked my parents, who were committed Christians, how it was possible that Christians had participated in this tragic extermination of the Jewish people. The answer, in addition to the recognition of deep-seated anti-Semitism in Europe, was that these Christians believed that they were obligated by the teaching of the Bible to obey the dictates of the state.[18]

Similarly Robert Bates also recounts the various ways in which the Bible was re-interpreted to affirm German "National Socialist ideas, teachings and terminology."[19]

All these examples highlight how a reader's identity and ideology can be reaffirmed as they read the Bible. However, this tendency to read in self-affirming ways is not limited to the Bible. Elizabeth Flynn's study of male and female readers, noted that the men were more likely to dominate a text, holding it at arm's length and imposing "a previously established structure on the text" and so reducing the possibility of learning.[20] David Smith similarly commented on his students' tendency to dominate texts in a particular way. He was teaching German to a class of students at a North American Evangelical college, and gave them poetry by Ernst Jandl to read, observing that the students:

> Were lured by Jandl's poem into a reading clearly rooted in personal resonances, yet also shaped by standard cultural schemata and communal interpretive strategies. In the process they came up with a reading that is both hermeneutically and theologically dubious.[21]

Smith argues that the poem's intertextual allusions contradicted the readings undertaken by the students. With critical questioning the group of students would eventually reject their earlier reading of the poem.[22]

Strictly speaking, aside from the German socialist Christian readings of the Bible, these examples should not be thought of as ideological or theological readings, for that is not what the readers understood themselves to be doing. An ideological or theological reading is one where the reader is able to name an ideology (such as Marxism), or a theological concept (such as liberation) and engages with a text in the light of it. What these examples

---

18. Brauch, *Abusing Scripture*, 54.
19. Bates, "'In Our Image'?," 31.
20. Flynn, "Gender and Reading," 268.
21. Smith, "The Poet, the Child and the Blackbird," 148–49.
22. Ibid., 150. See also Smith, "Misreading through the Eyes of Faith."

demonstrate is that the Bible can be read in such a way as to uphold the reader's sense of identity or ideological and theological presuppositions without realizing it.

A note of caution should be raised, for many of the scholars quoted above are Christians and are reflecting upon the church's use of the Bible, in other words Christians are aware of this tendency and have warned against it. In the year before Hitler's rise to power (1933), at a lecture entitled *The Church is Dead*, Dietrich Bonhoeffer argued:

> Has it not become terrifyingly clear again and again, in everything that we have said here to one another, that we are no longer obedient to the Bible? We are more fond of our own thoughts than of the thoughts of the Bible. We no longer read the Bible seriously, we no longer read it against ourselves, but for ourselves. If the whole conference here is to have any great significance, it may be perhaps that of showing us that we must read the Bible in quite a different way, until we find ourselves again.[23]

More popularly, Christian scholars have suggested various ways of limiting the inclination to read in self-affirming ways,[24] one of which is reading in community. For instance, Stanley Hauerwas provocatively argues that:

> *The Bible is not and should not be accessible to merely anyone, but rather it should only be made available to those who have undergone the hard discipline of existing as part of God's people.*[25]
> (Emphasis in original)

This, he suggests, would limit the tendency of Christians to read the Bible in denominationally and politically affirming ways. What these examples and the corresponding corrective advice nonetheless demonstrate is that there is a ring of truth about the medieval Catholic saying: "This is the book in which everyone looks for his own convictions-and everyone likewise finds his own convictions."[26]

This phenomenon of a reader unconsciously reading in a self-affirming way was seen in my case study, as chapters 5 to 9 have recounted. Sam's readings presented in the Introduction are a good example of this, for they resulted in every text echoing the formula: do X, or Y will happen.

---

23. Bonhoeffer, *No Rusty Swords*, 185–86.

24. Brauch, *Abusing Scripture*; McKnight, *The Blue Parakeet*; Powell, *What do they Hear?*; Stack-Nelson, "Beyond Biblical Literacy"; Thiselton, *New Horizons in Hermeneutics*.

25. Hauerwas, *Unleashing Scripture*, 9.

26. Congar, *Tradition and Traditions*, 385.

Anthony's Christian reading of the five texts is another one, for he was able to find a positive message in the most hopeless of texts. However, it was also the case that in some instances the reader consciously decided to read the Bible in such a way as to uphold a particular ideology or expectation, such as Victor deciding he was going to "be fair" when reading the texts. Nevertheless, whether a reader consciously or unconsciously upholds a particular presupposition the result is the same, the reader is preeminent in the reading transaction, and the reading often affirms their conscious or unconscious expectations. This was seen in my readings outside the church, but the examples contained in the last few pages demonstrate that it also occurs inside the church.

The Reader-response Theory of Stanley Fish

The pre-eminence of the reader as they engaged with the text fits comfortably with reader-response criticism, for it emphasizes the role of the reader in reading. However, some reader-response theories, such as the transactional theory, allow for the possibility of a reading dominated by the reader but indicate that this is not always the case. Others, such as that proposed by Stanley Fish, insist that the reader (and the community of which they are a part) will always dominate the reading and there is no alternative.[27] This is because, according to Fish, reality can never be known objectively, what exists must be interpreted in order for it to have any significance or meaning. Therefore, any significance or meaning that is attributed to reality is composed by ourselves.[28] Fish has a constructivist ontology and interpretivist epistemology, and so with reference to reading he argues that a text does not exist in itself rather it only exists in the mind of the reader. He is not claiming that the page with black squiggles on it is not real, instead he is pointing out that a person will never know what that object with squiggles on it is until she or he attempts to read it. However, as all reading involves the act of interpretation and it is the reader who does the interpreting, the text only takes shape in the mind of the reader. Therefore, he concludes that "the text as an entity independent of interpretation [. . .] drops out and is replaced by the texts that emerge as the consequence of our interpretive activities."[29] For Fish, texts do not exist as external objects; they only exist in the reader:

---

27. Fish, *Is There a Text in This Class?*
28. Ibid., 11.
29. Ibid., 13.

> Interpretive strategies are not put into execution after reading; they are the shape of reading, and because they are the shape of reading, they give texts their shape, making them rather than, as is usually assumed, arising from them. . . . In other words, these strategies exist prior to the act of reading and therefore determine the shape of what is read rather than, as is usually assumed, the other way around.[30]

Of particular importance to my case study is Fish's understanding that the text does not evoke a response from a reader or contribute to the reading. He makes this point forcefully when arguing against Wolfgang Iser, who posits that both text and reader contribute to the meaning produced in a reading.[31] Fish counters that "there is no distinction between what the text gives and what the reader supplies; he [the reader] supplies *everything*."[32] (Emphasis in original). This theory is a popular one and has been applied to Bible reading. For example, Eryl Davies traces the emergence of reader-response criticism within literary theory and biblical studies. He suggests one of the contributions of this "turn to the reader" is a greater appreciation that a single text can have multiple meanings, for different readers bring different presuppositions to the text which uniquely shape the reading and meaning produced. Davies then considers the question: are all readings/meanings equally valid or are some better than others?

> The question was, however, who decides? Whose reading counts? Who had the competence and authority to validate a given interpretation? The answer to this imponderable was provided by Stanley Fish.[33]

For Davies, Fish's theory, that the reader's interpretive community validates and limits the potentially endless plurality of meanings, solved the problem. Thus, the church (one interpretive community) can read the Bible in a certain way, and the academy (another interpretive community) can read it in a different way. Both these interpretive communities act in different ways to restrict which readings of the Bible are considered acceptable. Davies writes:

> The community will determine the range of meanings a given text can accommodate, and will adjudicate between readings that are admissible and those that are misguided. Each

---

30. Ibid., 13–14.
31. Iser, *The Implied Reader*
32. Fish, "Why No One's Afraid of Wolfgang Iser," 7.
33. Davies, *Biblical Criticism*, 20.

interpretative community will have its own criteria of evidence and its own measures of adequacy, and any given interpretation will be deemed to be valid when the interpretative community agrees it is valid. Such agreement is vital, for there is no objective criteria by which to judge the validity of a given interpretation apart from the assent of the interpretative community from which it emerged.[34]

In Davies' case, and so too Stephen Moore's,[35] he is persuaded that Fish's theory adequately describes and informs how real readers read the Bible. Other scholars have used Fish to argue for the validity of the Christian interpretive community,[36] or the need for inter-community dialogue and friendship with reference to Bible reading.[37] However, what follows calls into question Fish's claim that the reader contributes everything to a reading and the text brings nothing, for it explores three occasions in which the reader did not dominate the text, rather the text led the reader. This is to say, the reader's relationship with the five biblical texts shaped their reading of those texts, but not always in a way which conformed to the reader's assumptions.

The Influence of the Text

Fish's claim not only contrasts Iser's thinking, but also that of Hans-Georg Gadamer. Gadamer argued for the place of the reader's prejudices in reading, but went on to suggest that the reader is not trapped by those prejudices, but rather is open to allowing the text to "assert its own truth against one's own fore-meaning."[38] The transactional theory also contends that texts can and do shape a reading. The text contributes something, for it is in the transaction between it and the reader that meaning emerges. Rosenblatt argues that a text can stir up a reader, by this she understands that particular signs (squiggles) on the page stimulate particular memories, experiences, concepts and so on.[39] Moreover, the text not only stimulates, but also "helps to regulate what shall be held in the forefront of the reader's attention."[40]

34. Ibid., 28.
35. Moore, "Negative Hermeneutics."
36. Clines, *The Bible and the Modern World*; Petric, "The Reader(s) and the Bible(s) 'Reader Versus Community' in Reader-Response Criticism and Biblical Interpretation."
37. Jasper, "How Can We Read the Bible?"
38. Gadamer, *Truth and Method*, 238.
39. Rosenblatt, *Making Meaning with Texts*, xxv, 9, 31.
40. Rosenblatt, *The Reader, the Text, the Poem*, 11.

To that end, reading can have a liberating effect, whereby readers can vicariously participate in a time, culture, or context with which they and their interpretive community are unfamiliar. Rosenblatt writes:

> The physical signs of the text enable him to reach through himself and the verbal symbols to something sensed as outside and beyond his own personal world. The boundary between inner and outer world breaks down, and the literary work of art, as so often remarked, leads us into a new world.[41]

In other words, the text has the potential to lead the reader into unknown territory or an interpretation he or she had not anticipated.

A central difference between Rosenblatt's view of reading and Fish's, concerns the question: How is reality known? Fish understands that, as humans located in time and space, all our engagement with the world is interpreted; an interpretation only made possible, but also limited by, our social networks that have shaped us, that is our interpretive communities. Rosenblatt also assumes that all engagement with the world is interpretive, but adds that those objects that are being interpreted are able to inform and shape that interpretation. Thus, she contends that a text is able to guide the reader and influence what meaning emerges. Accordingly, this results in some interpretations being better than others, reflecting a critical realist ontology.

The three examples that follow demonstrate the way in which readers can approach the texts with a set of assumptions only to find that they are challenged by the text. Unlike Victor, these were not occasions when the readers had consciously decided to suspend particular preconceptions. Instead, these were men who found that the text evoked in them a response they had not anticipated, one outside of their expectations.

Stuart's "Powerful" Reading

Stuart is a forty-one-year-old welder, who identifies as "not at all religious." He is married and has two young daughters whom he enjoys spending time with, to that end life outside of work was mainly taken up with family. Stuart was quick-witted and usually the source of much banter during my visits. He is the younger brother of Dave, who I noted read "bitterly" (in chapter 5) and like Dave, he spoke negatively about his past, though in his case it was his Dad rather than the churches they attended which he focused upon:

---

41. Ibid., 21.

> I mean I was, we were pretty much dragged to church. Well my Dad had a few problems to be honest with you. And eh, I don't know. His Dad went to the way of God and 'cause he was in the Navy and he, he felt guilty about what he did in the Navy during the war. He kinda, that affected him. Which kinda affected my Dad, which he just, I don't know what, make himself feel better I suppose. But, dragged us along with him. I never wanted to go. Things like Sunday School and all the rest. [. . .] You grow up in an environment like that you can't wait to get away from it.

Stuart read most of the texts from an efferent standpoint and in a detached way, much as Gary had done (in chapter 5). He described the Bible as a moral guide, one that may be of relevance to others, but not to him. Accordingly, he did not annotate any text and described most of them as irrelevant and not worth remembering. When asked about this in our interview he said it was "because I do know it is never going to play a part of my life." He would later say that the texts have "not affected me, anything that was to affect me regarding religion was done when I was younger anyway, no, it could never affect me." Stuart's detached reading of the texts was one shaped by his prior experiences of religion.

However, there was one text he did not read in a detached way—Psalm 88. Stuart did not annotate this text, but his answers in the accompanying questionnaire suggested that he had found this text stimulating. For example, when asked: What, if anything, "jumped out at you" as you read through the passage? Stuart wrote: "It was very powerful." When asked what his gut reaction was to this passage he wrote: "I think it was very powerful." In the remainder of the questionnaire Stuart did not elaborate as to how or why he found the psalm "powerful," thankfully though in the interview he was more forthcoming.

> David: This was the psalm, what did you make of that one?
>
> Stuart: Sad, it's sad. That someone. It's quite funny that it was used in the Bible to be honest. It's sad that someone could trust a God and then realise the path they are going down and not being answered. So someone, say, who was very, very ill or very, very poorly and in pain or can't understand what they have done wrong to deserve what they got. That's quite powerful that one.
>
> David: OK, powerful in what way?
>
> Stuart: Powerfulness in, in it rings true to life really, sometimes.

[The conversation continues onto 2 John, before returning to Psalm 88]

David: Can I just clarify for my own sake. So you think this one was powerful [indicating Psalm 88] because you feel it relates to you?

Stuart: Well, I, it's related to parts of my life.

David: OK.

Stuart: I used to have a "Jesus Loves Us" sticker on the side of our bed and used to listen to me Mum and Dad row at night and then hide behind the church where everything was good and everyone was happy and everyone. And I used to cry looking at that sticker, and I still at times, when I get down, when I think about that. Although I haven't had the pain when religion was put on me, eh, I can understand someone that believes in the Lord and feels let down. I was a very frightened child.

Contrasting Stuart's indifferent and efferent reading of the other four texts, this had been a stimulating read, Stuart had been drawn into the world of the poem/song. He had read it from an aesthetic standpoint, focusing on what he was "living through during his relationship with that particular text."[42] Specifically, he found he could identify with the psalmist and the pain that was expressed. This resulted in him finding himself immersed in the psalm. "Powerful" was the word that summed up his reading. My field notes record that contrasting his usual jovial self, Stuart was unusually quiet and reflective after reading it.

This is an example of the way in which a text can lead a reader to an unexpected interpretation, one significantly different to their established reading pattern. As Stuart engaged with Psalm 88 he responded to the emerging reading with surprise and empathy. The difference between his responses to this text and the detached reading of the other four demonstrates the role that the text can play in leading a reader into unknown territory. In all five readings the same painful experiences and assumptions played a significant role, what resulted in a powerful rather than detached reading was the specific content of Psalm 88.

My suggestion that Stuart was led by and responded to Psalm 88 is a more coherent understanding of what took place than that implied by Fish. He would argue that Stuart had constructed for himself a stimulating

---

42. Rosenblatt, *The Reader, the Text, the Poem*, 25.

text using his socially produced assumptions, that is, his interpretive community. Such an explanation raises the question, why did Stuart not construct the other texts in a similarly stimulating way? Fish's theory places too much weight on the reader's socially produced assumptions. When recounting teaching a seminar on literary theory, Fish suggests that "theories always work and they will always produce exactly the results they predict."[43] Therefore his class "did not concentrate on what theories can do (since they will always generate the texts demanded by their assumptions)."[44] Such a belief does correspond with most of the examples in this case study. However, Stuart's reading of Psalm 88 was one contrary to the assumptions and theories that had shaped his reading of the other four texts. His engagement with Psalm 88 was informed by those assumptions but did not reaffirm them rather it challenged them. The same experiences that resulted in his detached reading of the other texts were vital for this powerful reading, for he found that the subject matter of the Psalm related to those experiences in an unforeseen way. Louise Rosenblatt writes: "powerful personal reverberations and moments of intensity or illumination may be the result of the coming-together of the reader and the text at an especially propitious moment."[45] This was the case in Stuart's reading transaction with Psalm 88, one where the text provoked, stimulated, and guided him into an unexpected reading, one which contrasted his reading of the other four texts.

Others who have engaged with Fish's work have raised a similar question.[46] John Barton is one of a number of scholars who note that according to Fish a text is not something a reader responds to, rather it is something they construct for themselves, and so asks:

> How can a text ever surprise or inform us, if we ourselves bring the meaning to it, if the text is nothing but an occasion for us to formulate ideas which we ourselves find unexceptionable?[47]

In this way then, Stuart's reading of Psalm 88 problematizes Fish's theory for it suggests that the text contributes something to the reading.

---

43. Fish, *Is There a Text in This Class?* 68.
44. Ibid., 68.
45. Rosenblatt, *The Reader, the Text, the Poem*, 157–58.
46. Eagleton, *The Event of Literature*, 39–41; Osborne, *The Hermeneutical Spiral*, 478–82; Thiselton, *New Horizons in Hermeneutics*, 549–50; Wright, "'Get thee behind me Satan,'" 30.
47. Barton, "Thinking about Reader-Response Criticism," 149.

Ethan's Skeptical Readings

The following two examples are briefer and demonstrate that a reading informed by the text does not always result in a positive or coherent experience for the reader. Ethan is a forty-year-old engineer who got married during my time at the Chemical Industrial Plant. He described himself as "not at all religious" but an "open minded" and spiritual person. Until his late teenage years he and his family attended church on occasion, significantly though he did not know how many gospels there were in the Bible, and did not describe this earlier church contact as personally meaningful. He was a strongly skeptical reader, tending to focus on the parts of the texts he felt were wrong.

During our interview I pointed out to him that most of his annotations were comments highlighting a contradiction or discrepancy, they appeared to focus on aspects of the texts he disagreed with. His reply surprised me.

> Ethan: I didn't expect anything negative.
>
> David: Sorry?
>
> Ethan: That's my preconception of what may be in the Bible is a positive way to look at life. I didn't expect that negativity and in that degree as well.

Earlier in our conversation he had indicated a number of times, how "negative" he found various aspects of the texts. For instance, when asked if anything surprised him about the passages he said:

> Some of the texts were quite negative. Em, they gave maybe a sort of sandwich between good comments about this is maybe what you should do and then if you don't, this will happen. And I'm thinking, that shouldn't, that wasn't expected.

I followed up this question by asking Ethan if there was a passage that particularly stood out to him for any reason and he replied:

> There's two of them and I'm just trying to remember which one they are. It was the song and it was the, it was the last one we did, was it the letter to, that they wrote. And it was for those reasons [the negativity]. The song, I think it was quite condemning, if you didn't do or behave in a way it was stating and the same for the last passage [. . .] I didn't expect it to, it cast aside or it gave the ability to cast aside people and I didn't expect that from a religion or the Bible. I thought it was believe in forgiveness and understanding.

Ethan's expectation was that the Bible would contain a "positive way to look at life" and he did not expect it would have statements condemning people. At the end of our interview he reflected on whether the Bible has developed through the years, and said:

> Because then you could say that these negative statements may have been true then [when the texts were written] although they aren't in the modern world, or they aren't in my impression of the modern world today.

Contrasting many of the men, Ethan's expectations were not imposed upon the texts and did not result in a reading that affirmed them. Contrary to Fish's claim that theories "will always generate the texts demanded by their assumptions,"[48] Ethan found that his theory, that the Bible was a book containing a "positive way to look at life," fell short of the texts he read, and resulted in a reading at odds with that theory. Ethan's reading was one in which his theory, or assumption, did not have a preeminent role rigidly enforcing a reading in which that theory was upheld. The content of the texts were such that those assumptions were called into question and an unexpected reading occurred. His assumptions certainly informed his reading, for when finding that those assumptions were not confirmed, Ethan read strongly skeptically. Tellingly, when asked if he had any over-all impressions about the Bible passages he said: "it showed me I don't know what's in the Bible."

Phil's Confused Reading

The third example that challenges the view that a text contributes nothing to a reading concerns the confusion which one of the men expressed towards Psalm 88. I noted in chapter 8 that the men assumed an efferent stance towards the five passages because they believed the Bible to be a didactic text. To that end, there were examples of men who read Psalm 88 efferently and found that their reading affirmed that efferent stance, leaving them feeling they had successfully understood the Psalm, even if they rejected it. For example, Peter described the Bible as "a book of stories and interpretations of how we should behave." In the questionnaire accompanying Psalm 88 he described it as an "evil" and "bullying" text, one that acted as "threat" or "warning" that "if you do not do as you are told, 'God' will not see you." In our interview this was the text which he said stood out to him due to its threatening message and he "didn't like it, didn't like it at all." Peter had assumed an efferent stance towards this text and so read it seeking

---

48. Fish, *Is There a Text in This Class?* 68.

information, in this case a central message. Having been able to claim that he had grasped this central message, Peter's efferent stance towards this text was confirmed and vindicated. Peter was not the only one to read this psalm in this particular way, Dave, Tony, Ethan, and Sam all concluded that this text was a warning to any reader that if they ignore God their life would be miserable and God would not help them even if they ask.

However, as I highlighted with Stuart, not all men read this psalm from an efferent standpoint. Phil is a forty-eight-year-old electrician at the Plant, who described himself as "slightly religious," and found this Psalm confusing. He was a strongly skeptical reader who, with most of the men, assumed an efferent stance towards all the texts. With most of the texts Phil was able to articulate what he felt each was claiming and why he disagreed with it, but not with Psalm 88. Phil did not annotate the psalm but he spoke about it in this way:

> Mmm, it, it's more confusing than anything else. It doesn't seem to give. I can't see a clear message in that. There's no, em, there doesn't seem to be. It's almost like a poem. Does that make sense?

Phil expected this text to conform to the efferent reading stance he had assumed by having a clear message or directive. However, his assumption did not lead him to find such a message, rather the assumption was found wanting. Phil was able to identify the text as a poem, and this is perhaps due to the short descriptor I included where the psalm was described as a "song". Nonetheless, Phil still read it from an efferent standpoint, expecting it to have "a clear message." This is a further example of the way in which a reader's expectations did not always result in a reading that conformed to them. It also demonstrates the strength of those expectations, for although Phil was able to identify the genre of this text as poetry he did not attempt to read it aesthetically. Once again, a reader's assumptions did not produce the phenomenon he expected to find, all of which troubles Fish's theory, which seems to reduce the text to the function of a Rorschach ink blot upon which the viewers/readers projects themselves. Instead, with Rosenblatt, I would contend that a literary text is not a neutral inkblot, but a series of patterns and symbols a reader engages with.

> The transactional view, whilst insisting on the importance of the reader's contribution, does not discount the text and accepts a concern for validity of interpretation. Misinterpretations may thus provide clues to the reader's preoccupations, but responses

may also be a function of characteristics of the text, viewed in the light of the peculiar complex nature of the literary encounter.[49]

Summary

Stuart, Ethan, and Phil did not actively choose to suspend their preconceptions towards the biblical texts, as Victor had, rather it was in the reading transactions themselves that the text challenged those preconceptions, leading the reader to an unexpected reading. In Stuart's case one he would describe as "powerful," in Ethan's one resulting in a skeptical reading, and for Phil the consequence was confusion. These examples suggest that a reader is not limited by their preconceptions, assumptions, interpretive community, or particular theory they hold, for the transaction with the text was able to produce an atypical or unknown reading. These three examples are in a minority however, for most of the men read in such a way that their assumptions, expectations and so on were affirmed in their reading, as explored in the previous five chapters. This does not lessen the significance of Stuart, Ethan, and Phil's readings, instead it demonstrates that Fish's theory does adequately describes the majority of the readings, but not all. Rosenblatt's transactional theory however, does account for all the readings that took place.

Fish may not agree with this conclusion and might argue that this is my interpretation of the data, one shaped and limited by my interpretive community. He, being shaped and limited by his, would interpret the data differently. To his way of thinking, what is more important is whether our interpretive communities accept our different retellings of this case study. Such a response shows the difficulty in arguing against such a relativistic theory, for any evidence presented is considered an interpretation of the data, one no better or worse than an opposing interpretation. Terry Eagleton describes the impasse in this way: if Fish "cannot understand you, this is probably because you inhabit an interpretive community incommensurable with his own, and your criticism may thus safely be ignored."[50] The difference again concerns how reality is known. To that end, a more fruitful discussion may be to contrast the implications of the transactional theory and Fish's theory for the biophysical world where universal "laws" are spoken of, and the ethical world with its concept of human rights or virtues. Such a comparison would not only prove fruitful in further clarifying differences between both

---

49. Rosenblatt, *The Reader, The Text, the Poem*, 151.
50. Eagleton, *The Event of Literature*, 44.

theories, but may progress the apparent stalemate which exists by showing one theory to be more robust or workable than the other.

These three examples therefore are a further way in which the reader's relationship with the five biblical texts shaped their readings of those texts. While the majority of the men dominated their reading transactions, the examples of Stuart, Ethan, and Phil demonstrate that the text was able to lead the reader in an unexpected direction, to an unforeseen reading.

Conclusion

In this chapter I have contended that a text is able to guide a reader into an unexpected reading, one which is a result of, but does not conform to, her or his relationship with the text. This is the third strand of my central argument that the reader's relationship with the five biblical texts shaped his or her reading of those texts. The first strand was the theorizing of my argument using the transactional theory of reading. The second strand evidenced my central argument by demonstrating how my readers' experiences, identities, attitudes, and beliefs shaped their reading of the texts. What these examples also illustrated was the way in which a reader can assume a controlling position towards a text, a phenomenon that has been noted within Christian readings of the Bible as well.

Finally, my third strand has shown that although the readers' relationship with the texts shaped their reading, it did not always result in a reading which reaffirmed the readers' preconceptions. In other words, the reader did not always dominate the text, on occasion the text led the reader into an unforeseen reading. This was noted in Stuart's powerful reading of Psalm 88 that contrasted his detached reading of the other four texts. In Ethan's case the result of his expectations not being met was a skeptical reading, and for Phil it was confusion. In all three cases the reader's attitudes towards, or expectations of, the texts played a significant role, but they did not result in a reading that reaffirmed them. These three examples trouble the literary theory of Stanley Fish, who argues that the reader will always read in conformity to their interpretive community and its assumptions. For him, the text is unable to stimulate, guide, provoke, or lead. However, I would posit that the examples of Stuart, Ethan, and Phil have illustrated how a text is able to stimulate a reader into the unexpected. Thus, the reader's relationship with the five biblical texts was indeed a relationship, understood as the transaction between two parties, one where the reader often dominated, but not always.

Conclusion

Implications of Relational Bible Reading

I HAVE BEEN EXPLORING the way a reader's relationship with a text shapes their reading of that text, with reference to a particular group of readers and a particular group of texts. This final chapter will trace the three strands of the central argument I have been making in last seven chapters. I will also revisit the five insights from this case study that problematize various assumptions in the academic and Christian world. Having done so, I will then note the three specific ways in which this work is an original contribution to knowledge, before reflecting upon four implications of it for Bible reading studies and practice. This chapter concludes by discussing three limitations of the work and the potential for further research they stimulate.

Summary of Argument

It has been my contention that the men's relationships with the five biblical texts shaped their readings of those texts. That is to say, all that a reader is in relation to a text—his or her presuppositions, beliefs, fears, hopes, attitudes, past experiences, and sense of identity—shaped his or her reading of it. I have argued this in three ways. First, I theorized this relational view of reading using Louise Rosenblatt's transactional theory, for she postulated that readers and texts co-exist in a dynamic matrix and that all that a reader is in relation to a text shapes her or his reading of that text. She writes:

> The reader, drawing on past linguistic and life experience, links the signs on the page with certain words, certain concepts, certain sensuous experiences, certain images of things, people, actions, scenes. The special meanings and, more particularly, the submerged associations that these words and images have for the individual reader will largely determine what the work communicates to him. The reader brings to the work

> personality traits, memories of past events, present needs and preoccupations, a particular mood of the moment, and a particular physical condition. These and many other elements in a never-to-be-duplicated combination determine his inter-fusion with the peculiar contribution of the text.[1]

Furthermore, she then contends that through the process of selective attention certain aspects of a reader's relationship with a text will be considered more salient to the reading than others. Those aspects that are considered salient will shape the reading more than those that are not.

Having provided a theoretical foundation for my central claim, the second strand of my argument involved demonstrating its reality in the readings that occurred in the Chemical Industrial Plant. First, I highlighted the influence of the reader's prior experiences of religion upon their readings, by recounting Dave's bitter, and Gary's detached readings. Second, in order to demonstrate the link between my readers' sense of religious identity and the skeptical or accepting nature of their readings I explored John's atheist and Anthony's Christian readings of the texts. Third, I considered the role of the participants' attitudes towards the Bible, for in the case of Victor and Paul their attitudes informed their readings more than their sense of religious identity. Fourth, I explored two ways in which these men's beliefs about the Bible shaped their reading of the biblical texts. What I argued was that these men believed the Bible was in some way an instruction manual and so assumed an efferent stance towards the texts. They also believed it was transformative and so many participants counter-read in order to disarm this apparent threat.

This second strand also showed that the readers' relationship with the texts was often reinforced by their reading of the texts. For example, believing the text to be a moral guide, they read it attempting to extract ethical directives from the text, which in turn reinforced their belief that it is a moral guide. However, the third strand of my argument examined ways in which the texts influenced the readings, challenging some part of the pre-existing relationship. Stuart's "powerful" reading of Psalm 88, Ethan's expectations that the Bible contained a "positive way to look at life," and Phil's confusion when attempting to read Psalm 88 efferently, all demonstrate this. Although these examples were in a minority they illustrate that both the reader and the text have the potential to contribute, for that is the nature of a relationship. In these three ways I have argued that my readers' relationships with the five biblical texts shaped their readings of those texts.

---

1. Rosenblatt, *Literature as Exploration*, 30.

I also presented five smaller arguments in addition to my central claim. In these instances, I was bringing certain insights from my case study to bear on a number of different assumptions found within the academic or Christian world. First, I noted that contextual Bible reading approaches, such as CBS, believe that the geographical setting of the reading will significantly inform how the text is read.[2] In my case though, there was minimal linking of the biblical texts, or ideas, to the Chemical Industrial context in which these Bible readings were located. This suggests that some influences are more significant than others, in the case of my participants their sense of religious identity had a greater impact on the readings than the workplace setting. Second, those who identified as "not at all religious" typically read skeptically whilst those who identified as "religious" in some way, were more likely to read acceptingly. However, this skeptical/accepting binary which I used, and reflects similar pairings found within academia,[3] was itself brought into scrutiny for amongst these men a clear binary did not exist rather a spectrum of readings could be seen. Moreover, on occasion, the men's religious identity did not always correspond to the skeptical or accepting reading anticipated, cautioning against the use of an over simplistic binary. Third and fourth, some, such as Vincent[4] and Aichele,[5] have argued that the Bible has retained very little authority or power in the western world, and others, such as Bible Society,[6] contend that it is a text with agency-like qualities, capable of transforming the reader. My case study challenges both views, for on the one hand my participants read the biblical texts as if they had a transformative potential. On the other hand though, this was a potential they felt threatened by and so counter-read, disempowering the perceived threat. Finally, although most of the men read the texts in such a way that their preconceptions were affirmed, not all did. The three occasions in which an unexpected reading occurred problematizes the reader-response theory of Stanley Fish.[7] He contends that the reader contributes everything to the reading and the text brings nothing, but in these cases the content of the text provoked the readers to an atypical reading, one beyond the assumptions and expectations derived from their interpretive communities.

2. Lawrence, *The Word in Place*; Peden, "Contextual Bible Study at Cornton Vale Women's Prison, Stirling"; Riches, *What Is Contextual Bible Study?*
3. Davies, *Whose Bible Is It Anyway?*; Volf, *Captive to the Word of God*.
4. Vincent, "The Death and Resurrection of the Bible in Church and Society."
5. Aichele, *The Control of Biblical Meaning*.
6. Engelke, *God's Agents*, 4–5.
7. Fish, *Is There a Text in This Class?*

Contribution of Research

Every scholar hopes that their work will positively contribute to the wider subject they have been investigating and there are three ways in which my case study has done this. First, this case study is unique, principally because it has directly examined how British people who do not regularly read the Bible or go to church, read the Bible. There are those, like Village,[8] or Rogers,[9] who have considered how regular Bible readers read the Bible. Others, such as Macdonald,[10] and Webster,[11] have engaged with those who are not regular churchgoers, but the aim of these works was to consider the use of *Lectio Divina* (Macdonald) or CBS (Webster). Le Grys similarly used nonreligious participants in his Bible reading study but they acted as a comparison with his larger group of religious readers upon whom he focused.[12] There is plenty of quantitative and qualitative research that has considered nonreligious peoples' attitudes to and beliefs about the Bible.[13] However, none of these works has directly explored how the Bible is read by nonregular Bible readers. This is therefore the principal contribution which my work makes, as it is the first to directly describe how British men who are not regular Bible readers, read the Bible.

Second, in doing so, I have linked together the belief that the Bible is an instruction manual with the adoption of an efferent stance. Researchers have noted that the Bible is commonly viewed as an instruction manual,[14] and Rosenblatt's efferent/aesthetic spectrum has been explored and promoted, mainly by literary and education scholars.[15] By bringing these two components together I have illuminated a particular aspect of Bible reading that lay in shadow. This linking of concepts across academic disciplines also demonstrates the usefulness of interdisciplinary research, where connections can be made and insights gained as different fields of study are traversed.

Third, no one has described or defined "counter-reading" as I do: a reading style emanating from a reader's personal response to an assumed

8. Village, *The Bible and Lay People*.
9. Rogers, *Congregational Hermeneutics*.
10. Macdonald, "The Psalms and Spirituality."
11. Webster, "When the Bible Meets the Black Stuff."
12. Le Grys, *Shaped by God's Story*.
13. For example see: Spencer, *Beyond the Fringe*; Theos, *Post-Religious Britain?*
14. Beal, *The Rise and Fall of the Bible*; Engelke, *God's Agents*; Le Grys, *Shaped by God's Story*; Spencer, *Beyond the Fringe*; Theos, *Post-Religious Britain?*
15. Harvey and Goudvis, *Strategies that Work*; Karolides, "The Transactional Theory of Literature"; Kesler, "Evoking the World of Poetic Nonfiction Picture Books."

threat which is posed by a text's assumed transformative potential. Some make use of the term "resisting reading,"[16] "reading against the grain,"[17] or "hermeneutics of suspicion,"[18] and others highlight the texts historical legacy.[19] These four overlapping concepts lack the personal sense of threat and defensive response seen in my case study. In introducing this term I have extended scholarly understanding of how readers' respond to texts.

Implications of Research

Research such as this not only describes a previously unexplored area, but it also has implications for Bible reading. While it has been suggested that the findings from a case study cannot be generalized or applied to another context, this is a contested claim.[20] I would argue that there are at least two reasons why my findings are not limited to these men and this research project. First, by identifying the transactional theory as one that suitably explains and describes the readings I observed, my case study and this theory are linked. This theory claims to be generalizable and my project has demonstrated this in the case of my readers. Second, I have consistently shown that other studies have reach similar conclusions to my own. For instance, not only did my participants typically dominate their readings, but so have lay Christians,[21] church leaders,[22] academics,[23] politicians,[24] and university students.[25] The comparable research that I have presented throughout this work validates the theory I build upon and indicates that my findings are not unique but rather represent a more common phenomenon.

Therefore, in light of my central argument and the claim that this case study has a degree of generalizability, there are at least four implications for the study or practice of Bible reading. First, the claim made to read the

16. Fetterley, *The Resisting Reader*; Harding, "In the Name of Love."

17. Clines, *Interested Parties*; Domeris, "Reading the Bible against the Grain"; West, "Taming Texts of Terror."

18. Aichele et al., *The Postmodern Bible*, 272–308; Fiorenza, *Bread Not Stone*; Volf, *Captive to the Word of God*.

19. Fiorenza, *Searching the Scriptures,* 11; Braun, "Resisting John," 63.

20. Steinmetz, "Odious Comparisons," 384–90.

21. Malley, *How the Bible Works*; McKnight, *The Blue Parakeet*; Murphy, "The Trouble with Good News."

22. Powell, *What do they Hear?* 38–60; Thiselton, *New Horizons in Hermeneutics*, 8.

23. Stack-Nelson, "Beyond Biblical Literacy"; Williams, "Contextual influences in Readings of Nehemiah 5."

24. Crossley, "What the Bible Really Means"; Bates, "'In our Image'?"

25. Smith, "The Poet, the Child and the Blackbird."

Bible from a specific social location, such as a feminist, African, or disabled reading, should be qualified, for there are other aspects of these readers' relationships with the Bible that will also shape the reading. Second, study into biblical literacy should focus less on Bible knowledge or cultural appropriations of biblical tropes, and more on people's relationship with the Bible. Third, in Bible-reading settings, such as the church, an aesthetic reading of the Bible should be promoted. Fourth, all readers of the Bible should be aware of the potential, perhaps tendency, for the reader to dominate the reading. In highlighting these implications, I am aware that some readers of this book may well note others, reflecting their own backgrounds, training, and interests. However, in light of the ethical parameters of my study along with my own interests and training, I will focus on these four.

First, as chapter 1 documented, it is relatively common in the subfield of contextual Bible reading for the scholar/reader to identify the social location from which she or he is reading the text. For instance, I presented John Hull as someone who reads the Bible in light of his blindness and there are many other examples of contextual Bible reading.[26] However, my central finding that the reader's relationship with a text shapes his or her reading of that text challenges the neatness of the claim to read from a particular social location. Instead, it suggests that the reader's relationship with the text informs the reading, a relationship that includes various social locations (such as attitudes, assumptions, beliefs, preoccupations, and personality). Not all of these will have a significant impact upon the reading that takes place, selective attention means that some will inform the reading more than others. Nevertheless, it will never be only one social location that shapes a reading, it will be many.

To put it starkly, just as there is no such thing as a neutral or objective reading of a text, so too there is no such thing as a blind, feminist, African, or, in my case, Scottish reading of the Bible. Rather, there are readings undertaken by blind, feminist, African, or Scottish readers who bring all that they are to the biblical text—that is their personality, attitudes, expectations, beliefs, interests, motivations, and so on, along with the particular social location they are choosing to publicly identify with. These other aspects of their relationship with the Bible will also shape their reading to a greater or lesser degree, and so should be acknowledged as well. Hull, for example, is a Christian and this religious identity and related attitudes and beliefs also permeate his book, as does his gender, academic training, western lifestyle, personality, temperament, and a myriad of other factors I suspect. He does not claim that these other components have not influenced his reading of

---

26. Hull, *In the Beginning there was Darkness*, see chapter 1 for further examples.

the Bible, but his work is principally identified with one social location, his blindness. Hull is not alone, for a cursory glance at contextual Bible reading titles and at the labels that scholars adopt (such as "black," "postmodern," "postcolonial," "Latin American," and so on) indicates that many of them identify with one social location, ignoring or playing down other aspects of their relationship with the Bible.

This is not always the case. Gregory Jenks's intertextual reading of Jonah, is an example of a contextual reading, but one undertaken only after a detailed description of his own upbringing, experiences, interests, and sense of identity.[27] The emergence of autobiographical biblical criticism further demonstrates awareness that all that a reader is shapes their reading. These examples, however, are in the minority; more often than not scholars concentrate on one particular social location, marginalizing other aspects of their relationship with the text. My case study suggests that if a reader's relationship with a text shapes his or her reading of that text, then a wider identification of the social locations or influences upon the reading transaction should be acknowledged.

Second, I also highlighted in chapter 1 that "biblical literacy" is a contested term, one that some have used to refer to Bible knowledge,[28] whilst others have used to describe the presence of biblical tropes and images in popular culture.[29] For this reason, surveys often consider three, four, or five aspects of biblical literacy, not just one. Clive Field's meta-analysis is one example of this, for he addressed five different areas: ownership of the Bible, readership of the Bible, knowledge of the Bible's content, belief in the Bible's veracity, and influence of the Bible in everyday life.[30] This demonstrates the way in which biblical literacy research is being subdivided into component parts, each with its own research question, such as: How many people own a Bible? or How often is the Bible read? This fragmentation of biblical literacy and the study attached to it is troubled by my central finding, for if a reader's relationship with a text shapes his or her reading of that text, then the central question which should be asked is: What is the British public's relationship with the Bible? The answer to this would not only encompass established areas of biblical literacy such as Bible knowledge, belief, and so on, but it would also consider other areas like a reader's experiences, hopes, and hurts

27. Jenks, "The Sign of Jonah."
28. Davies, "Whose Bible? Anyone's?"
29. Edwards, *Rethinking Biblical Literacy*.
30. Field, "Is the Bible Becoming a Closed Book?" He does not use the term "biblical literacy" rather he refers to "Bible-centrism," to describe how central the Bible is to British society. Nonetheless, the content of his paper addresses subjects which have been labeled "biblical literacy."

in regard to the Bible, which rarely feature in biblical literacy research.[31] In this way, both a more holistic appreciation of the British public's biblical literacy, and a clearer insight into a central tenet of it would be gained.

Third, I found that most of the men in my study read most of the texts efferently, doing so because they viewed the Bible as a guide or didactic text and I suspect that within the British church the Bible is handled in a very similar way. For example, Andrew Rogers explored how the Bible was used from the pulpit in two English evangelical churches (one reformed and one charismatic) and described observing a "one-way hermeneutics" comprised of exegesis or engagement with the text and then application.[32] To handle the Bible in this way is to read it for information, as some sort of slightly obscure instruction manual whose instructions are explained by the expert (the preacher) to the laity. Rogers also describes one of the evangelical church's view of Bible reading as being "teaching, training, instructing, informing, and learning, but also rebuking and challenging,"[33] and it's "tendency to treat the Bible propositionally, with the category of 'story' being eschewed."[34] Nancy Ammerman found something very similar in her earlier work with what she described as a "fundamentalist" church in the USA. There she noted that the pastor's sermon "explains what the Bible means and tells the people how the Bible says they should live."[35] In both cases, to handle the Bible in this way requires an efferent stance.

Ann Christie's research into how Anglican lay people in North Yorkshire view Jesus, something she labeled: "ordinary Christology,"[36] highlighted how the Bible is used with reference to Christ. She writes:

> The data show that when people say "Jesus shows us how to live" they are primarily casting Jesus in the role of moral exemplar: Jesus is the model for moral behavior (because he was morally

---

31. Scott McKnight similarly suggests the tone of a Christian's relationship with the Bible shapes their reading of it. In his case, he further adds that behind this lies the type of relationship they have to the God read of in the Bible. See: McKnight, *The Blue Parakeet*, 83–84.

32. Rogers, "Congregational Hermeneutics," 496.

33. Ibid, 495. This echoes 2 Tim 3:16 "All Scripture is God-breathed and is useful for teaching, rebuking, correcting and training in righteousness," (NIV).

34. Rogers, *Congregational Hermeneutics*, 133. Rogers highlights that the other, more charismatic evangelical church viewed the goal of Bible reading "in the language of encounter with God." See Rogers, "Congregational Hermeneutics," 495–96.

35. Ammerman, *Bible Believers*, 121.

36. Christie, *Ordinary Christology*.

"totally perfect" and "never did anything wrong") whom they "should always aspire and strive to be like."[37]

Christie links this exemplarist view of Jesus to how her participants read the Bible. Such a reading is not uncommon, in 1957 Richard Hoggart summarized the Christian (or religious) aspect of working class culture in England in this way: "they will say, without a sense of contradiction, that science has taken the place of religion, but that we ought all to try to 'live according to Christ's teaching.'"[38] In 1984 Robert Towler suggested there were five different types of religiousness in Britain and exemplarism was one of them, where a person "sees in Jesus, in his life and death, and in his teaching, an example for all to follow."[39] In light of some of these works, Jeff Astley describes exemplarism as "a particularly English form of Christianity."[40] The point I am making is that this exemplar way of viewing Jesus is a further illustration of how the Bible is read efferently within a British church setting.

If my participants' tendency to read the biblical texts from an efferent standpoint reflects British church practice as well, as seen in these examples, then there is surely a need to nurture aesthetical readings of the Bible within the church as well.[41] In *Encouraging Biblical Literacy*, Margaret Killingray argues against engaging with the Bible as one would an instruction manual. She writes: "A reading of John 1.1, Genesis 1.1 and Hebrews 1.1 should prepare us for a great deal more than the 'handbook' or 'manual' view of Scripture."[42] The promotion of narrative biblical criticism,[43] reading the Bible as a story,[44] imaging it as a drama,[45] along with meditative Bible reading approaches like *Lectio Divina*,[46] and the direct call for Bible engagement from an aesthetic stance,[47] all affirm this. Indeed most recent-

37. Christie, "Jesus as Exemplar," 78.
38. Hoggart, *The Uses of Literacy*, 116.
39. Towler, *The Need for Certainty*, 19.
40. Astley, "'Non-Realism for Beginners?'" 101.
41. Similar calls have been made regarding how the Bible is used in school. For example see: Pike, "Reading and Responding to Biblical Texts"; Esther Reed et al., "Narrative Theology in Religious Education." My thanks to Susannah Cornwall who alerted me to this.
42. Killingray, *Encouraging Biblical Literacy*, 14.
43. Alter, *The Art of Biblical Narrative*.
44. McKnight, *The Blue Parakeet*.
45. Bartholomew and Goheen, *The Drama of Scripture*; Wright, *The New Testament and the People of God*. 139–43.
46. Macdonald, "Engaging the Scriptures"; Webber, *The Younger Evangelicals*, 184–85.
47. Pike, "The Bible and the Reader's Response."

ly, the rise in popularity of reader's Bibles further emphasizes this. Those who argue for the use of the reader's Bible format, such as Glenn Paauw, claim that traditional Bible formats have encouraged an efferent style of engagement (although he does not use the word "efferent") but a reader's Bible lends itself more to an aesthetic reading style, one lost to the present day Bible reader.[48]

With reference to the predominant weight that is given to reading texts efferently in schools, Rosenblatt suggests aesthetic readings should be nurtured by:

1. Do not generate an efferent stance when presenting texts as poems or stories or plays.
2. Do not use the texts being read aesthetically for the explicit teaching of reading skills.
3. Do not preface aesthetic reading with requests for information or analysis that require predominantly efferent reading.[49]

It may be worth those within the church reflecting on their use of the Bible and rebalancing a prevailing efferent reading stance by incorporating some of Rosenblatt's suggestions and reading the Bible from an aesthetic standpoint as well.[50]

Finally, as many of my participants demonstrated, a reader can dominate the reading of a text. For example, Sam believed that the Bible's central message could be summed up in the equation: do X or Y will happen. That equation was then what he found when reading the texts, thus confirming his original belief. This shows how a reader's relationship with the text can shape her or his reading and result in the affirmation of that prior relationship. However, my participants were not alone in this act, as highlighted by Bonhoeffer's accusation to Christians of his day that "we no longer read the Bible seriously, we no longer read it against ourselves, but for ourselves."[51]

---

48. Paauw, *Saving the Bible from Ourselves*.

49. Rosenblatt, *Making Meaning with Texts*, 102–3. She also suggests: "4. Do not hurry the young reader away from the lived-through aesthetic experience by too quickly demanding summaries, paraphrases, character analyses, explanations of broad themes. 5. Do not hurry the young reader into substituting literacy terminology or definitions for the lived-through work." These last two suggestions appear less relevant to contemporary British church practice.

50. With David Smith, I am not advocating a purely aesthetical reading of the Bible, rather in light of the possibility that the Bible is normally read from an efferent stance provision should be made for engaging with it from an aesthetical standpoint as well. See: Smith, "The Poet, the Child and the Blackbird."

51. Bonhoeffer, *No Rusty Swords*, 185.

The ease with which my participants (un)consciously read the Bible affirming their prior expectations or assumptions should act as a warning to those of us, myself included, who read the Bible regularly. I would suggest that it is just as easy for a regular Bible reader to read the Bible in this reaffirming way, as it was for my participants.

This need not be the case, on occasion it may be that the text leads us into an unexpected reading which does not conform to our prior expectations, as was the case for Stuart, Ethan, and Phil. It is also possible for the reader to decide to "be fair," and to some degree withhold their expectations and assumptions, allowing the text to play a fuller role in the reading transaction. This latter option was one that required a conscious decision on Victor's part and is perhaps one way in which the Bible can be read lessening the chances of reading it "for ourselves." Miroslav Volf makes a similar point when discussing how to read the Bible as scripture:

> We can continue to engage the text without suppressing puzzlement or even negative judgement, while patiently waiting for the sense to emerge, either as a result of a new insight or of a personal transformation. In our encounter with the Bible, tarrying in persistent non-understanding is often the condition of the possibility of genuine disclosure, in which we hear more than just the echo of our own internal voice.[52]

Volf is arguing for the need of a reader's patience when engaging with the Bible and critical judgment that assumes the text is neither corrupt nor passively accepts all that it claims.

Limitations and Further Research

There were of course various limitations with my case study, some of which I have noted earlier, and there are three more worth considering now. First, my case study significantly focused on four aspects of a reader's relationship with a text, his or her experiences, identity, attitudes, and beliefs. I concentrated on these four areas because they emerged as main themes in my data and presenting them individually enabled me to explore each in greater depth. However, as I explained in chapter 4, I am not suggesting that these are the only aspects that make up a reader's relationship with a text. This highlights the need for further research into the relational nature of reading, encompassing aspects I did not address. For example, I did not attempt to formally consider the role of the reader's personality, nor did I consider

---

52. Volf, *Captive to the Word of God*, 35.

the participant's temperament on any particular day, or the influence they had upon each other as they spoke about the project outside my lunchtime visits. These are all part of a reader's relationship with a text that could be expected to influence their reading.

Furthermore, although the four aspects that I noted significantly informed the readings that took place they should not be thought of as being unconnected or mutually exclusive, rather two, three, or all four of them will have played a significant role in any one participant's reading. Rosenblatt notes "the various strands of response are often simultaneous, often interwoven, and often interacting."[53] For instance, Gary read the texts in a detached way because of his prior experiences of Christianity. However, his sense of a religious identity ("not at all religious") and beliefs about the Bible (that it is a guidebook and was going to try to convert him) also informed his reading. These three different aspects were all part of Gary's relationship with the five biblical texts and shaped that reading; each reinforcing or working in tandem with the other, so his experiences informed his sense of identity and that identity reinforced the irrelevance with which he treated the texts, and so on. My decision to present the four aspects as distinct components does not do justice to their interlacing nature.

This suggests there is scope for further research, perhaps addressing the question: What is the British public's relationship with the Bible? Unlike other research into biblical literacy that has subdivided it into different parts or in my own case compartmentalized the reader's relationship with the Bible, I would advocate an approach that is able to respond and appreciate the flowing, contradictory, and interweaving nature of people's relationships with the Bible. Ethnography would be one such approach, as would undertaking a single case study, as Mike Jennings did,[54] for both would provide the degree of depth required to trace the various components of the reading transactions.

Another limitation of this study is that although all the participants volunteered to take part, they did so at my request, reading texts that I had chosen for them. This is one of the particularities of my case study and raises the question: How would these men have read the Bible if they had personally chosen to pick it up, say in a hotel room, and read it in the privacy of that setting? Would their readings have been any different? Phil suggested that reading the Bible in such a context (that is out of his own volition) would have resulted in a "completely different" reading. He felt the research setting had encouraged him to "nit-pick," or highlight "the negatives."

---

53. Rosenblatt, *The Reader, the Text, the Poem*, 69.
54. Jennings, "Word and Spirit."

Phil: It's only because we've been asked to provide answers that you nit-pick in a sense, if I was reading without this kind of influence, I'd have just sat, read it, and I'd read it and I'd put it back down.

David: OK, yep.

Phil: But I think that's just a natural reaction, people are picking out the negatives.

I would agree with Phil, in that I too think if my participants were to have read the five texts out of their own volition, the results would have been different. Perhaps the degree of counter-reading would have been less, and as Phil suggests the readers would not have nit-picked as much. My presence, along with my associated "religious" identity, and the research materials doubtless influenced the readings that took place. However, I disagree that the research personnel, setting, and tools inevitably resulted in the men reading skeptically. If, as Phil suggests, they strongly encouraged the participants to focus on the negative parts of the text then I would have expected all the readers to have done this, but they did not. The data shows that those who identified as "religious" were less likely to "nit-pick," whilst those who were "not religious" were more likely to "nit-pick." The participants' religious identity correlated with the degree to which they read skeptically, suggesting this was a bigger factor.

The influence of my research methods upon the readings undertaken raises five different research avenues which may be worth subsequent exploration. First, much as the GOMA Bible annotation was undertaken in a setting where the public could choose to read and write on the Bible. So too, providing a series of similar sanctioned contexts where the public could read and respond to the Bible would be one way of removing the need to ask specific people to volunteer. Second, contrasting Bible readings in two different settings would be a further way of exploring the influence of the research materials and context upon the reading. For instance, if someone were to read a text out of a large black Bible in a Cathedral would they read it differently to one accessed from a smartphone in a coffee shop? Furthermore, simply asking "what did you make of that?" rather than inviting the reader to annotate and fill in a questionnaire would also add to the normalcy of the event rather than reinforcing its research nature. Third, if readers' relationships with the Bible shape their reading of it, a comparison between how people read a text unaware that it was from the Bible and read it aware that it is a biblical text would shed light on how people view the Bible. Fourth, a similar comparison could be carried out with other

CONCLUSION: IMPLICATIONS OF RELATIONAL BIBLE READING   217

sacred texts, where the same reader is asked to read something from the Qu'ran, the Bible, the Vedas (the sacred texts from the three largest religious groups in Britain) along with a text written by an atheist or agnostic. This again would reveal something of the reader's relationship with these various groups. Fifth, all of these examples are snapshots of people's relationships with the Bible, and this raises the need for a longitudinal component similar to Webster,[55] Jennings,[56] and Macdonald.[57] How would reading an entire book from the Bible over a series of weeks inform the reader's relationship with the text? Would the relationship change, and if so in what way?

Finally, my case study assumed a reader-response and sociological approach to this subject. However, in doing so I was not claiming that my findings would fully explain the readings that took place; rather I was providing one particular perspective on them. This is a further limitation, for these readings could have been considered from a psychological, historical, philosophical, or Christian theological perspective. For instance, as I noted in chapter 1, in biblical studies the historical-critical method is still widely used.[58] However, because of the reader-response nature of this project I did not consider the implied authorial intent. Also, within Christian theology the Holy Spirit is understood to illuminate readers, convincing them of the significance and implications of the biblical text.[59] Due to the approach I have adopted though I did not reflect on the role of the Holy Spirit but rather focused on the participants own recounting of their readings.[60] Thus, there is the need to re-examine Bible reading by those who are non-regular Bible readers but from different theoretical perspectives, complementing my own work.

Conclusion

I began with a question: How would British people, who are not regular Bible readers, read the Bible? My attempt to answer this took me to a Chemical Industrial Plant and to twenty men who worked there. Kindly, they volunteered to read through five biblical texts, sharing their readings

55. Webster, "When the Bible meets the Black Stuff."
56. Jennings, "Word and Spirit."
57. Macdonald, "The Psalms and Spirituality."
58. Clines, "Historical Criticism."
59. Achtemeier, *Inspiration and Authority*, 122–26; Klooster, "The Role of the Holy Spirit in the Hermeneutics Process"; Vanhoozer, *Is There a Meaning in This Text?* 407–31.
60. Village's *The Bible and Lay People*, considers both of these aspects.

with me. Led by the data produced, one overriding theme emerged, that these men's relationships with the five biblical texts shaped their reading of those texts. In other words, the associations evoked in these readers by these biblical texts, heavily informed the readings which followed. Louise Rosenblatt's transactional theory of reading provided the wider theoretical foundation upon which this could be presented for she had argued that a person brings all that he or she is to the reading of a text. In particular, my participants' experiences, identities, attitudes, and beliefs were seen to shape the readings they undertook, and in doing so those same readerly elements were often reaffirmed in the process. This was not always the case however, for there were a few occasions when the texts stimulated the reader to an atypical or unforeseen reading. In this way, I have been arguing that reading is a relational act.

Bibliography

Achtemeier, Paul J. *Inspiration and Authority: Nature and Function of Christian Scripture*. Peabody, MA: Hendrickson, 1999.
Agar, Michael H. *The Professional Stranger: An Informal Introduction to Ethnography*. 2nd ed. Bingley, UK: Emerald Group, 1996.
Aichele, George. *The Control of Biblical Meaning: Canon as Semiotic Mechanism*. Harrisburg, PA: Trinity, 2001.
Aichele, George, et al. *The Postmodern Bible: The Bible and Culture Collective*. New Haven, CT: Yale University Press, 1995.
Alaghbary, Gibreel S. "A Feminist Counter-Reading of 'Indian Women.'" *International Journal of English Linguistics* 3.3 (2013) 23–30. http://www.ccsenet.org/journal/index.php/ijel/article/view/27557/16711
Alter, Robert. *The Art of Biblical Narrative*. 2nd ed. New York: Basic, 2011.
Ammerman, Nancy T. *Bible Believers: Fundamentalist in the Modern World*. New Brunswick, NJ: Rutgers University Press, 1987.
Anderson, Arnold A. *2 Samuel*. Word Biblical Commentary. Dallas, TX: Word, 1989.
———. *The Book of Psalms: Volume 2*. Somerset, UK: Oliphants, 1972.
Anderson, Jance C., and Jeffrey L. Staley, eds. *Taking it Personally: Autobiographical Biblical Criticism*. Atlanta: Scholars, 1995.
Archer, Margaret, et al., eds. *Critical Realism: Essential Readings*. London: Routledge, 1998.
Arweck, Elizabeth. "'I've been christened, but I don't really believe in it': How Young People Articulate Their (Non-)Religious Identities and Perceptions of (Non-)Belief." In *Social Identities between the Sacred and the Secular*, edited by Abby Day et al., 103–25. Farnham, UK: Ashgate, 2013.
Astley, Jeff. "Non-Realism for Beginners?" In *God and Reality: Essays in Christian Non-Realism*, edited by Colin Crowder, 100–113. London: Mowbray, 1997.
———. *Ordinary Theology: Looking, Listening and Leaning in Theology*. Farnham, UK: Ashgate, 2002.
Astley, Jeff, and Leslie J. Francis. *Exploring Ordinary Theology: Everyday Christian Believing and the Church*. Farnham, UK: Ashgate, 2013.
Ault, James M. *Spirit and Flesh: Life in a Fundamentalist Baptist Church*. New York: Knopf, 2004.
Avalos, Hector. "In Praise of Biblical Illiteracy." *The Bible and Interpretation*. (2010). http://www.bibleinterp.com/articles/literate357930.shtml.
Avalos, Hector, et al., eds. *This Abled Body: Rethinking Disabilities in Biblical Studies*. Atlanta: Society of Biblical Literature, 2007.

Bal, Mieke, ed. *Anti-Covenant: Counter-Reading Women's Lives in the Hebrew Bible.* Sheffield, UK: Almond, 1989.

Barber, Cyril J. *Nehemiah and the Dynamics of Effective Leadership.* Neptune, NJ: Loizeaux Brothers, 1976.

Barbour, John D. *Versions of Deconversion: Autobiography and the Loss of Faith.* Charlottesville, VA: The University Press of Virginia, 1994.

Barna. *Transforming Scotland: The State of Christianity, Faith and the Church in Scotland.* Ventura, CA: Barna Group, 2015.

Baron, Akesha. "'The Man Is the Head': Evangelical Discourse and the Construction of Masculinities in a Tzotzil Village." In *The Social Life of Scriptures: Cross-Cultural Perspectives on Biblicism,* edited by James. S. Bielo, 44-63. New Brunswick, NJ: Rutgers University Press, 2009.

Baron, Robert A., and Donn R. Byrne. *Social Psychology.* 9th ed. Needham Heights, MA: Allyn & Bacon, 2000.

Barthes, Roland. "The Death of the Author." In *The Rustle of Language,* edited by Roland Barthes, 49-55. Translated by R. Howard. Berkeley, CA: University of California Press, 1989.

Bartholomew, Craig G., and Michael W. Goheen. *The Drama of Scripture: Finding Our Place in the Biblical Story.* Grand Rapids: Baker Academic, 2004.

Barton, John. "Historical-Critical Approaches." In *The Cambridge Companion to Biblical Interpretation,* edited by John Barton, 9-20. Cambridge: Cambridge University Press, 1998.

———. "Thinking about Reader-Response Criticism." *The Expository Times* 113 (2002) 147-51.

Bates, Robert G. "'In Our Image'? The A. S. Peake Memorial Lecture." *Epworth Review* 36.4 (2009) 30-47.

Bazeley, Patricia. *Qualitative Data Analysis: Practical Strategies.* London: SAGE, 2013.

Beach, Richard. "Critical Issues: Reading and Responding to Literature at the Level of Activity." *Journal of Literacy Research* 32.2 (2000) 237-51.

Beal, Timothy. *The Rise and Fall of the Bible: The Unexpected History of an Accidental Book.* New York: Mariner, 2011.

Beaman, Lori G., and Peter Beyer. "Betwixt and Between: A Canadian Perspective on the Challenges of Researching the Spiritual But Not Religious." In *Social Identities Between the Sacred and the Secular,* edited by Abby Day et al., 127-144. Farnham, UK: Ashgate, 2013.

Begoray, Deborah, et al. "Adolescent Reading/Viewing of Advertisements: Understandings from Transactional and Positioning Theory." *Journal of Adolescent & Adult Literacy* 51.2 (2013) 121-30.

Bell, Judith. *Doing Your Research Project: A Guide for First-Time Researchers in Education, Health and Social Science.* 4th ed. Maidenhead, UK: Open University Press, 2005.

Bennett, Andrew. *Readers and Reading.* Harlow, UK: Longman, 1995.

Bergen, Robert D. *1, 2 Samuel.* The New American Commentary. Nashville, TN: Broadman & Holman, 1996.

Bible Society. "About us." https://www.biblesociety.org.uk/about-us/

———. *Pass It On.* United Kingdom: Bible Society, 2014. http://www.biblesociety.org.uk/press/uploads/final-copy-of-Pass-it-On-research-report_02070706.pdf

Bickley, Paul. *The Problem of Proselytism.* London: Theos, 2015.

Bielo, James S., ed. *The Social Life of Scriptures: Cross-Cultural Perspectives on Biblicism*. New Brunswick, NJ: Rutgers University Press, 2009.

———. *Words upon the Word: An Ethnography of Evangelical Group Bible Study*. New York: New York University Press, 2009.

Bissett, Will. *Outside In: Exploring the View of People in Britain Who Do Not Attend Church Regularly or at All*. Bloomington, IN: WestBow, 2016.

Black, Fiona. C. ed. *The Recycled Bible: Autobiography, Culture and the Space Between*. Atlanta: Society of Biblical Literature, 2006.

Bleich, David. "Epistemological Assumptions in the Study of Response." In *Reader-Response Criticism: From Formalism to Post-Structuralism*, edited by Jane P. Tompkins, 134–63. Baltimore, MD: Johns Hopkins University Press, 1980.

———. "The Identity of Pedagogy and Research in the Study of Response to Literature." In *Researching Response to Literature and the Teaching of Literature Points of Departure*, edited by Charles R. Cooper, 253–72. Norwood, NJ: Ablex, 1985.

———. "Gender Interests in Reading and Language." In *Gender and Reading: Essays on Readers, Texts, and Contexts*, edited by Elizabeth. A. Flynn, and Patricia P. Schweickart, 234–66. Baltimore, MD: Johns Hopkins University Press. 1986

———. *Subjective Criticism*. Baltimore, MD: Johns Hopkins University Press, 1978.

Bonhoeffer, Dietrich. *No Rusty Swords: Letters, Lectures and Notes 1928–1936*. Translated by Edwin H. Robertson and John Bowden. London: Collins, 1965.

Booth, Wayne C. "Foreword." In *Literature as Exploration,* 5th ed., by Louise M. Rosenblatt, vii–xiv. New York: Modern Language Association of America, 1995.

———. *The Rhetoric of Fiction*. 2nd ed. Chicago: University of Chicago Press, 1983.

Boulton, David, and Martyn Hammersley. "Analysis of Unstructured Data." In *Data Collection and Analysis*, 2nd ed., edited by Roger Sapsford and Victor Jupp, 243–59. London: SAGE, 2006.

Brauch, Manfred T. *Abusing Scripture: The Consequences of Misreading the Bible*. Downers Grove, IL: InterVarsity, 2009.

Braun, Willi. "Resisting John: Ambivalent Redactor and Defensive Reader of the Fourth Gospel." *Studies in Religion/Sciences Religieuses* 19 (1990) 59–71.

Brenner, Athalya, and Carole Fontaine, eds. *A Feminist Companion to Reading the Bible: Approaches, Methods and Strategies*. Sheffield, UK: Sheffield Academic Press, 1997.

Brierley, Peter. *Pulling Out of the Nose Dive: A Contemporary Picture of Churchgoing— What the 2005 English Church Census Reveals*. London: Christian Research, 2006.

Briggs, Melody R. *How Children Read Biblical Narrative: An Investigation of Children's Readings of the Gospel of Luke*. Eugene, OR: Wipf & Stock, 2017.

Briggs, Richard. S. *Reading the Bible Wisely: An Introduction to Taking Scripture Seriously*. Rev. ed. Eugene, OR: Cascade, 2011.

———. *The Virtuous Reader: Old Testament Narrative and Interpretive Virtue*. Grand Rapids: Baker Academic, 2010.

British Sociological Association. "Statement of Ethical Practice for the British Sociological Association." http://www.britsoc.co.uk/media/27107/StatementofEthicalPractice.pdf?1432648169491

Britt, Brian. "Male Jealousy and the Suspected Sotah: Toward a Counter-Reading of Numbers 5:11–31". *The Bible and Critical Theory* 3.1 (2007) 5.1–5.19.

Britton, James. *Language and Learning*. Harmondsworth, UK: Penguin, 1970.

British Social Attitudes. "British Social Attitudes 28." http://ir2.flife.de/data/natcen-social-research/igb_html/index.php?bericht_id=1000001&index=&lang=ENG

Brown, Callum. *The Death of Christian Britain: Understanding Secularisation 1800–2000*. 2nd ed. Abingdon, UK: Routledge, 2009.

Brown, Callum, and Gordon Lynch. "Cultural Perspectives." In *Religion and Change in Modern Britain*, edited by Linda Woodhead and Rebecca Catto, 329–51. Abingdon, UK: Routledge, 2012.

Brown, Raymond E. *The Epistles of John*. Anchor Bible. Garden City, NY: Doubleday, 1982.

Brown, Robert M. *Gustavo Gutierrez: An Introduction to Liberation Theology*. Maryknoll, NY: Orbis, 1990.

Bruce, Steve. "The Demise of Christianity in Britain." In *Predicting Religion: Christian, Secular and Alternative Futures*, edited by Grace Davie et al., 53–63. Aldershot, UK: Ashgate, 2003.

Brueggemann, Walter. *The Bible and Postmodern Imagination: Texts under Negotiation*. London: SCM, 1993.

———. *First and Second Samuel*. Interpretation. Louisville, KY: John Knox, 1990.

———. *The Psalms & the Life of Faith*. Edited by Patrick Miller. Minneapolis, MN: Augsburg Fortress, 1995.

———. "The Re-Emergence of Scripture: Post-Liberalism." In *The Bible in Pastoral Practice: Readings in the Place and Function of Scripture in the Church*, edited by Paul Ballard and Stephen R. Holmes, 153–73. London: Darton, Longman and Todd, 2005.

Bullivant Stephen, and Lois Lee. "Interdisciplinary Studies of Non-Religion and Secularity: The State of the Union." *Journal of Contemporary Religion* 27.1 (2012) 19–27.

Bultmann, Rudolf. "Is Exegesis without Presuppositions Possible?" In *The Hermeneutics Reader*, edited by Kurt Mueller-Vollmer, 241–55. New York: Continuum, 1985.

Burgess, Robert G. "Sponsors, Gatekeepers, Members, and Friends: Access in Educational Settings." In *Experiencing Fieldwork: An Inside View of Qualitative Research*, edited by William B. Shaffir and Robert A. Stebbins, 43–52. London: SAGE, 1991.

Bushman, Brad J. "Does Venting Anger Feed or Extinguish the Flame? Catharsis, Rumination, Distraction, Anger, and Aggressive Responding." *Personality and Social Psychology Bulletin* 28.6 (2002) 724–31.

Camery-Hoggatt, Jerry. *Reading the Good Book Well: A Guide to Biblical Interpretation*. Nashville, TN: Abingdon, 2007.

Cardany, Audrey B. "A Transactional Approach to "Sing" by Raposo and Lichtenheld." *General Music Today* 27.3 (2014) 28–32.

Carroll, Robert P. *Wolf in the Sheepfold: The Bible as Problematic for Theology*. 2nd ed. London: SCM, 1997.

Cartledge, Mark J. *Testimony of the Spirit: Rescripting Ordinary Pentecostal Theology*. Farnham, UK: Ashgate, 2010.

Castelli, Elizabeth A., et al., eds. *The Postmodern Bible: The Bible and Culture Collective*. New Haven, CT: Yale University Press, 1995.

Catholic Biblical Federation. "Scriptures Reading." http://www.c-b-f.org/documents/survey_population_general.pdf

Chandler, Siobhan. "The Social Ethic of Religiously Unaffiliated Spirituality." *Religion Compass* 2.2 (2008) 240–56.

Christian Research. *Bible Engagement in England and Wales.* Swindon, UK: Bible Society, 2011.

Christie, Ann. "Jesus as Exemplar." In *Exploring Ordinary Theology: Everyday Christian Believing and the Church,* edited by Jeff Astley and Leslie J. Francis, 77–85. Aldershot, UK: Ashgate, 2013.

———. *Ordinary Christology: Who Do You Say I Am? Answers from The Pews.* Aldershot, UK: Ashgate, 2012.

Clements, Ben. *Surveying Christian Beliefs and Religious Debates in Post-War Britain.* Basingstoke, UK: Palgrave Macmillan, 2016.

Clines, David J. A. *The Bible and the Modern World.* Sheffield, UK: Sheffield Academic Press, 1997.

———. "Historical Criticism: Are its Days Numbered?" *Teologinen Aikakauskirja* 6 (2009) 542–58.

———. *Interested Parties: The Ideology of Writers and Readers of the Hebrew Bible.* Sheffield, UK: Sheffield Academic Press, 1995.

———. *What Does Eve do to Help? And Other Readerly Questions to the Old Testament.* Sheffield, UK: Sheffield Academic Press, 1990.

Collins, Matthew A. "Loss of the Bible and the Bible in *Lost*: Biblical Literacy and Mainstream Television." In *Rethinking Biblical Literacies,* edited by Katie B. Edwards, 71–94. London: Bloomsbury, 2015.

Congar, Yves. M.-J. *Tradition and Traditions: An Historical and Theological Essay.* Translated by Michael Naseby and Thomas Rainborough. London: Burns & Oates, 1966.

Connell, Jeanne M. "The Emergence of Pragmatic Philosophy's Influence on Literary Theory: Making Meaning with Texts from a Transactional Perspective." *Educational Theory* 58.1 (2008) 103–22.

Coolican, Hugh. *Research Methods and Statistics in Psychology.* 6th ed. Hove, UK: Psychology, 2014.

Cornwall, Susannah. "British Intersex Christians' Accounts of Intersex identity, Christian Identity and Church Experience." *Practical Theology* 6.2 (2013) 220–36.

———. "Contextual Bible Study: Characteristics and Challenges." *Modern Believing* 53.1 (2012) 14–22.

Cornwall, Susannah, and David Nixon. "Readings from the Road: Contextual Bible Study with a Group of Homeless and Vulnerably-Housed People." *The Expository Times* 123 (2011) 12–19.

Costantino, Tracie E. "Constructivism." In *The SAGE Encyclopedia of Qualitative Research Methods, Vol. 2,* edited by Lisa M. Given, 116–20. Thousand Oaks, CA: SAGE, 2008.

Crapanzano, Vincent. *Serving the Word: Literalism in America from the Pulpit to the Bench.* New York: New Press, 2000.

Crawford, Mary, and Roger Chaffin. "The Reader's Construction of Meaning: Cognitive Research on Gender and Comprehension." In *Gender and Reading: Essays on Readers, Texts, and Contexts,* edited by Elizabeth A. Flynn, and Patricia P. Schweickart, 3–30. Baltimore, MD: Johns Hopkins University Press, 1983.

Creswell, John W. *Research Design: Qualitative, Quantitative, & Mixed Methods Approaches.* 4th ed. Thousand Oaks, CA: SAGE, 2014.

Crossley, James G. "Biblical Literacy and the English King James Liberal Bible: A Twenty-First Century Tale of Capitalism, Nationalism and Nostalgia." *Postscripts* 7.2 (2011) 197–211.

———. "Brexit Barrow: Real-Time Receptions of the Bible during a Summer of Political Chaos." *Relegere* 6.1 (2016) 19–60.

———. *Harnessing Chaos: The Bible in English Politics and Culture Since 1968*. London: Bloomsbury, 2014.

———. "What the Bible Really Means: Biblical Literacy in English Political Discourse." In *Rethinking Biblical Literacy*, edited by Katie B. Edwards, 23–46. London: Bloomsbury, 2015.

Culler, Jonathan. *The Pursuit of Signs: Semiotics, Literature, Deconstruction*. Ithaca, NY: Cornell University Press, 1981.

Curtis, Andrew. "An Encounter with Ordinary Real Readers Reading the Gospels: Implications for Mission." In *To Cast Fire upon the Earth: Bible and Mission Collaborating in Today's Multicultural Global Context*, edited by Teresa Okure, 126–34. Pietermaritzburg, South Africa: Cluster, 2000.

Damico, James S., et al. "Transactional Theory and Critical Theory in Reading Comprehension." In *Handbook of Research on Reading Comprehension* edited by Susan E. Israel and Gerald G. Duffy, 177–88. New York: Routledge, 2009.

Darr, John A. *On Character Building: The Reader and the Rhetoric of Characterization*. Louisville, KY: Westminster John Knox, 1992.

David, Matthew, and Caroline D. Sutton. *Social Research: An Introduction*. 2nd ed. Thousand Oaks, CA: SAGE, 2011.

Davie, Grace. *Religion in Britain: A Persistent Paradox*. Chichester, UK: Wiley Blackwell, 2015.

———. "Vicarious Religion: A Methodological Challenge." In *Everyday Religion: Observing Modern Religious Lives*, edited by Nancy T. Ammerman, 21–35. Oxford: Oxford University Press, 2007.

Davie, Grace, and Tony Walter. "The Religiosity of Women in the Modern West." *British Journal of Sociology* 49.4 (1998) 640–59.

Davie, Jody S. *Women in the Presence: Constructing Community and Seeking Spirituality in Mainline Protestantism*. Philadelphia: University of Pennsylvania Press, 1995.

Davies, Andrew. *Double Standards in Isaiah: Re-Evaluating Prophetic Ethics and Divine Justice*. Leiden: Brill, 2000.

Davies, Eryl W. *Biblical Criticism: A Guide for the Perplexed*. London: Bloomsbury, 2013.

Davies, Martin. B. *Doing a Successful Research Project: Using Qualitative or Quantitative Methods*. Basingstoke, UK: Palgrave Macmillan, 2007.

Davies, Philip R. "Whose Bible? Anyone's?" *The Bible and Interpretation* (2009). http://www.bibleinterp.com/opeds/whose.shtml

———. *Whose Bible is it Anyway?* 2nd ed. London: T. & T. Clark, 2004.

Davies, William D., and Dale C. Allison. *Matthew: A Shorter Commentary*. London: T. & T. Clark, 2004.

Dawson, Andrew. "The Origins and Character of the Base Ecclesial Community: A Brazilian Perspective." In *The Cambridge Companion to Liberation Theology*, edited by Christopher Rowland, 109–28. Cambridge: Cambridge University Press, 1999.

Day, Abby. *Believing in Belonging: Belief & Social Identity in the Modern World*. Oxford: Oxford University Press, 2011.

Day, Abby, et al., eds. *Social Identities Between the Sacred and the Secular*. Farnham, UK: Ashgate, 2013.

Denscombe, Martyn. *The Good Research Guide: For Small-Scale Social Research Projects*. 3rd ed. Maidenhead, UK: Open University Press, 2007.

Denzin, Norman K. *Interpretive Ethnography: Ethnographic Practices for the 21st Century*. Thousand Oaks, CA: SAGE, 1997.

Detweiler, Robert. "What is a Sacred Text?" *Semeia* 31 (1985) 213–30.

Dewey, John. *Logic: The Theory of Inquiry*. New York: Holt, Rienhart and Winston, 1938.

———. "Propositions, Warranted Assertibility, and Truth." *The Journal of Philosophy* 38.7 (1941) 169–86.

Dewey, John, and Arthur F. Bentley. *Knowing and the Known*. Boston: Beacon, 1949.

Dickson, J. N. Ian. "The Bible in Pastoral Ministry: The Quest for Best Practice." *Journal of Adult Theological Education* 4.1 (2007) 103–21.

Dillard, Annie. *Living By Fiction*. New York: Harper & Row, 1982.

Domeris, William R. "Reading the Bible Against the Grain." *Scriptura* 37 (1991) 68–81.

Dube, Musa W. *Postcolonial Feminist Interpretation of the Bible*. St. Louise, MO: Chalice, 2000.

Dugan, JoAnn. "Transactional Literature Discussions: Engaging Students in the Appreciation and Understanding of Literature." *The Reading Teacher* 51.2 (1997) 86–96.

Eagleton, Terry. "The Estate Agent." *London Review of Books* 22.5 (2000) 10–11.

———. *The Event of Literature*. New Haven, CT: Yale University Press, 2012.

Edwards, Katie. B. *Admen and Eve: The Bible in Advertising*. Sheffield, UK: Sheffield Phoenix, 2012.

———, ed. *Rethinking Biblical Literacy*. London: Bloomsbury, 2015.

Eiser, J. Richard. "Accentuation Revisited." In *Social Groups & Identities: Developing the Legacy of Henri Tajfel*, edited by William P. Robinson, 121–42. Oxford: Butterworth Heinemann, 1996.

Engelke, Matthew. *God's Agents: Biblical Publicity in Contemporary England*. Berkeley, CA: University of California Press, 2013.

———. *A Problem of Presence: Beyond Scripture in an African Church*. Berkeley, CA: University of California Press, 2007.

Esler, Philip. *New Testament Theology: Communion and Community*. Minneapolis, MN: Fortress, 2005.

Fee, Gordon D., and Mark L. Strauss. *How to Choose a Translation for All Its Worth: A Guide to Understanding and Using Bible Versions*. Grand Rapids: Zondervan, 2007.

Fetterley, Judith. *The Resisting Reader: A Feminist Approach to American Fiction*. Bloomington, IN: Indiana University Press, 1978.

Field, Clive D. "Is the Bible Becoming a Closed Book? British Opinion Poll Evidence." *Journal of Contemporary Religion* 29.3 (2014) 503–28.

Fiorenza, Elisabeth S. *Bread Not Stone: The Challenge of Feminist Biblical Interpretation*. Boston: Beacon, 1984.

———, ed. *Searching the Scriptures: A Feminist Introduction*. London: SCM, 1993.

Fiorenza, Francis S. "Systematic Theology: Tasks and Methods." In *Systematic Theology: Roman Catholic Perspectives*, 2nd ed., edited by Francis S. Fiorenza and John P. Galvin, 1–88. Minneapolis, MN: Fortress, 2011.

Fish, Stanley E. "Interpreting the "Variorum."" *Critical Inquiry* 2.3 (1976) 465–85.

———. *Is There A Text in This Class? The Authority of Interpretive Communities.* Cambridge: Harvard University Press, 1980.

———. *Surprised by Sin: The Reader in Paradise Lost.* 2nd ed. Cambridge: Harvard University Press, 1997.

———. "Why No One's Afraid of Wolfgang Iser." *Diacritics* 11.1 (1981) 2–13.

Flynn, Elizabeth A. "Gender and Reading." In *Gender and Reading: Essays on Readers, Texts, and Contexts,* edited by Elizabeth A. Flynn and Patrocinio P. Schweickart, 267–88. Baltimore, MD: Johns Hopkins University Press, 1986.

Flyvbjerg, Bent. "Case Study." In *The SAGE Handbook of Qualitative Research,* edited by Norman K. Denzin and Yvonna S. Lincoln, 301–16. Thousand Oaks, CA: SAGE, 2011.

Ford, David F. "An Interfaith Wisdom: Scriptural Reasoning between Jews, Christians and Muslims." *Modern Theology* 22.3 (2006) 345–66.

Fowler, Robert M. *Let the Reader Understand: Reader-Response Criticism and the Gospel of Mark.* Rev. ed. Harrisburg, PA: Trinity, 2001.

———. "Who is "the Reader" in Reader Response Criticism?" *Semeia* 31 (1985) 5–23.

Francis, Leslie J. "Monitoring the Christian Development of the Child." In *Family, School and Church in Religious Education* edited by Leslie J. Francis et al., 1–25. Edinburgh: Department of Christian Ethics and Practical Theology, University of Edinburgh, 1984.

———. "Ordinary Readers and Reader Perspectives on Sacred Texts: Drawing on Empirical Theology and Jungian Psychology." In *Exploring Ordinary Theology,* edited by Jeff Astley and Leslie J. Francis, 87–96. Aldershot, UK: Ashgate, 2013.

———. *Personality Type and Scripture: Exploring Mark's Gospel.* London: Mowbray, 1997.

———. "What Happened to the Fig Tree? An Empirical Study in Psychological Type and Biblical Hermeneutics." *Mental Health, Religion & Culture* 15.9 (2012) 873–91.

Francis, Leslie J., and Andrew Village. *Preaching with All Our Souls: A Study in Hermeneutics and Psychological Type.* London: Continuum, 2008.

Francis, Leslie J., and Jeff Astley. "The Quest for the Psychological Jesus: Influences of Personality on Images of Jesus." *Journal of Psychology and Christianity* 16 (1997) 247–59.

Francis, Leslie J., and William K. Kay. "Attitude towards Religion: Definition, Measurement and Evaluation." *British Journal of Educational Studies* 32 (1984) 45–50.

Franzosi, Roberto P. "Content Analysis." In *Handbook of Data Analysis,* edited by Melissa Hardy and Alan Bryman, 547–65. London: SAGE, 2004.

Freathy, Rob J. K. "Gender, Age, Attendance at a Place of Worship and Young People's Attitudes towards the Bible." *Journal of Beliefs and Values* 27.3 (2006) 327–39.

Fuller, Robert C. *Spiritual But Not Religious: Understanding Unchurched America.* New York: Oxford University Press, 2001.

Gadamer, Hans-Georg. *Truth and Method.* London: Sheed and Ward, 1979.

Garrett, Duane A. *Proverbs Ecclesiastes Song of Songs.* The New American Commentary. Nashville, TN: Broadman, 1993.

Gerring, John. *Case Study Research: Principles and Practices.* Cambridge: Cambridge University Press, 2007.

Gibson, Walker. "Authors, Speakers, Readers, and Mock Readers." In *Reader-Response Criticism: From Formalism to Post-Structuralism*, edited by Jane P. Tompkins, 1–6. Baltimore, MD: Johns Hopkins University Press, 1980.

Gill, Robin, et al. "Is Religious Belief Declining in Britain?" *Journal for the Scientific Study of Religion* 37.3 (1998) 507–16.

Glaser, Barney G., and Anselm L. Strauss. *The Discovery of Grounded Theory: Strategies for Qualitative Research*. New York: Aldine de Gruyter, 1967.

Goldstein, Daniel M. "Desconfianza and Problems of Representation in Urban Ethnography." *Anthropological Quarterly* 75.3 2002 485–517.

Gorman, Michael J. *Elements of Biblical Exegesis: A Basic Guide for Students and Ministers*. Rev. ed. Peabody, MA: Hendrickson, 2009.

Gottwald, Norman K., and Richard A. Horsley, eds. *The Bible and Liberation: Political and Social Hermeneutics*. Rev. ed. London: SPCK, 1993.

Gray, David E. *Doing Research in the Real World*. 2nd ed. London: SAGE, 2009.

Greil, Arthur L., and Lynn Davidman. "Religion and Identity." In *The SAGE Handbook of the Sociology of Religion*, edited by James A. Beckford and Jay Demerath III, 549–65. London: SAGE, 2007.

Guest, Deryn, et al., eds. *The Queer Bible Commentary*. London: SCM, 2006.

Guy, Pat. *Transforming Reading Skills in the Secondary School: Simple Strategies for Improving Literacy*. Abingdon, UK: Routledge, 2015.

Hagner, Donald A. *Matthew 14–28*. Word Biblical Commentary. Dallas, TX: Word, 1995.

Hamberg, Eva. M. "Unchurched Spirituality." In *The Oxford Handbook of The Sociology of Religion*, edited by Peter B. Clarke, 742–57. Oxford: Oxford University Press, 2009.

Hammersley, Martyn, and Paul Atkinson. *Ethnography: Principles in Practice*. 3rd ed. Abingdon, UK: Routledge, 2007.

Hammersley, Martyn, and Roger Gomm. "Introduction." In *Case Study Method: Key Issues, Key Texts*, edited by Roger Gomm et al., 1–16. London: SAGE, 2000.

Hampson, Daphne. *After Christianity*. London: SCM, 1996.

Handler, Richard. "The Uses of Incommensurability in Anthropology." *New Literary History* 40.3 (2009) 627–47.

Hankle, Dominick D. "The Therapeutic Implications of the Imprecatory Psalms in the Christian Counseling Setting." *Journal of Psychology and Theology* 38.4 (2010) 275–80.

Harding, James E. "In the Name of Love: Resisting Reader and Abusive Redeemer in Deutero-Isaiah." *The Bible and Critical Theory* 2.2 (2006) 14.1–14.15.

Harding, Jamie. *Qualitative Data Analysis from Start to Finish*. London: SAGE, 2013.

Harrison, Jan. *Attitudes to Bible, God, Church: Research Report*. London: Bible Society, 1983.

Hartley, Jenny. *Reading Groups*. Oxford: Oxford University Press, 2001.

Harvey, Stephanie, and Anne Goudvis. *Strategies That Work: Teaching Comprehension for Understanding and Engagement*. Portland, ME: Stenhouse, 2007.

Hauerwas, Stanley. *Unleashing the Scripture: Freeing the Bible from Captivity to America*. Nashville, TN: Abingdon, 1993.

Havea, Jione, et al., eds. *Bible, Borders, Belonging(s): Engaging Readings from Oceania*. Atlanta: Society of Biblical Literature, 2014.

Hay, David, and Kate Hunt. "Understanding the Spirituality of People Who Don't Go to Church: A Report on the Findings of the Adults' Spirituality Project at the University of Nottingham." http://www.churchofscotland.org.uk/__data/assets/pdf_file/0006/3678/understanding_spirituality_report.pdf

Heelas, Paul, and Linda Woodhead. *The Spiritual Revolution: Why Religion is Giving Way to Spirituality*. Oxford: Blackwell, 2005.

Heidegger, Martin. *Supplements: From the Earliest Essays to Being and Time and Beyond*. Translated by J. van Buren. 1919/21. Albany, NY: State University of New York, 2002.

Hermes, Joke. *Reading Women's Magazines: An Analysis of Everyday Media Use*. Cambridge: Polity, 1995.

Herriot, Peter. *Religious Fundamentalism and Social Identity*. London: Routledge, 2007.

Hess, David. *Science in the New Age: The Paranormal, Its Defenders and Debunkers, and American Culture*. Madison, WI: University of Wisconsin Press, 1993.

Higton, Mike. "Scriptural Reasoning." *Conversations in Religion and Theology* 7.2 (2009) 129–33.

Higton, Mike, and Rachel Muers. *The TEXT in PLAY: Experiments in Reading Scripture*. Eugene, OR: Cascade, 2012.

Hine, Iona C., et al. "Practicing Biblical Literacy: Case Studies from the Sheffield Conference." *Postscripts* 7.2 (2011) 173–96.

Hirsch, E. D. *Validity of Interpretation*. New Haven, CT: Yale University Press, 1967.

Hogg, Michael A., and Dominic Abrams. *Social Identifications: A Social Psychology of Intergroup Relationship and Group Processes*. London: Routledge, 1998.

Hogg, Michael A., and Graham M. Vaughan. *Social Psychology*. 6th ed. Harlow, UK: Pearson Education Limited, 2011.

Hoggart, Richard. *The Uses of Literacy: Aspects of Working-Class Life with Special Reference to Publications and Entertainments*. Harmondsworth, UK: Penguin, 1957.

Hoggarth, Pauline. *The Seed and the Soil: Engaging with the Word of God*. Carlisle, UK: Global Christian Library, 2011.

Holland, Norman N. *The Nature of Literary Response: Five Readers Reading*. 2nd ed. New Brunswick, NJ: Transaction, 2011.

———. *Poems in Persons: An Introduction to the Psychoanalysis of Literature*. New York: Norton, 1973.

———. "Re-Covering 'The Purloined Letter': Reading as a Personal Transaction." In *The Reader in the Text: Essays on Audience and Interpretation*, edited by Susan R. Suleiman, and Inge Crosman, 350–70. Princeton, NJ: Princeton University Press, 1980.

———. "Unit Identity Text Self." In *Reader-Response Criticism: From Formalism to Post-Structuralism*, edited by Jane P. Tompkins, 118–33. Baltimore, MD: Johns Hopkins University Press, 1980.

Horrell, David G. *The Bible and the Environment: Towards a Critical Ecological Biblical Theology*. London: Equinox, 2010.

Horrell, David G., et al., eds. *Ecological Hermeneutics: Biblical, Historical and Theological Perspectives*. London: T. & .T Clark, 2010.

Horrell, David G., et al., eds. *Greening Paul, Rereading the Apostle in a Time of Ecological Crisis*. Waco, TX: Baylor University Press, 2010.

Hossfeld, Frank-Lothar, and Erich Zenger. *Psalms 2*. Hermeneia. Minneapolis, MN: Augsburg Fortress, 2005.

Hull, John. *In the Beginning There Was Darkness*. London: SCM, 2001.

Hutchings, Tim. "E-Reading and the Christian Bible." *Studies in Religion/Sceinces Religieuses* 44.4 (2012) 423–40.

Ipsen, Avaren. *Sex Working and the Bible*. London: Equinox, 2009.

Iser, Wolfgang. *The Act of Reading: A Theory of Aesthetic Response*. Baltimore, MD: The John Hopkins University Press, 1978.

———. *The Implied Reader: Patterns of Communication in Prose Fiction from Bunyan to Beckett*. Baltimore, MD: Johns Hopkins University Press, 1974.

———. *Prospecting: From Reader Response to Literary Anthropology*. Baltimore, MD: Johns Hopkins University Press, 1989.

———. "The Reading Process: A Phenomenological Approach." In *Reader-Response Criticism: From Formalism to Post-Structuralism*, edited by Jane P. Tompkins, 50–69. Baltimore, MD: Johns Hopkins University Press, 1980.

James, William. *Principles of Psychology*. 1890. Reprint. Cambridge: Harvard University Press, 1981.

Jamieson, Alan. *A Churchless Faith: Faith Journeys beyond the Churches*. London: SPCK, 2002.

Janesick, Valerie J. *"Stretching" Exercises for Qualitative Researchers*. 2nd ed. Thousand Oaks, CA: SAGE, 2004.

Jasper, David. "How Can We Read the Bible?" In *English Literature, Theology and the Curriculum*, edited by Liam Gearon, 9–26. London: Cassell, 1999.

———. *A Short Introduction to Hermeneutics*. Louisville, KY: Westminster John Knox, 2004.

Jemmer, Patrick. "Abreaction—Catharsis: Stirring Dull Roots with Spring Rain." *European Journal of Clinical Hypnosis* 7.1 (2006) 26–36.

Jenks, Gregory C. "The Sign of Jonah: Reading Jonah on the Boundaries and from the Boundaries." In *Engaging Readings from Oceania*, edited by Jione Havea et al., 223–38. Atlanta: Society of Biblical Literature, 2014.

Jennings, Mike. "Word and Spirit: Reading Stance and Selected Emerging-Adult Reader Attributions of Experience of God in Church-Situated Readings of the Bible." PhD diss., University of Leeds, 2011.

Karolides, Nicholas J. "The Transactional Theory of Literature." In *Reader Response in Secondary and College Classrooms*, edited by Nicholas J. Karolides, 3–24. Mahwah, NJ: Lawrence Erlbaum Associates, 2000.

Keener, Craig S. *A Commentary on the Gospel of Matthew*. Grand Rapids: Eerdmans, 1995.

Keller, Eva. *The Road to Clarity: Seventh-Day Adventism in Madagascar*. New York: Palgrave MacMillan, 2005.

Kendall, Carol. *The Gammage Cup*. New York: Hardcourt, Brace, 1959

Kendall, Elizabeth. *Myers-Briggs Type Indicator: Step 1 Manual Supplement*. Palo Alto, CA: Consulting Psychologists, 1998.

Kesler, Ted. "Evoking the World of Poetic Nonfiction Picture Books." *Children's Literature in Education* 43.4 (2012) 338–54.

Killingray, Margaret. *Encouraging Biblical Literacy*. Cambridge: Grove, 1997.

King, Ursula. *The Search for Spirituality: Our Global Quest for Meaning and Fulfilment*. Norwich, UK: Canterbury, 2009.

Kitzberger, Ingrid R., ed. *Autobiographical Biblical Criticism: Between Text and Self.* Leiden, Netherlands: Deo, 2002.

———, ed. *The Personal Voice in Biblical Interpretation.* London: Routledge, 1999.

Klooster, Fred H. "The Role of the Holy Spirit in the Hermeneutics Process: The Relationship of the Spirit's Illumination to Biblical Interpretation." In *Hermeneutics, Inerrancy, and the Bible*, edited by Earl D. Radmacher, and Robert D. Preus, 451–72. Grand Rapids: Zondervan, 1984.

Koptak, Paul. E. *Proverbs.* The NIV Application Commentary. Grand Rapids: Zondervan, 2003.

Krahé, Barbara. "Aggression." In *An Introduction to Social Psychology*, 5th ed., edited by Miles Hewstone, et al., 273–312. Chichester, UK: Wiley & Sons, 2012.

Kümmel, Werner. G. *The New Testament: The History of the Investigation of its Problems.* 2nd ed. Translated by S. McLean Gilmour and Howard C. Kee. London: SCM, 1973.

Kvale, Steinar, and Svend Brinkmann. *InterViews: Learning the Craft of Qualitative Research Interviewing.* 2nd ed. Thousand Oaks, CA: SAGE, 2009.

Langer, Judith A. *Envisioning Knowledge: Building Literacy in the Academic Disciplines.* New York: Teachers College, 2011.

Lau, Peter H. W. *Identity and Ethics in the Book of Ruth: A Social Identity Approach.* Berlin, Germany: de Gruyter GmbH & Co, 2011.

Lawrence, Louise J. *The Word in Place: Reading the New Testament in Contemporary Contexts.* London: SPCK, 2009.

Le Grys, Alan. *Shaped by God's Story: Making Sense of the Bible.* London: Lulu, 2010.

Lee, Lois. "Research Note: Talking about a Revolution: Terminology for the New Field of Non-Religion Studies." *Journal of Contemporary Religion* 27.1 (2012) 129–39.

———. "Secular or Nonreligious? Investigating and Interpreting Generic 'Not Religious' Categories and Populations." *Religion* 44.3 (2014) 466–82.

Leland, Christine, et al. "Reading from Different Interpretive Stances: In Search of a Critical Perspective." *Journal of Adolescent & Adult Literacy* 55.5 (2012) 428–37.

Leonard, Alison. *Living in Godless Times: Tales of Spiritual Travellers.* Edinburgh: Floris, 2001.

Leslie, Lauren, and JoAnne S. Caldwell. "Formal and Informal Measures of Reading Comprehension." In *Handbook of Research on Reading Comprehension*, edited by Susan E. Israel, and Gerald G. Duffy, 403–27. New York: Routledge, 2009.

Levison, John. R., and Priscilla Pope-Levison, eds. *Return to Babel: Global Perspectives on the Bible.* Louisville, KY: Westminster John Knox, 1999.

Lewis, Cynthia. "Limits of Identification: The Personal, Pleasurable, and Critical in Reader Response." *Journal of Literacy Research* 32.2 (2000) 253–66.

Lewis, Hannah. *Deaf Liberation Theology.* Aldershot, UK: Ashgate, 2007.

Llewellyn, Dawn. *Reading, Feminism, and Spirituality: Troubling the Waves.* London: Palgrave Macmillan, 2015.

Logan, Sarah, and Rhona Johnston. "Investigating Gender Differences in Reading." *Educational Review* 62.2 (2010) 175–87.

Loman, Susan E., and Leslie J. Francis. "The Loman Index of Biblical Interpretation: Distinguishing between Literal, Symbolic and Rejecting Modes among 11 to 14 Year Olds." *British Journal of Religious Education* 28.2 (2006) 131–40.

Longman III, Tremper. *Proverbs.* Baker Commentary on the Old Testament. Grand Rapids: Baker Academic, 2006.

Lynch, Gordon. *Losing My Religion? Moving on from Evangelical Faith.* London: Darton, Longman and Todd, 2003.

Lyons, Evanthia. "Social Psychology 1." In *Psychology: An Integrated Approach,* edited by Michael W. Eysenck, 323–55. Harlow, UK: Pearson Education Limited, 1998.

Macdonald, Fergus A. J. "Engaging the Scriptures: The Challenge to Recover Biblical Literacy." *Scottish Bulletin of Evangelical Theology* 27.2 (2009) 192–213.

———. "The Psalms and Spirituality: A Study of Meditative Engagement with Selected Psalms among Edinburgh Students." PhD diss., University of Edinburgh, 2007.

Magonet, Jonathan. *A Rabbi's Bible.* London: SCM, 1991.

Major, Brenda, and Laurie T. O'Brien. "The Social Psychology of Stigma." *Annual Review of Psychology* 56.1 (2005) 393–421.

Malley, Brian. *How the Bible Works: An Anthropological Study of Evangelical Biblicism.* Walnut Creek, CA: Altamira, 2004.

Mann, Leon. "The Baiting Crowd in Episodes of Threatened Suicide." *Journal of Personality and Social Psychology* 41.4 (1981) 703–9.

Mardel. "Bible Translation Guide." http://www.mardel.com/bible-translation-guide.aspx.

Marler, Penny L., and C. Kirk Hadaway. ""Being Religious" or "Being Spiritual" in America: A Zero Sum Proposition?" *Journal for the Scientific Study of Religion* 41.2 (2002) 289–300.

Marshall, I. Howard. *The Epistles of John.* The New International Commentary on the New Testament. Grand Rapids: Eerdmans, 1978.

Mason, Jennifer. *Qualitative Researching.* London: SAGE, 2002.

McCallum, Nema. "Anonymity Desirable, Bibliography Not Required: A Journey from Psychiatry to Theology." *Theology & Sexuality* 14.1 (2007) 29–52.

McCutcheon, Russell T. *The Insider/Outsider Problem in the Study of Religion: A Reader.* London: Cassell, 1999.

McKnight, Edgar V. *Postmodern Use of the Bible: Emergence of Reader-Oriented Criticism.* Nashville, TN: Abingdon, 1988.

———. "Reader-Response Criticism." In *To Each Its Own Meaning: An Introduction to Biblical Criticisms and Their Application,* edited by Steven L. McKenzie, and Stephen R. Haynes, 197–220. London: Chapman, 1993.

McKnight, Scott. *The Blue Parakeet: Rethinking How you Read the Bible.* Grand Rapids: Zondervan, 2008.

McLaughlin, Maureen, and Glenn DeVoogd. "Critical Literacy as Comprehension: Expanding Reader Response." *Journal of Adolescent & Adult Literacy* 48.1 (2004) 52–82.

Meredith, Christopher. "A Big Room for Poo: Eddie Izzard's Bible and the Literacy of Laughter." In *Rethinking Biblical Literacy,* edited by Katie B. Edwards, 187–212. London: Bloomsbury, 2015.

Mesters, Carlos. *Defenseless Flower: A New Reading of the Bible.* Translated by Francis McDonagh. 1983. Maryknoll, NY: Orbis, 1989.

Mézié, Nadège. ""WI, se kretyènn mwen ye" (Yes, I am Christian): Methodological Falsehood in Fieldwork." *Fieldwork in Religion* 5.2 (2010) 180–192.

Middlebrook, Patricia N. *Social Psychology & Modern Life.* 2nd ed. New York: Knopf, 1980.

Miller, Samuel D., and Beverly S. Faircloth. "Motivation and Reading Comprehension." In *Handbook of Research on Reading Comprehension*, edited by Susan E. Israel and Gerald G. Duffy, 307–22. New York: Routledge, 2009.

Miller, Patrick D. *Interpreting the Psalms*. Philadelphia: Fortress, 1986.

Milne, Pamela J. "Toward Feminist Companionship: The Future of Feminist Biblical Studies and Feminism." In *A Feminist Companion to Reading the Bible: Approaches, Methods and Strategies*, edited by Athalya Brenner, and Carole Fontaine, 39–60. Sheffield, UK: Sheffield Academic Press, 1997.

Morgan, F. "Raising Awareness of the Bible in Contemporary British Society: A Case Study of Young Adults Who Are Not Involved in a Faith Community." *Encounters Mission Ezine* 27 (2008) 1–18.

Morris, Wayne. *Theology without Words: Theology in the Deaf Community*. Aldershot, UK: Ashgate, 2008.

Moore, Stephen D. "Negative Hermeneutics, Insubstantial Texts: Stanley Fish and the Biblical Interpreter." *Journal of the American Academy of Religion* 54.4 (1986) 707–19.

———. "Revolting Revelations." In *The Personal Voice in Biblical Interpretation*, edited by Ingrid R. Kitzberger, 183–200. London: Routledge, 1999.

Moore, Zoe B. *Introducing Feminist Perspectives on Pastoral Theology*. Sheffield, UK: Sheffield Academic Press, 2002.

Morf, Carolyn, C., and Sander L. Koole. "The Self." In *An Introduction to Social Psychology* edited by Miles Hewstone et al., 6th ed., 123–70. Chichester, UK: Wiley & Sons, 2015.

Murphy, Roland E. *Proverbs*. Word Biblical Commentary. Nashville, TN: Thomas Nelson, 1998.

Murphy, Liam D. "The Trouble with Good News: Scripture and Charisma in Northern Ireland." In *The Social Life of Scriptures: Cross-Cultural Perspectives on Biblicism*, edited by James S. Bielo, 10–29. New Brunswick, NJ: Rutgers University Press, 2009.

Murray, Stuart. *Biblical Interpretation in the Anabaptist Tradition*. Kitchener, ON: Pandora, 2000

———. *Post-Christendom: Church and Mission in a Strange New World*. Milton Keynes, UK: Paternoster, 2004.

Muskus, Eddy J. *The Origins and Early Development of Liberation Theology in Latin America*. Carlisle, UK: Paternoster, 2002.

Myers, Isabel B., and Peter B. Myers. *Gifts Differing: Understanding Personality Type*. Mountain View, CA: CPP, 1995.

Meyerstein, Israela, and Gila Ruskin. "Spiritual Tools for Enhancing the Pastoral Visit to Hospitalized Patients." *Journal of Religion and Health* 46.1 (2007) 109–22.

Neal, Lynn S. *Romancing God: Evangelical Women and Inspirational Fiction*. Chapel Hill, NC: The University of North Carolina Press, 2006.

Nida, Eugene A., and Charles R. Taber. *The Theory and Practice of Translation*. Leiden: Brill, 1982.

Nienhuis, David R. "The Problem of Evangelical Biblical Illiteracy: A View from the Classroom." *Modern Reformation* 19.1 (2010) 10–13.

Nolland, John. *The Gospel of Matthew*. The New International Greek Testament Commentary. Grand Rapids: Eerdmans, 2005.

Odağ, Özen. "Emotional Engagement during Literary Reception: Do Men and Women Differ?" *Cognition and Emotion* 27.5 (2013) 856–74.
Office of National Statistics. "Religion in England and Wales 2011." http://www.ons.gov.uk/ons/dcp171776_290510.pdf
Olesberg, Lindsay. *The Bible Study Handbook: A Comprehensive Guide to an Essential Practice*. Downers Grove, IL: InterVarsity, 2012.
Oppenheim, A. N. *Questionnaire Design, Interviewing and Attitude Measurement*. 2nd ed. London: Cassell, 1992.
Osborne, Grant R. *The Hermeneutical Spiral: A Comprehensive Introduction to Biblical Interpretation*. Rev. ed. Downers Grove, IL: InterVarsity, 2006.
———. "Hermeneutics/Interpreting Paul." In *Dictionary of Paul and his Letters*, edited by Gerald F. Hawthorne et al., 388–97. Downers Grove, IL: InterVarsity, 1993.
Owens, Donna C. "The Psalms: 'A Therapy of Words.'" *Journal of Poetry Therapy* 18.3 (2005) 133–52.
Paauw, Glen. R. *Saving the Bible from Ourselves: Learning to Read and Live the Bible Well*. Downers Grove, IL: InterVarsity, 2016.
Parker, Andrew. *Painfully Clear: The Parables of Jesus*. Sheffield, UK: Sheffield Academic Press, 1996.
Patte, Daniel. "Acknowledging the Contextual Character of Male, European-American Critical Exegesis: An Androcritical Perspective." In *Reading from This Place: Social Location and Biblical Interpretation in the United States*, Vol. 1., edited by Fernando F. Segovia, and Mary A. Tolbert, 35–55. Minneapolis, MN: Augsburg Fortress, 1995.
———. "Critical Biblical Studies from a Semiotic Perspective." *Semeia* 81 (1998) 3–26.
Paulson, Eric J., and Sonya L. Armstrong. "Situating Reader Stance within and beyond the Efferent-Aesthetic Continuum." *Literacy Research and Instruction* 49.1 (2009) 86–97.
Pearce, Lynne. *Feminism and the Politics of Reading*. London: Arnold, 1997.
Pearson, Jo. "'Going Native in Reverse': The Insider as Researcher in British Wicca." In *Theorizing Faith: The Insider/Outsider Problem in the Study of Ritual*, edited by Elisabeth Arweck, and Martin D. Stringer, 97–114. Birmingham, UK: University of Birmingham Press, 2002.
Pearson, P. David. "The Roots of Reading Comprehension Instruction." In *Handbook of Research on Reading Comprehension*, edited by Susan E. Israel, and Gerald G. Duffy, 3–31. New York: Routledge, 2009.
Peden, Alison. "Contextual Bible Study at Cornton Vale Women's Prison, Stirling." *Expository Times* 117.1 (2005) 15–18.
Pelikan, Jaroslav. *Jesus through the Centuries: His Place in the History of Culture*. New Haven, CT: Yale University Press, 1985.
Pendry, Louise. "Social Cognition." In *An Introduction to Social Psychology*, 5th ed., edited by Miles Hewstone, et al., 91–120. Chichester, UK: Blackwell, 2012.
Perdue, Leo G. *Proverbs*. Interpretation. Louisville, KY: John Knox, 2000.
Perrin, Ruth H. *The Bible Reading of Young Evangelicals: An Exploration of the Ordinary Hermeneutics and Faith of Generation Y*. Eugene, OR: Pickwick, 2016.
Petric, Paulian-Timotei. "The Reader(s) and the Bible(s) 'Reader Versus Community' in Reader-Response Criticism and Biblical Interpretation." *Sacra Scripta* X.1 (2012) 54–68.

Pietersen, Lloyd. *Reading the Bible After Christendom*. Milton Keynes, UK: Paternoster, 2011.

Pike, Mark A. "The Bible and the Reader's Response." *Journal of Education and Christian Belief* 7.1 (2003) 37–51.

———. *From Personal to Spiritual Transaction: The Potential of Aesthetic Reading.* Unpublished lecture given at Calvin College, Grand Rapids, MI, 2004.

———. "Reading and Responding to Biblical Texts: Aesthetic Distance and the Spiritual Journey." In *Spiritual Education: Literary, Empirical and Pedagogical Approaches*, edited by Cathy Ota and Clive Erricker, 189–201. Brighton, UK: Sussex Academic Press, 2005.

Plate, S. Brent. "Looking at Words: The Iconicity of the Page." *Postscripts* 6.1–3 (2010) 67–82.

Porter, Sam. "Critical Realist Ethnography." In *Qualitative Research in Action*, edited by Tim May, 53–72. London: SAGE, 2002.

Porter, Stanley E. "Why Hasn't Reader-Response Criticism Caught on in New Testament Studies?" *Journal of Literature & Theology* 4.3 (1990) 278–92.

Porter, Stanley E., and Kent D. Clarke. "What is Exegesis? An Analysis of Various Definitions." In *Handbook to Exegesis of the New Testament*, edited by Stanley E. Porter, 3–22. Leiden: Brill, 1997.

Povinelli, Elizabeth A. "Radical Worlds: The Anthropology of Incommensurability and Inconceivability." *Annual Review of Anthropology* 30 (2001) 319–34.

Powell, Mark A. *Chasing the Eastern Star: Adventures in Biblical Reader-Response Criticism*. Louisville, KY: Westminster John Knox, 2001.

———. *What Do They Hear? Bridging the Gap between the Pulpit & Pew*. Nashville, TN: Abingdon, 2007.

Prothero, Stephen. *American Jesus: How the Son of God Became a National Icon*. New York: Farrar, Straus and Giroux, 2003.

Pyper, Hugh S. "The Bible as a Children's Book: The Metrical Psalms and *The Gammage Cup*." In *The Recycled Bible: Autobiography, Culture, and the Space Between*, edited by Fiona C. Black, 143–60. Atlanta: Society of Biblical Literature, 2006.

Radway, Janice A. *Reading the Romance: Women, Patriarchy and Popular Literature*. Chapel Hill, NC: The University of North Carolina Press, 1984.

Rajan, Rajeswari S. *Real & Imagined Women: Gender, Culture and Postcolonialism*. London: Routledge, 1993.

Reed, Esther D., et al. "Narrative Theology in Religious Education." *British Journal of Religious Education* 35.3 (2013) 297–312.

Resseguie, James L. "Reader-Response Criticism and the Synoptic Gospels." *Journal of the American Academy of Religion* 52.2 (1984) 307–24.

Riches, John, ed. *What Is Contextual Bible Study? A Practical Guide with Group Studies for Advent and Lent*. London: SPCK, 2010.

Ricoeur, Paul. *Hermeneutics & the Human Sciences: Essays on Language, Action and Interpretation*. Translated by John B. Thompson. Cambridge: Cambridge University Press, 1981.

———. *A Ricoeur Reader: Reflection and Imagination*. Edited by Mario J. Valdes. Hemel Hempstead, UK: Harvester Wheatsheaf, 1991.

Ritblatt, Shulamit, and Janet H. Ter Louw. "The Bible as Biblio-Source for Poetry Therapy." *Journal of Poetry Therapy* 5.2 (1991) 95–103.

Robbins, Mandy, and Leslie J. Francis. "All Are Called, But Some Psychological Types Are More Likely to Respond: Profiling Churchgoers in Australia." *Research in the Social Scientific Study of Religion* 22 (2011) 212–29.

Robson, Colin. *Real World Research: A Resource for Users of Social Research Methods in Applied Settings*. 3rd ed. Chichester, UK: Wiley & sons, 2011.

Rodriguez, Rafael. "Bible Illiteracy and the Contribution of Biblical Higher Education." *The Bible and Interpretation*. (2014) http://www.bibleinterp.com/opeds/2014/03/rod388028.shtml

Roen, Duane, and Nicholas Karolides. "Louise Rosenblatt: A Life in Literacy." *The Alan Review* 32.3 (2005) 59–61.

Rogers, Andrew P. "Congregational Hermeneutics: A Tale of Two Churches." *Journal of Contemporary Religion* 28.3 (2013) 489–506.

———. *Congregational Hermeneutics: How Do We Read?* Farnham, UK: Ashgate, 2015.

———. "Ordinary Biblical Hermeneutics and the Transformation of Congregational Horizons within English Evangelicalism: A Theological Ethnographic Study." PhD diss., King's College, London, 2009.

———. "Ordinary Hermeneutics and the Local Church." *The Bible in Transmission*, Summer (2007) 18–21.

Rosen, Monica. "Gender Difference in Reading Performance on Documents across Countries." *Reading and Writing* 14 (2001) 1–38.

Rosenblatt, Louise M. *Literature as Exploration*. 5th ed. New York: The Modern Language Association, 1995.

———. *Making Meaning with Texts: Selected Essays*. Portsmouth, NH: Heinemann, 2005.

———. *The Reader, the Text, the Poem: The Transactional Theory of the Literary Work*. Rev. ed. Carbondale, IL: Southern Illinois University Press, 1994.

Rowland, Chris, and John Vincent, eds. *Bible and Practice*. Sheffield, UK: Urban Theology Unit, 2001.

Rowland, Christopher, and Jonathan Roberts. *The Bible for Sinners: Interpretation in the Present Time*. London: SPCK, 2008.

Sandell, Richard, et al. "An Evaluation of Sh[out]—The Social Justice Programme of the Gallery of Modern Art, Glasgow 2009–2010." (2010) http://www2.le.ac.uk/departments/museumstudies/rcmg/projects/sh-out/An%20evaluation%20of%20shOUT.pdf

Sapsford, Roger. *Survey Research*. London: SAGE, 2007.

Sarantakos, Sotirios. *Social Research*. 4th ed. New York: Palgrave MacMillan, 2013.

Sawyer, Joy. "Toward a Pastoral Psychotherapeutic Context for Poetry Therapy: A Poetry Therapy Process Adaptation of the Hynes and Hynes-Berry Biblio/Poetry Therapy Model." *Journal of Poetry Therapy* 17.3 (2004) 155–63.

Sayer, Andrew, *Realism and Social Science*. London: SAGE, 2000.

Schwáb, Zoltán. "Mind the Gap: The Impact of Wolfgang Iser's Reader-Response Criticism on Biblical Studies—A Critical Assessment." *Literature and Theology* 17.2 (2003) 170–81.

Schneiders, Sandra M. *The Revelatory Text: Interpreting the New Testament as Sacred Scripture*. 2nd ed. Collegeville, MN: Liturgical, 1999.

———. *Written That You May Believe: Encountering Jesus in the Fourth Gospel*. Rev. ed. New York: Crossroad, 2003.

Schweitzer, Albert. *The Quest of the Historical Jesus*. Translated by John Bowden. 1906. Reprint. London: SCM, 2000.

Scottish Bible Society and The Contextual Bible Study Group. *Conversations: The Companion*. Scottish Bible Society.

Segovia, Fernando F., and Mary A. Tolbert, eds. *Reading from this Place: Social Location and Biblical Interpretation in the United States*. Vol. 1. Minneapolis, MN: Augsburg Fortress, 1995.

———, eds. *Reading from This Place: Social Location and Biblical Interpretation in Global Perspective*. Vol. 2. Minneapolis, MN: Augsburg Fortress, 1995.

Seul, Jeffrey R. "'Ours Is the Way of God': Religion, Identity, and Intergroup Conflict." *Journal of Peace Research* 36.5 (1999) 553–69.

Shaffir, William B. "Managing a Convincing Self-Presentation: Some Personal Reflections on Entering the Field." In *Experiencing Fieldwork: An Inside View of Qualitative Research*, edited by William B. Shaffir, and Robert A. Stebbins, 72–82. London: SAGE, 1991.

Sheard, Matt. "Ninety-Eight Atheists: Atheism among the Non-Elite in Twentieth Century Britain." *Secularism and Nonreligion* 3.6 (2014) 1–16.

Sherwood, Yvonne. *Biblical Blaspheming: Trials of the Sacred for a Secular Age*. Cambridge: Cambridge University Press, 2012.

———. *A Biblical Text and Its Afterlives: The Survival of Jonah in Western Culture*. Cambridge: Cambridge University Press, 2000.

———. "Bush's Bible as a Liberal Bible (Strange Though that Might Seem)." *Postscripts* 2.1 (2006) 47–58.

Silva, Moisés. *Has The Church Misread the Bible? The History of Interpretation in the Light of Current Issues*. Grand Rapids: Zondervan, 1987.

Silverman, David. *Doing Qualitative Research: A Practical Handbook*. 3rd ed. Thousand Oaks, CA: SAGE, 2010.

Simons, Helen. *Case Study Research in Practice*. Thousand Oaks, CA: SAGE, 2009.

Slee, Nicola. *Women's Faith Development: Patterns and Processes*. Aldershot, UK: Ashgate, 2004.

Sloan, Glenna. "Reader Response in Perspective." *Journal of Children's Literature* 28.1 (2002) 22–31.

Smallbones, Jackie L. "Teaching Bible for Transformation." *Christian Education Journal* 4.2 (2007) 293–307.

Smalley, Stephen S. *1, 2, 3 John*. Word Biblical Commentary. Waco, TX: Word, 1984.

Smith, Christian. *The Bible Made Impossible: Why Biblicism Is Not a Truly Evangelical Reading of Scripture*. Grand Rapids: Brazos, 2011.

Smith, David I. "Misreading through the Eyes of Faith: Christian Students' Reading Strategies as Interlanguage." *The Journal of Education and Christian Belief* 11.2 (2007) 53–66.

———. "The Poet, the Child and the Blackbird: Aesthetic Reading and Spiritual Development." *International Journal of Children's Spirituality* 9.2 (2004) 143–54.

Smith, Groum. "'God's Word Changed My Life,' says Former Street Kid." http://www.biblesociety.org/

Snape, Dawn, and Liz Spencer. "The Foundations of Qualitative Research." In *Qualitative Research Practice: A Guide for Social Science Students and Researchers*, edited by Jane Ritchie, and Jane Lewis, 1–23. London: SAGE, 2003.

Snodgrass, Klyne R. *Stories with Intent: A Comprehensive Guide to the Parables of Jesus.* Cambridge: Eerdmans, 2008.

Sorensen, Christine K., and Daniel C. Robinson. "Gender and Psychological Type: Implications for Serving Nontraditional Students." *Continuing Higher Education Review* 56.1–2 (1992) 35–47.

Soter, Anna O., et al. "Deconstructing 'Aesthetic Response' in Small-Group Discussions about Literature: A Possible Solution to the 'Aesthetic Response' Dilemma." *English Education* 42.2 (2010) 204–25.

Spencer, Nick. *Beyond Belief? Barriers and Bridges to Faith Today.* London: LICC, 2003.

———. *Beyond the Fringe: Researching a Spiritual Age.* Hope Valley, UK: Cliff College, 2005.

Stack-Nelson, Judith. "Beyond Biblical Literacy: Developing Readerly Readers in Teaching Biblical Studies." *Dialog* 53.4 (2014) 293–303.

Stein, Robert H. "The Genre of the Parables." In *The Challenge of Jesus' Parables*, edited by Richard N. Longenecker, 30–50. Grand Rapids: Eerdmans, 2000.

Steiner, George. "Critic"/"Reader." *New Literary History* 10.3 (1979) 423–52.

Steinmetz, George. "Odious Comparisons: Incommensurability, the Case Study, and 'Small N's' in Sociology." *Sociological Theory* 22.3 (2004) 371–400.

Stetzer, Ed, et al. *Lost and Found: The Younger Unchurched and the Churches That Reach Them.* Nashville, TN: B&H, 2009.

Stewart, Allison. "Case Study." In *Qualitative Methodology: A Practical Guide*, edited by Jane Mills, and Melanie Birks, 145–60. London: SAGE, 2014.

Streib, Heinz. "Deconversion." In *Oxford Handbook of Religious Conversion*, edited by Lewis R. Rambo, and Charles E. Farhadian, 271–96. Oxford: Oxford University Press, 2012.

Strhan, Anna. *Aliens and Strangers? The Struggle for Coherence in the Everyday Lives of Evangelicals.* Oxford: Oxford University Press, 2015.

Suler, John. "The Online Disinhibition Effect." *Cyber Psychology and Behavior* 7.3 (2004) 321–26.

Sugirtharajah, R. S. *Exploring Postcolonial Biblical Criticism.* Chichester, UK: Wiley & Sons, 2012.

———, ed. *Voices from the Margin: Interpreting the Bible in the Third World.* London: SPCK, 1991.

Suleiman, Susan R., and Inge Crosman, eds. *The Reader in the Text: Essays on Audience and Interpretation.* Princeton, NJ: Princeton University Press, 1980.

Summers, Gene F. "Introduction." In *Attitude Measurement*, edited by Gene F. Summers, 1–20. London: Kershaw, 1970.

Summers, Kate. "Adult Reading Habits and Preferences in Relation to Gender Differences." *Reference & User Services Quarterly* 52.3 (2013) 243–49.

Swinton, John, and Harriet Mowat. *Practical Theology and Qualitative Research.* London: SCM, 2006.

Tacey, David. *The Spiritual Revolution: The Emergence of Contemporary Spirituality.* London: Routledge, 2004.

Tajfel, Henri. *Differentiation between Social Groups: Studies in the Social Psychology of Intergroup Relations.* London: Academic Press, 1978.

Tate, Marvin E. *Psalms 51–100.* Word Biblical Commentary. Dallas, TX: Word, 1990.

Tate, W. Randolph. *Biblical Interpretation: An Integrated Approach.* Rev. ed. Peabody, MA: Hendrickson, 1997.

Tearfund. "Churchgoing in the UK: A Research Report from Tearfund on Church Attendance in the UK." http://news.bbc.co.uk/1/shared/bsp/hi/pdfs/03_04_07_tearfundchurch.pdf

"The Bible Changed My Life." *Idea* Nov/Dec (2010) 19–23. http://www.eauk.org/idea/nov-dec-2010-issuu.cfm

Theos. *Post-Religious Britain? The Faith of the Faithless*. London: Theos, 2012.

Todd, Andrew J. "The Interaction of Talk and Text: Re-contextualising Biblical Interpretation." *Practical Theology* 6.1 (2013) 69–85.

Thiselton, Anthony C. *New Horizons in Hermeneutics: The Theory and Practice of Transforming Biblical Reading*. Grand Rapids: Zondervan, 1992.

Thompson, Marianne M. *1–3 John*. The IVP New Testament Commentary Series. Leicester, UK: InterVarsity, 1992.

Tompkins, Jane P., ed. *Reader-Response Criticism: From Formalism to Post-Structuralism*. Baltimore, MD: Johns Hopkins University Press, 1980.

Towler, Robert. *The Need for Certainty: A Sociological Study of Conventional Religion*. London: Routledge & Kegan Paul, 1984.

Trzebiatowska, Marta, and Steve Bruce. *Why Are Women More Religious Then Men?* Oxford: Oxford University Press, 2012.

Tucker, J. Brian, and Coleman A. Baker, eds. *T. & T. Clark Handbook to Social Identity in the New Testament*. London: Bloomsbury, 2014.

Tutu, Desmond. *The Rainbow People of God: The Making of a Peaceful Revolution*. New York: Image Doubleday, 1994.

Unger, Rhoda K. "Using the Master's Tools: Epistemology and Empiricism." In *Feminist Social Psychologies; International Perspectives*, edited by Susan Wilkinson, 165–81. Buckingham, UK: Open University Press, 1996.

Vanhoozer, Kevin. J. *Is There a Meaning in This Text? The Bible, the Reader and the Morality of Literary Knowledge*. Grand Rapids: Zondervan, 1998.

———. "The Reader in New Testament Interpretation." In *Hearing the New Testament: Strategies for Interpretation*, edited by Joel B. Green, 259–88. Grand Rapids: Eerdmans, 2010.

Village, Andrew. *The Bible and Lay People: An Empirical Approach to Ordinary Hermeneutics*. Aldershot, UK: Ashgate, 2007.

Village, Andrew, and Leslie J. Francis. "The Relationship of Psychological Type Preferences to Biblical Interpretation." *Journal of Empirical Theology* 18.1 (2005) 74–89.

Vincent, Ray. "The Death and Resurrection of the Bible in Church and Society." *Modern Believing* 53 (2012) 159–66.

Voas, David, and Siobhan McAndrew. "Three Puzzles of Non-Religion in Britain." *Journal of Contemporary Religion* 27.1 (2012) 29–48.

Volf, Miroslav. *Captive to the Word of God: Engaging the Scriptures for Contemporary Theological Reflection*. Grand Rapids: Eerdmans, 2010.

Wachob, Phyllis. "Critical Friendship Circles, the Cultural Challenge of Cool Feedback." *Professional Development in Education* 37.3 (2011) 353–72.

Walker, David. "The Religious Beliefs and Attitudes of Rural Anglican Churchgoers." *Rural Theology* 8 (2010) 159–72.

Wann, Daniel. L. et al. "Beliefs in Symbolic Catharsis: The Importance of Involvement with Aggressive Sports." *Social Behavior and Personality* 27.2 (1999) 155–64.

Waters, Guy. P. *Justification and the New Perspective: A Review and Response.* Philipsburg, NJ: Presbyterian and Reformed, 2004.

Watson, Francis. *Text, Church and World: Biblical Interpretation in Theological Perspective.* London: T. & T. Clark, 1994.

Weaver-Zercher, Valerie. *Thrill of the Chaste: The Allure of Amish Romance Novels.* Baltimore, MD: John Hopkins University Press, 2013.

Webber, Robert E. *The Younger Evangelicals: Facing the Challenges of the New World.* Grand Rapids: Baker, 2002.

Webster, Tiffany. "When the Bible Meets the Black Stuff: A Contextual Bible Study Experiment." PhD diss., University of Sheffield, 2017.

Weiser, Artur. *The Psalms.* London: SCM, 1962.

Weiss, Robert S. *Learning from Strangers: The Art and Method of Qualitative Interview Studies.* New York: Free, 1994.

Wengraf, Tom. *Qualitative Research Interviewing: Biographic Narrative and Semi-Structured Methods.* London: SAGE, 2001.

West, Gerald O. *The Academy of the Poor: Towards a Dialogical Reading of the Bible.* Sheffield, UK: Sheffield Academic Press, 1999.

———. *Contextual Bible Study.* Pietermaritzburg, South Africa: Cluster, 1993.

———. "Do Two Walk Together? Walking with the Other through Contextual Bible Study." *Anglican Theological Review* 93.3 (2011) 431–49.

———. "Taming Texts of Terror: Reading (Against) the Gender Grain of 1 Timothy." *Scriptura* 86 (2004) 160–73.

West, Jim. "The Bible in the Pew: Congregations and Critical Scholarship from the Pastor's Perspective." *The Expository Times* 116.10 (2005) 330–33.

Westermann, Claus. *The Psalms: Structure Content and Message.* Minneapolis, MN: Augsburg, 1980.

Williams, Gary R. "Contextual Influences in Readings of Nehemiah 5: A Case Study." *Tyndale Bulletin* 53.1 (2002) 57–74.

Wharton-McDonald, Ruth W., and Shannon Swiger. "Developing Higher Order Comprehension in the Middle Grades." In *Handbook of Research on Reading Comprehension,* edited by Susan E. Israel, and Gerald G. Duffy, 510–30. New York: Routledge, 2009.

Wimsatt, William K., and Munro C. Beardsley. "The Affective Fallacy." In *The Verbal Icon: Studies in the Meaning of Poetry,* edited by William K. Wimsatt, 21–39. 1946. Reprint. London: Methuen, 1970.

Wimsatt, William K., and Munro C. Beardsley. "The Intentional Fallacy." In *The Verbal Icon: Studies in the Meaning of Poetry,* edited by William K. Wimsatt, 3–18. 1946. Reprint. London: Methuen, 1970.

Wink, Walter. *The Bible in Human Transformation.* 2nd ed. Minneapolis, MN: Fortress, 2010.

Wolf, Daniel R. "High-Risk Methodology: Reflections on Leaving an Outlaw Society." In *Experiencing Fieldwork: An Inside View of Qualitative Research,* edited by William B. Shaffir, and Robert A. Stebbins, 211–23. London: SAGE, 1991.

Wood, David. *Let the Bible Live: Report from the North Yorkshire Dales Biblical Literacy Project.* Durham, UK: CODEC, 2013.

Wooden, R. Glenn. "The Role of "the Septuagint" in the Formation of the Biblical Canons." In *Exploring the Origins of the Bible: Canon Formation in Historical,*

Literary, and Theological Perspective, edited by Craig A. Evans, and Emanuel Tov, 129–46. Grand Rapids: Baker, 2008.

Woodside, Arch G. *Case Study Research: Theory, Methods, Practice.* Bingley, UK: Emerald Group, 2010.

Wright, Christopher J. H. *The Mission of God: Unlocking the Bible's Grand Narrative.* Leicester, UK: InterVarsity, 2006.

Wright, N. T. *The New Testament and the People of God.* London: SPCK, 1992.

Wright, Terence R. "'Get thee behind me Satan': On Resisting Fishy Models of Reading." In *English Literature, Theology and the Curriculum,* edited by Liam Gearon, 27–34. London: Cassell, 1999.

Wright, Bradley R. E., et al. "Explaining Deconversion from Christianity: A Study of Online Narratives." *Journal of Religion & Society* 13 (2011) 1–17.

Wurst, Shirley J. J. "Dancing on the Minefield: Feminist Counter-Readings of Women in Proverbs 1–9." PhD diss., University of South Australia, 1999.

Wuthnow, Robert. *Sharing the Journey: Support Groups and America's New Quest for Community.* New York: Free, 1994.

Yin, Robert K. *Case Study Research: Design and Methods.* 5th ed. Thousand Oaks, CA: SAGE, 2014.

Zondervan. "Bible Translation Chart." http://www.zondervan.com/m/bibles/translation_chart_poster.pdf

Zuckerman, Phil. *Faith No More: Why People Reject Religion.* New York: Oxford University Press, 2012.

Index

Aichele, George, 91, 172, 181
analysis, 84-85
attitude, 94, 135-36

Bible reading surveys, 33-34, 36-37, 47-49, 166-67, 210
biblical literacy, 34-35, 210-11
Bielo, James, 25, 45, 46, 124, 143
belief, 149-50
Braun, Willi, 178-79
Brueggemann, Walter, 23, 28

churchgoing surveys, 36, 48
Clines, David, 28, 178, 179, 182
Crossley, James, 37, 107, 189
confessional/non-confessional reading, 100-101, 146
contextual Bible reading, 27-30, 132-33, 207, 209-210
Contextual Bible Study method, 31-32, 39-40, 53, 54, 72, 119-20, 132-33, 169-70, 206
Cornwall, Susannah, 32, 53, 119
counter-reading the Bible, 176-83, 206, 207-8, 216
critical realism, 66, 195

Davies, Eryl, 22-23, 193-94
Davies, Philip, 35, 100-101
deconstructive literary criticism, 179
defensive reader, 178-79
Detweiler, Robert, 107, 130, 170-71, 180

Engelke, Matthew, 112-14, 167-68, 171

Fetterley, Judith, 177-78
Field, Clive, 34, 48, 51, 210
fieldwork, 69-71, 81-84, 162-63, 173-74, 175-76
 Andy G, 6, 70, 150, 165
 Andy K, 6, 156
 Anthony, 7, 70-71, 127-30, 143, 192, 205
 Bob, 7, 131, 154, 180, 181-82
 Dave, 7, 99-108, 115-17, 130-31, 148, 166, 205
 Derek, 7, 131-32, 153, 165, 183
 Ethan, 7, 174, 199-200, 202-3
 Gary, 7, 109-114, 115-17, 130, 174, 181, 205, 215
 John, 7, 120-27, 148, 165, 174, 182, 205
 Matty, 7, 172-73, 174, 182
 Mick, 7, 150, 166, 172, 173
 Paul, 7, 140-44, 205
 Peter, 7, 151, 166, 173, 200-201
 Phil, 7, 165, 173, 200-202, 215-16
 Richie, 7, 151
 Sam, 1-3, 8, 151-53, 165, 174, 191, 213
 Stuart, 8, 195-98, 202
 Tony, 8, 153, 166, 175-76
 Victor, 8, 136-40, 180-81, 192, 205
 Zadok, 8, 70, 166, 173, 174, 181
Fish, Stanley, 20-21, 24, 96, 192-94, 195, 197-98, 200, 202-3, 206
Francis, Leslie, 76, 135-36, 163

Gadamer, Hans-Georg, 21-22, 139, 194
gatekeeper, 81-82

gender and Bible reading, 47–50, 163–65, 167–68
GOMA Bible, 74–75, 105–6

hermeneutics of suspicion and faith, 101, 146
Holland, Norman, 19–20
Horrell, David, 28–29
Hull, John, 29, 209–210

interpretive community, 20–21, 24, 96–97, 192–95, 197–98, 202–3, 206
Iser, Wolfgang, 20, 24, 95–96, 139, 193

Jennings, Mike, 45–46, 76, 79, 98, 215

Lawrence, Louise, 120, 170
Le Grys, Alan, 38–39, 46, 166

Macdonald, Fergus, 37–38, 44, 46, 171–72
Malley, Brian, 43, 72–73, 186–87
manual view of Bible, 150–55, 165–68, 186, 206, 207, 211–13
Masowe weChishanu Church, 111–14
methodology, 42–47
    case study, 44–45
    sampling, 47–51, 82
    choice of texts, 51–64
methods, 71–72, 73–81
    mixed-method approach, 74–78
    annotation, 74–76
    questionnaires, 76–77, 78–80
    semi-structured interview, 77–78
    pilot study, 80–81
    limitations, 214–17
Murphy, Liam, 124, 187–88

no religion, 33, 50–51, 130, 145–46

Peden, Alison, 32, 54, 119–20, 132, 165
Perrin, Ruth, 26
Practical theology and Bible reading, 37–39, 46
    ordinary hermeneutics, 26–27
    ordinary Christology, 211–12
Pyper, Hugh, 29–30

reader-response criticism, 18–22, 157–58
    and the Bible, 22–25
reader shaped Bible readings, 185–92
    accepting readings, 100, 127–30, 137–38, 153, 205
    aesthetic readings, 196–98, 201, 212–13
    atheist readings, 120–27, 205
    'Bible has agency' readings, 172–84, 205, 206
    'Bible is a manual' readings, 150–56, 165–68, 205
    bitter readings, 99–108, 115–17, 205
    Christian readings, 127–30, 205
    confused reading, 156–57, 200–202, 205
    detached readings, 109–114, 115–17, 196, 205
    doubting readings, 140–44, 205
    efferent readings, 149–68, 186, 200–201, 211–13
    fair readings, 136–40, 205, 214
    powerful reading, 195–98, 205
    skeptical readings, 100–104, 109–111, 115–17, 120–27, 130, 140–45, 172–84, 199–200, 200–202, 205
    skeptical and accepting readings, 136–40, 144–46, 206
reading against the grain, 177–78
reflexivity, 65–73, 208–210
    Christian identity, 67–73, 175–76
    influence of materials, 71–72, 161–63, 174–75
resisting reader, 177–78
Riches, John, 119
Ricoeur, Paul, 101, 157–58
Rogers, Andrew, 26, 43, 66, 211
Rosenblatt, Louise, 4–5, 90–98, 115–17, 123–24, 139, 157–61, 167, 179–80, 194–95, 198, 201–2, 204–5, 207, 213, 215

Schneiders, Sandra, 158, 183
Sherwood, Yvonne, 34, 74–75, 105–6, 107, 189

Social-scientific study of Bible readers, 25, 45–46, 186–90
Social psychology
    catharsis, 107–8
    disinhibition, 106–7
    self-schema theory, 126–27, 129
    social identity theory, 124–26, 129
Spencer, Nick, 37, 166–67, 182–83
spiritual but not religious, 1, 79
Steiner, George, 157

transactional theory of reading, 4–5, 89–98, 115–16, 158–61, 194, 204–5, 214–15
    reader/text relationship, 92–93, 94, 115–17, 133–34, 146–47, 165–68, 194–95, 198, 205, 213–14
    reader, 93–94
    text, 94–95
    text/reader relationship, 194–203, 205, 214
    selective attention, 5, 95–96, 148, 205
    limitations, 96–98, 160–61
    efferent/aesthetic spectrum, 91, 95, 157–61, 197, 200–202, 207, 211–13

transformative potential of Bible reading, 169–84, 194–98, 206

Village, Andrew, 26, 43, 53, 94, 149
Volf, Miroslav, 101, 182, 214

Webster, Tiffany, 39–40, 50

Zuckerman, Phil, 111

Printed in Great Britain
by Amazon